The Optimistic Classroom

Creative Ways to Give Children Hope

> **By** Deborah Hewitt and Sandra Heidemann

> **Illustrated by** Stéphanie Roth

 Redleaf Press

Book design by Cathy Spengler Design
Illustrations by Stéphanie Roth

Published by: Redleaf Press
                 a division of Resources for Child Caring
                 450 N. Syndicate, Suite 5
                 St. Paul, MN 55104

Distributed by: Gryphon House
                 Mailing Address:
                 P.O. Box 207
                 Beltsville, MD 20704-0207

Library of Congress Cataloging-in-Publication Data

Hewitt, Debbie, 1958-
    The optimistic classroom : creative ways to give children hope /
by Deborah Hewitt and Sandra Heidemann ; illustrations by Stéphanie
Roth.
       p.   cm.
    Includes bibliographical references (p.   ).
    ISBN 1-884834-60-4
    1. School children—Psychology. 2. Early childhood education—
Activity programs. 3. Hope—Study and teaching (Early childhood)
4. Nurturing behavior—Study and teaching (Early childhood)
I. Heidemann, Sandra, 1946-   . II. Title.
LB1117.H458   1998
305.234—DC21
                                                    98-30927
                                                    CIP

We dedicate this book to . . .

our parents

Harold and Vivian, Maynard and Justine

our siblings

Barb and Dave, Joann and Caroline

our communities

Castlewood, SD and Mankato, MN

who surrounded us as children

and to . . .

our families

Jim, Jeff

Carrie and Daniel, Marcie and Reid

who encircle us now.

Contents

Preface

What will children of today remember of their childhood? Will they remember the guns brought to school by classmates? Will they recall times when they were scared to talk with someone they didn't know? Will they express the fears they had about their parents getting a divorce? Will they remember the lack of food in their homes or the times they were stopped and threatened by police? Will they remember times when violence between their parents threatened their security and safety?

Many books and much publicity have focused on the difficulties facing children today. Children and our society have a myriad of issues with which to deal. How do we help our children? This burning question drove our search for answers. We looked at historical examples of hardships and advocacy. We thought about the importance of hope and determination. We recognized the need for strong policies and protections for our nation's children. And we researched the strengths individuals need to thrive in a variety of circumstances. We came to the following conclusions:

1. Every generation has faced challenges that threatened the survival and healthy growth of its children.

2. History provides us with inspiration and hope; sometimes it gives us concrete strategies, and at other times the push to solve the problem.

3. Solutions need to address societal issues, fortify community supports, and build strengths within individual children.

4. We must equip children with skills to solve complex personal and social dilemmas in the twenty-first century and provide the protections they need to thrive.

5. Caregivers have a pivotal role in planning for and implementing strategies that provide external support and teach internal strengths.

6. Hope will sustain us when we falter and provide us with inspiration to keep going. We must model and impart our hope to children.

This book recognizes the need for action on a number of levels and offers concrete steps to take. In chapter 1 we build rationale for the importance of supporting children in a variety of ways.

Chapter 2 considers historical examples of problems children have faced. The examples show us the difficulties children have experienced and the supports adults put in place to protect them.

The components of hope are described in the third chapter. Hope gives us both a vision for the future and motivation to keep moving.

Steps we can take to help today's children are outlined in chapter 4. They include actions we can take on a national level and within our communities to support families and children.

Chapter 5 provides a list of ten strengths that are essential for the children of this nation. They are drawn from research on resiliency and are of benefit to every child.

Chapter 6 highlights activities that teach these strengths. It looks at the importance of structuring the environment, catching teachable moments, and being a role model. It provides the caregiver with a variety of activities that teach the ten strengths. These are not meant as a curriculum but a compilation of activities you can utilize to fit the needs of your group.

To make this book gender fair, we have tried to refer to children as a group. The alternating use of *he* and *she* has been used when necessary.

It is difficult to find a single term for all those who might be interested in the information in this book. We use *early childhood educator*, *caregiver*, and *provider* for those providing direct care, whether it is in a family child care setting, a child care center, preschool, family support program, or Head Start. Others who may find this book useful include center directors and administrators, trainers, and resource and referral staff.

As we wrote, we found the scope of the book to be far-reaching. What began as a series of simple questions expanded and became more elaborate. The results of our research on the historical examples, advocacy work, and resiliency could each provide the foundation for a book in itself. We found ourselves working to be thorough and yet purposeful in our focus. In doing this, we had to prioritize what we would include.

We struggled to write about the very real and sometimes painful experiences of people in the past without trivializing them. The comments our initial readers gave us on the historical examples were of particular interest. The historical events we studied were not dry facts to them, but were alive in their hearts and in their experiences. They felt very strongly about the situations we described. The readers helped us understand the importance of the information and the differing perspectives people bring to history. Each example tells only a small piece of the total picture. There is much more to tell. We would hope that others would explore these topics in other venues.

Our vision for the future led our inquiry, our research, our questions, and our answers. When we became overwhelmed, we remembered the faces of many children, both those we care for and our own.

At the end of this process we have discovered that we are more committed to finding effective ways to advance children's issues. We are dedicated to making our communities places where children flourish. We are determined to build upon the strengths of the families we encounter. And we renew our pledge to foster hope in each individual. We hope this book will inspire you to work toward a future that holds more opportunity, is more inclusive, ensures adequate food and shelter, guarantees safe places for children to grow and play, supports families, and provides excellent education for all children.

Debbie Hewitt
Sandy Heidemann

Acknowledgments

We are grateful to the many people who have been helpful to us throughout the writing of this book. First are our husbands, Jim and Jeff. They lent their support, encouragement, and belief that this is an important undertaking. They listened as we discussed ideas and provided valuable feedback as they read half-written chapters and partially developed ideas.

Thanks to our children—Marcie, Reid, Carrie, and Daniel—for their patience, their humor, and the inspiration they bring us. They push us to tell the truth and to care deeply about the events taking place around us.

Many people read the manuscript and responded with ideas that helped to strengthen it. We are thankful to Joyce Frett, Nancy Johnson, Joe Kingbird, Barbara O'Sullivan, Sue Springer-Hewitt, Jim Stengel, Karol Underwood, Caroline Winget, and Eva Zygmunt. Joe, Joyce, and Nancy's added resources, ideas, and advice on the historical examples brought them to life. Many people provided us with personal stories that gave the manuscript a human face: the woman still walking fifty-four years after polio, Risa Tritabaugh, Marcy Whitebook, and Nedra Robinson. Eva Zygmunt researched the resource list found in the appendix. Mary Burns adapted the original activities to better meet the needs of toddlers, and Diane Lerberg adapted the activities for schoolagers. Their contributions are greatly appreciated. Others who have been influential in the process include Kathy Kolb at Partnership to Address Violence Through Education and Marilyn Wolkerstorfer, Kris Greer, and Sue Manion at Anoka-Hennepin Learning Readiness. Thanks to Southside Family Nurturing Center staff who tried activities, asked clarifying questions, and shouldered extra responsibility during the writing of this book. They truly demonstrate the ten strengths in their work to help children overcome challenges. We appreciate the work Caroline Winget did to field-test many of the activities. We are grateful to Deb Strand for her resources and thoughts on resiliency, and to Eric Strand for his words of hope. Finally, we are indebted to Beth Wallace, Mary Steiner Whelan, and Eileen Nelson at Redleaf Press who saw the need for this book and have supported its development.

Chapter One

Is It Harder Now?

Early one morning Debbie and her young son were cuddling. He asked in a still-sleepy voice, "Momma, are we ever going to have another war?" She didn't have a good answer to that question, but she tried to calm his fears by saying, "I sure hope not. Lots of people are working hard to keep that from happening." It broke her heart that this kind of thought would occupy his mind at such a tender moment.

Like Debbie's son, we worry. We worry about the quality of schools, the accessibility of drugs, and finding places for children to play without the threat of violence. We worry about the children in our care who have already experienced the effects of lead exposure, sexual and physical abuse, disease and illness, and the harsh realities of living in poverty.

As we listen to news reports, read newspapers, and talk with others, we realize that children and providers throughout our country are struggling with these same issues. We are saddened by the fact that children are in trouble. We are also discouraged by the amount of blame placed on parents, teachers, and even the children themselves. We are surprised and disturbed by the degree of anger people express and the resignation they display.

It takes too much energy not to care.

—Lorraine Hansberry

People shrug their shoulders, throw up their hands, and sigh. "It's much harder to be a child now," they say. While most people are doing everything they can to ensure that children grow up under the best conditions, children and families face many hurdles. Millions of children are growing up in poverty as the income disparity between the rich and the poor continues to grow. The Census Bureau estimates that salaries for families making under $35,000 have only grown 3 to 7 percent in the past twenty years. Salaries for families making over $200,000 have jumped 63 percent in that same time period (Berg, 1998). Approximately one in five children—or 20 percent—live in poverty (Children's Defense Fund, 1996). Some go to bed without enough food to fill their stomachs. Others move from place to place without an address to call home. Their families depend on food shelves and makeshift arrangements for shelter. Babies are born having been exposed to alcohol or drugs, some to mothers who are barely more than children themselves.

Parents who work outside the home find themselves torn between their dedication to their families and the demands of their jobs. Children come home to empty houses after school and lack adequate supervision. When children are chronically sick, parents want to stay home with them, but they may be compelled to go to work. Many children are being raised by single parents who struggle to pay housing bills, food bills, and medical costs on their own. An unprecedented number of children experience the changes that come with divorce and their parents' subsequent remarriage, requiring adjustments to a new stepfamily. Some remain bitter and angry long after the physical separation.

Exposure to the media brings knowledge of such issues as hunger, sexuality, and violence. There are stories of shootings in and around schools, the murders of teenage boys of color, and kidnappings. Adults remark how unsafe and unpredictable the world is and hope that the violence doesn't touch their sons or daughters.

The picture looks bleak, and there are many risks for children. At first glance, the answer to our question—Is it harder now?—seems to be yes. But then we ask ourselves additional questions. What was it like for a child of color growing up thirty to fifty years ago? What was it like for a child whose family was poor? What was it like for a child one hundred years ago, or one hundred and fifty years ago?

When we think about whether or not it is harder to be a child in today's world from a broader perspective, we realize that historically it hasn't been easy for large numbers of people. Problems of poverty, unemployment, poor housing, and child neglect have plagued this nation for generations. Thirty to fifty years ago, an African American child was required to attend a segregated school, drink from separate fountains, and ride at the back of the bus. People of color were not included in the gains of white middle-class families in the 1950s. One third of American children were poor and did not have the benefit of food stamps and housing programs (Coontz, 1992).

We also know that adults recognized and worked to change unacceptable conditions for children. Thirty to fifty years ago, civil rights leaders marched to change the segregation laws in the South. Child advocates designed and implemented innovative programs for the education of young children. Reporting laws for child abuse and neglect were passed in all states. Food stamps and housing programs were provided for poor families starting in the 1960s as part of President Johnson's War on Poverty.

As we consider all these factors, it is impossible to answer the question "Is it harder now?" Instead the overriding issue is "What can we do now to help children?" It was hard then, and it is hard now. History tells us that many children faced unbearable conditions in the past, and the present brings pictures of children with great needs in our nation. Historically, people fought for change. Now it's our turn.

The good we secure for ourselves is precarious and uncertain...until it is secured for all of us and incorporated into our common life.

—Jane Addams

Circles of Support

As we move from the question "Is it harder now?" to "What can we do now to help our children?" we see how multifaceted this question is. We need to address issues at many levels.

When you throw a stone in a pond of water, it starts a chain reaction where ripples move outward from the initial splash to the edge of the pool. Each circle influences all the others. In much the same way, we envision the child as that first circle, needing the surrounding circles to flourish. With the inner circle being the child, the circles extend outward in the following order:

➤ Family: includes immediate family, extended family, and friends

➤ Child Care Programs and Schools: includes teachers, other personnel, and other children

➤ Community: includes neighborhood, city or town, ethnic group, religious community, and other supportive groups of adults

➤ National and State Level Government Supports: includes laws, policies, financial supports, and regulations

The child is most supported when all the circles are unbroken. However, a child's situation is rarely perfect. When circles are broken by violence, fear, poverty, or death, the child is always affected. Each child is affected differently, however, given varying external supports and internal make-ups.

Let's examine the situations of Maria and Jake, two children who live in an inner-city neighborhood in a large city. Both experience unpredictable violence in the neighborhood and witness drug deals on their block. However, the differences in both the external supports and the internal make-ups of the two children result in varying reactions to the stress in the neighborhood.

Maria lives with her mother and grandmother in a large security apartment building. She goes to a preschool in the local church, and her mother and grandmother encourage attendance. Maria visits her father every week and has a large number of supportive extended

Think of continuing generations of our families, think of our grandchildren and of those yet unborn, whose faces are coming from beneath the ground.

—Peacemaker, founder of the Iroquois Confederacy

In some situations, changing the environment may be most critical; in others changing the individual; in still others, it is the "transactional exchange" between the individual and the environment that is in need of alteration... we must know not just what to change but how.

—David Pellegrini

family members. Maria is temperamentally quite calm, self-confident, and persistent when faced with a problem. She enjoys reading and music. Maria has a number of external supports: her mother, father, and grandmother, her preschool, and a large extended family. Her internal make-up includes such strengths as self-esteem, perseverance, and confidence, which are reinforced and encouraged by her family's protection. The violence in the neighborhood is less likely to traumatize her because she has a number of protective circles in place.

Jake lives with his father and mother. He often stays in his bedroom when his parents fight because he has witnessed his father hitting his mother during conflicts. His mother is isolated from her extended family because of the domestic violence. Jake does not attend preschool because there are none in his neighborhood. His mother does not use public transportation and can't get him to school on her own. Jake plays outside alone and hangs around the street corner waiting for someone to talk to. He seems hungry for contact with others. Jake gets upset easily, throws frequent tantrums, and is difficult to comfort when he is anxious. His mother complains that he was difficult to comfort even as a baby. Like Maria, Jake has some external support from his mother and father, but because of the domestic violence in the family, his mother and father are not able to keep the support consistently in place. The circles of protection are not firmly in place for Jake. Unless adults are able to build in more protection, the violence and drug dealing in the neighborhood are likely to influence him more and more as he grows older and render his future as an adult less certain.

In each of the examples above, the children have circles of protection around them that can cushion the impact of neighborhood issues. In Maria's case, those circles are firmly in place. For Jake, the circles cannot adequately protect him from the violence around him. The obstacles Jake faces are both a lack of adequate protection and some internal fragility. He has a temperament that is sensitive to changes and stress. But if adults could put in extra supports for Jake, he would have a good chance to use his strengths. For instance, if he could go to a good preschool and be enrolled in community programs in art or sports, he might discover a talent that could help him succeed. He might also form a loving relationship with an adult, which would help to cushion the impact of his parents' inconsistency.

Maria and Jake have their own temperaments, learning styles, internal strengths, aptitudes, and birth histories. All children have these qualities. Some children are born with sunny, easy dispositions that draw adults to them. They gain strengths such as perseverance, coping skills, and empathy as they age. Even under distress, these children are able to cope and to gain support from adults who can help them recover from the trauma.

Other children may face challenges from the very beginning. For example, a mother may have ingested drugs or alcohol that affect the development of her child's brain. Or an infant may be prone to colic and difficult to comfort. Some children are born with special needs or genetic disorders. Clearly, these children will face challenges when learning to handle their emotions, learning to read, or overcoming their chronic health problems. But if the outer circles around the children are strengthened, they can meet those challenges. Given excellent medical care, special education, respite care, and family support, a child with Fetal Alcohol Syndrome can become an independent adult.

The Balance Scale

The balance scale also helps us envision how we can help children. The base of this balance scale is made up of the basic external supports that all children need. These include a family, home, food, medical care, sufficient family income, good education, and protection from violence and abuse. On one side of the scale are the individualized external supports that are provided by adults and needed by every child in order to thrive. On the other side are the strengths and challenges the individual child brings. The scale cannot be balanced without contributions on both sides. The balance of the scale changes with each child, due to the societal factors that make up the base and due to differences in each child's internal make-up and changing family situations.

All children need the protection that comes from good educational policies, anti-smoking laws, limited access to guns, and drug regulations. Other protections are needed by large subgroups of children, such as laws and programs to eliminate racism and increase opportunities for children of color or good bilingual education settings so children whose first language is not English are supported in maintaining their home language and culture. When we design and enact external supports for children, we need to envision a more systemic response, in addition to the family and community responses. This may mean lobbying for laws, practices, and regulations that will offer protection to large numbers of children. Disability laws are one recent example of laws that have improved the quality of life for many. They require adaptations, modifications, and special services in educational settings for children with special needs.

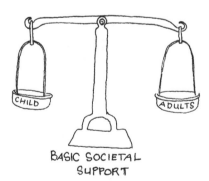

BASIC SOCIETAL
SUPPORT

By understanding the societal conditions, unique needs, and physical and emotional environments surrounding each child, we can put effective supports in place to construct optimum conditions for growth. Let's explore some different examples that illustrate the support a child might need to keep the scale in balance.

Some children maintain balance without much difficulty because they have both internal strengths and external supports. When a child has or is able to learn internal motivation, empathy, problem-solving skills, and good self-esteem, adults can easily foster internal strengths and provide the guidance, nurturance, and environment that builds success. Supports unique to the child's interests should be added to keep her involved in outside activities and successful in school.

Another child might be born with internal conditions that throw the balance off-kilter. A child may be born with a special need, such as a visual impairment, a hearing impairment, a difficult temperament, learning disabilities, or behavioral disorders. These internal conditions put the child at risk of failure. Although this child may have supports, such as an involved family, high-quality caregivers, and societal protections, he still needs more to achieve success. To offset the imbalance, adults must provide extra services in schools, such as interpreters, physical therapists, speech therapists, guidance counselors, and special education teachers. Adults must be committed to finding resources that build on the child's strengths and uphold any progress the child makes. Extra care and vigilance may be required of adults throughout the child's life.

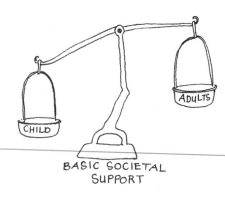

BASIC SOCIETAL
SUPPORT

For other children, the scale is off-kilter from the beginning because the societal elements that make up the base are deficient or lacking altogether. These children face challenges such as a difficult family life, a violent neighborhood, poorly funded schools, or the impact of racism and poverty. They may possess internal resources that help them bounce back from adversity and seek out other adults and activities to assist them. However, even a resilient child can flounder if sufficient individualized supports are not in place. Too many difficulties can chip away at her ability to cope. When experiences of failure or seemingly insurmountable problems erode her strength, adults must continue to replenish the scale to reestablish equilibrium.

Finally, a child may lack external supports *and* have internal challenges. Her family may be unable to advocate effectively for her special educational and health needs. She may be coping with the multiple stresses of living in poverty and attending a school where her home language and culture are not spoken or respected. She may have been separated from her parents and placed in foster care and also have Attention Deficit Disorder or a developmental disability. Children like this need extra support from their schools and communities and from society at large to bolster their self-esteem, learning, and resolve.

The equation for each child is complex. To come up with the right balance, our analysis must include societal factors, community supports, family conditions, and individual strengths.

What Does the Research Say?

Studies done by the Search Institute of Minneapolis in 1990 support this analysis of children's needs. They conducted research with 47,000 sixth- to twelfth-grade youth. This study was largely based in the Midwest and is yet to be nationally normed. They concluded that society, community, and family support are all necessary to raise a strong, healthy individual. The Search Institute has identified a list of internal and external assets that enable youth to be successful. Although this model was developed with research around the needs of youth, the concepts apply equally to young children. The Search Institute has just begun to apply its research model to younger children. Nancy Leffert and her colleagues have recently published research about the application of the Search Institute's model and younger children.

External assets identified by the Search Institute include parental communication and discipline, positive school climate, extracurricular activities, community activities, and positive religious involvement. These supports are provided in the community by institutions such as good schools, churches with strong youth programs, and outside activities like drama, music instruction, sports, and by the children's families. These assets offer support, control, and the structured use of time. For younger children, the Search Institute lists supportive family, caring out-of-home environment, religious community, and a caring neighborhood (Leffert, Benson, Roehlkepartain, 1997). One of the most vital external assets is the presence of caring adults. These caring adults can be family members, child care providers, coaches, teachers, ministers, or even neighbors. Youth do better with many caring adults surrounding them, but even one significant person can make a difference in a child's life.

Equally important, according to the Search Institute, are the youth's internal assets. Some of these qualities are achievement, motivation, empathy, responsibility, planning and decision making, good social skills, cultural competence, conflict resolution skills, good self-esteem, personal power (belief that "I have control over what happens to me"), and optimism about the future. Some of the internal assets they list for younger children are engagement in learning cultural practice and observations, self-esteem, and resistance skills. Societal support in the development of these assets is essential. Some children have been able to develop these assets using both their given aptitudes and institutional support. Others face barriers in developing the assets: institutional racism, special needs, family violence, poverty, frequent moves, instability in the home due to divorce or death of a parent, or lack of an excellent education. Whether children have many barriers or a few, all youth and children need adults to help them maintain these assets.

Emmy Werner's (1989) findings also uphold the metaphor of the circles of support or protection that will help children grow in positive ways. She has conducted a thirty-year study of racially diverse children in Hawaii. Many of the children were poor and under great family stress. Summarizing Werner's findings, Garmezy (1991) states that a child needs three types of protective factors to cushion the impact of stressful events:

1. Dispositional Attributes of the Child
   These can include activity level, sociability, average intelligence, competence in language and reading, and inner control.

2. Affectional Ties within the Family
   This includes emotional support in times of stress, whether from a parent, sibling, or other relative.

3. External Support Systems
   These include schools, caregiving environments, and churches that reward the individual's competencies and determination.

As both the Search Institute's research and Werner's study demonstrate, children need both positive internal assets and external support from caring adults, supportive institutions, and effective laws and policies.

The circle and the balance scale are metaphors we use to demonstrate the importance of providing external supports for and cultivating internal strengths in all children. Clearly, we must provide extra supports for children under duress. However, all children must have economic security, love, protective laws, perseverance, self-esteem, and the encouragement of adults. Although the stress or trauma children suffer may not always seem life-threatening or dramatic, any obstacle can block children's success. Children can have superior intelligence, but unless they have access to good schools, they will lack the skills to achieve. Children may have access to all the resources they need for their physical development, but lack time with their parents. As children grow older, they need the internal strengths to handle the experiences of death and grief, job changes, family transitions, and other kinds of emotional complications.

How Can We Help?

Throughout this book we ask the question "How can we help?" Our answers come from history, with its poignant stories of hardship and people's courageous attempts to overcome it, research about resiliency and the development of competence, and our own experiences. The answers seem simple and straightforward. For example, children need to have at least one caring adult in their lives to thrive, and children with special needs require the protection of laws to have equal access to schools and public settings. But the answers are complex and multilayered, given that societal conditions, family situations, and the internal make-up of children are all at play.

To counter problems, leaders and educators often choose to focus on either changing laws and societal practices or changing and educating individual children. While prioritizing one or the other is efficient, it is deceptive. Children must have both societal and individual support to succeed. All factors are interdependent and must be analyzed together when we plan our strategies. Similarly, as members of a child care community, we differ in our talents. We all have strengths and skills, and our knowledge, passion, and skills are all valuable and necessary. Some of us may feel more comfortable with advocacy, others with teaching individual children or small groups of children. However, we cannot effectively address the needs of children in our society without doing both.

Chapter Two

It Hasn't Been Easy

Earlier generations have faced what seem like insurmountable obstacles. These obstacles ranged from personal problems within the child or family and community and neighborhood issues to discriminatory laws affecting entire cultural or racial groups. But many people held fast to the belief that they could make life better for themselves and their children. They faced their problems with stubborn resolve as they struggled to ensure freedom and basic rights. Parents fought for education that would be meaningful to their children. People raised money, lobbied Congress, rebelled against unjust practices and laws, wrote books and reports, and continued addressing the issues even when initially defeated.

Tragic conditions and social issues have continually challenged our nation. Like previous generations, we are still dealing with such issues as poverty and unequal access to resources and opportunities, poor housing, disease, child neglect, crime, and prejudice. Looking at history and its lessons in personal and societal terms can give us assistance as we search for new solutions to our current problems. Historical study can help us:

> understand current problems and how they developed

> learn strategies that have worked for changing society

> learn individual coping strategies

> understand the urgency of our problems

> receive inspiration and hope as we face our own barriers

> heal from our often painful histories and build a more whole and inclusive community

The tireless efforts of those who went before us—some successful, some only partially so—can teach all of us. Potent examples of struggles against racism, disease, and poverty can be found throughout history. We have chosen to examine the impact that polio and child labor had on children and their families. To better understand racism's effect we examine two examples: Indian boarding schools and the enslavement of African people in America. We examine the problems as they affected children, the strategies used by those either working for change or coping with the conditions, and how the strategies created a better situation for children. Although these examples do not provide in-depth analysis of each problem, they do give us tools for understanding. They surround us with hope that we can also create a better world for children.

There are years that ask questions and years that answer.

– Zora Neale Hurston

Children and Polio

Polio is an acute viral infection caused by any one of three polio viruses. It is spread by contact with an infected person or with human feces that contain the polio virus. It can affect both children and adults, but those most at risk in the first part of this century were children from five to eight years old and pregnant women (Black, 1996). The first sizable polio epidemic in the United States was in 1894. In 1916 another epidemic occurred, with 28,767 cases reported. There were 6,000 deaths, 2,407 in New York City alone. People were so frightened they tried to flee the city, but police halted them on train platforms and roads. Hospitals wouldn't take polio patients because staff feared contagion (Cohn, 1976). The polio epidemic again dominated the news in the 1940s and 1950s, with the greatest epidemic occurring in 1946. Parents feared for their children. The summer months carried the highest risk of transmission. Consequently, children were kept inside and away from crowds. Swimming pools, beaches, and summer camps were closed. Any fever or illness was watched very closely. Children felt the curtailment of their normal activity levels and the increasing level of their parents' fear.

Years ago when a mother gave birth, she could not assume that she would see her child grow to become a strong, healthy adult. The death of an infant was so common that some parents waited to name a child until their second year when they were sure the baby had survived the greatest risks (Elkind, 1994). For example, in 1845 in New York City, one-fourth of the children died in their first year, one-third died before five, and one-half before age twenty (Bremner, 1970). Death and disease were constant threats.

By the 1940s and 1950s medical advances had reduced the occurrence of fatal diseases in children. However, polio continued to strike children and adults, and there was little hope for a cure.

A runny nose and a slight fever became cause for concern. For some, this is where it started and ended. For others, what appeared at first to be a case of the sniffles was followed by a ravaging fever, headache, and nausea. Next came a stiff neck and backache. If a doctor diagnosed polio, it conjured images parents couldn't bear to imagine. They had seen people who had polio and were suffering from contracted muscles that twisted and pulled their limbs into unnatural positions. They knew neighbors who had experienced the excruciating pain and paralysis that could result. They feared the pictures they had seen of those who could no longer breathe on their own and were dependent on an iron lung. Worst of all, they knew that the number of people dying from polio increased every day.

Some people fully recovered. Others required months of physical therapy to regain partial use of the afflicted muscles. Therapists applied hot compresses to alleviate pain and loosen joints and muscles so they could begin to massage them. Some children saw the moist warmth of the compresses as momentary relief. Others couldn't bear the weight, feeling, or temperature of the compresses and fought to take them off (Black, 1996). At first, a therapist tried to lift or bend a child's knee or ankle, until the child could endure no more. Each day the therapist attempted just a little more movement in an effort to improve the range of motion.

Children who contracted polio were quarantined for ten to twenty-one days. Parents were unable to comfort their sick children because of strict hospital visitation rules that stemmed from fear of contagion and a lack of knowledge of children's needs (Black, 1996). Parents became so desperate to catch a glimpse of their stricken children that some leaned ladders against hospital walls to peer in the windows (Black, 1996).

Some children were determined to ride their bikes and to play ball with others again. They were encouraged by those around them to move their legs or arms on their own. Any flicker of movement was seen as

Pain, fear, frustration, and hope are the words one polio survivor associates with her disease. She graduated from high school in 1944, just one week before developing a high fever and neck pain. She remembers the anxious looks of those around her, beside themselves with fear, as the doctors told them she had polio.

The right side of her body was affected extensively, and she was told she would never walk again. Young and positive, she refused to give up. Hot packs, hot pools, and exercises were prescribed for her twisted limbs. She wore a cast at night and an uncomfortable, unsightly, steel brace for walking during the day.

For six months she continued with the extensive, painful therapy. Throughout her experience, she vowed she would overcome and would walk again. Her therapists encouraged her and praised her efforts. She felt lucky to receive treatment in New York, where state-of-the-art rehabilitation methods had been developed to treat former governor Franklin D. Roosevelt. Her hope and determination drove her to shed her steel brace. Fifty-four years later, she still walks unaided.

hope for recovery. With lots of persistence, drive, and hard work, many were able to regain use of their limbs. Some were fitted for crutches and braces. Others used wheelchairs to get about. Expensive renovations were needed to make homes accessible to wheelchairs. When that wasn't possible, families were forced to find new housing that could better accommodate the needs of their children.

Without knowing a way to prevent this unpredictable disease, fear mounted as people worried that their loved ones might be the next to fall prey. The public cried out for a cure that would stop the horrible suffering of polio. Nationwide fund-raising efforts began with a number of Birthday Balls held throughout the country in honor of polio survivor Franklin D. Roosevelt. Fund-raising efforts continued when the public was asked to help in the fight against polio by contributing any amount of money they could, even if it was just a dime. The response was overwhelming, with dimes pouring into the White House in what was to be the first March of Dimes drive (Smith, 1990).

The funds helped to pay for the medical care of thousands of polio patients. They also helped support polio research. Jonas Salk and his team of researchers urgently conducted trial after trial to determine what would be an effective and safe vaccine. Finally, Salk believed he had the answer. In 1954 and 1955 children lined up to be "Pioneers" in field-testing the inoculation. The vaccine quickly came into wide use in 1955 and helped to reduce the incidence of polio. An even more effective oral vaccine was introduced by Albert Sabin in 1961. This unique combination of science, public support, government, and business had brought this potentially crippling or fatal disease to an end in this country (Smith, 1990).

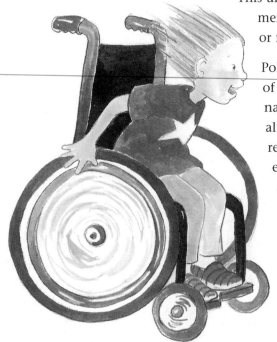

Polio was a frightening disease that threatened the health of thousands of children. However, with a concerted national effort, the incidence of polio has fallen to almost zero in this country. Dedicated scientists who researched vaccines won the battle against the virus, but equally inspiring were those who contracted the disease and those who treated them. The public was committed to giving money to support these two modalities, research and treatment. Because of these combined endeavors, children and their parents no longer need fear this deadly disease.

Children and Child Labor

Children have always worked. They often cared for animals, weeded fields, planted seed, picked cotton, cooked, cleaned, washed clothes, and helped to take care of their brothers and sisters. Usually all of this was done in the context of their families or through apprenticeships. The misuse of child labor became dangerous and problematic as the Industrial Revolution progressed, beginning in 1790. Children were working in food canneries, mills, coal mines, and glass factories. The work sites were more dangerous with the addition of machines and carried more health risks with the exposure to coal dust, glass fragments, and thread dust. The working conditions were abysmal. Children often worked twelve-hour days in dangerous, unhealthy conditions for very low wages. However, families needed the children's wages to survive because adults alone could not earn enough to support their families (Freedman, 1994). The numbers of children employed grew into the twentieth century. In 1870, 750,000 U.S. children from ten to fifteen years of age worked outside the home in nonagricultural settings. By 1910, 2,000,000 U.S. children were earning wages outside the home (Meltzer, 1994). In 1911 the country was shocked by the fire in the Triangle Shirtwaist factory in New York City. Nearly 150 workers, many of them young immigrant girls, were killed. Approximately 50 women jumped to their deaths. Others were burned or trampled to death. The building was a ten story loft. The sweatshop was on the three top floors. The doors by which the girls could have escaped were locked, and there was only one narrow fire escape. The tragedy highlighted the dangerous and inhumane conditions facing workers, especially child workers, in many factory settings.

Children as young as four years old were hired to work in mines, canneries, mills, and glass factories. Many rose before dawn to be at their jobs when the whistle blew at 5:00 a.m. They worked twelve to fourteen hours a day, six days a week, with only thirty minute breaks for breakfast and lunch (Bremner, 1970). Some jobs required children to be on their feet for most of the day. At other jobs they bent over their work for hours at a time. At 7:00 p.m., the end of the work day, tired children dragged themselves home, ate whatever meal was available, and fell into bed exhausted. Before fully rested, they woke again and returned to the same dull, repetitive tasks.

Children working in the cotton mills were given a variety of jobs: taking bobbins off the machines and replacing them, brushing lint from looms, and tying threads that broke. The workroom was kept uncomfortably hot and moist so that the threads didn't break as readily. Ventilation was poor and lint from the textiles filled the air. Many workers became ill with chronic respiratory difficulties.

In the coal mines, children were hitched to carts to pull the coal out of mines. They were also posted at doors, which they opened and closed as a cart came through. These "gatekeepers" waited in the dark for hours at a time with little to do before they were needed to open the door again. Other children worked as "coal breakers." They were seated over chutes that coal passed through. Their job was to sort the waste from the coal. They bent over chutes for hours at a time. The air they breathed was thick with black coal dust that covered their clothes and their bodies. Their fingers bled as they picked out the sharp pieces of slate and stone that didn't belong (Trattner, 1970).

Children worked under hazardous conditions whether they worked in the mills, the mines, or at other jobs. Some lost their lives, buried under the coal or burned by fire. Others suffered from disease, were stunted in growth, or sustained injuries that left them marred for life. The hours and physical demands of their work left little time, if any, for the children to devote to their education.

Many questions faced those adults who wanted to address reforms in child labor in the late 1800s and early 1900s. Beliefs at that time supported work and instilled a fear of idleness. Adults thought that hard work prepared children for the work they faced as they grew older. Poor families needed the wages of older children to feed and clothe the younger children. However, parents couldn't earn more as long as children could be hired for low wages. Manufacturers opposed attempts at reform due to the higher costs of hiring adults.

Reformers became concerned about the lack of education and the conditions under which children worked. They complained that children were not being prepared for future, meaningful work. Without time and energy to attend to their studies, these children would never have a chance at a better life. They argued that children were lacking the reading, writing, and reasoning skills needed to sustain a democracy. Education for citizenship became a focus.

To address both educational and safety concerns, the National Child Labor Committee (NCLC) was formed in 1904. Its stated purpose was to eliminate child labor. To get children the education and protection they needed, the NCLC conducted research on the numbers of children involved and conditions under which they worked. They also educated the public through lectures and publications, and they wrote and lobbied for effective legislation. The committee recognized that the problem of child labor was not taking place independent of other economic and social factors. They cooperated with educators to strengthen mandatory school attendance laws and to establish them where none existed. They worked with labor groups to write laws limiting the number of hours in a work week and to set minimum age requirements for employment. They collaborated with concerned organizations to advocate for support to families in need so they weren't dependent on their children's income (Trattner, 1970).

In 1908 the NCLC hired a photographer named Lewis Hines to assist in research and to photograph children at work. Hines was orphaned when he was fifteen years old and went to work in a furniture factory. There he worked fifteen hours a day, only to be rewarded at the end of the week with four dollars (Trattner, 1970). Even with these long hours and miserable wages, he was one of the determined who finished his education. He went on to obtain a master's degree. Although it was not his area of study, Hines had a special gift for photography and an interest in photographing poor people. He had a unique way of making people relax and capturing the essence of the scene.

The photographs he took of children working were meant to educate the public, enrage them about the conditions, and motivate them to support laws that protected children. Hines photographed children working in canneries, coal mines, glass factories, textile mills, on farms, and on the streets. Factory operators didn't want Hines to expose what was taking place. In order to gain entry into a factory, he sometimes had to hide his equipment. His photographs told a story that could not be denied. As they were published and reformers worked to make their cause known, a shift in philosophy slowly took place.

Even as the NCLC worked to raise public awareness about the conditions of child labor, the opposition the committee faced proved formidable. Many people continued to believe that work did not harm children. Mill operators argued they were supplying salaries to children whose families would be destitute without them (Trattner, 1970). Families continued to believe that children should and could contribute to the family's financial well-being, just as they always had. Children even signed petitions stating that they were satisfied with their work and wanted to be left alone (Trattner, 1970).

Although the opposition was strong and unbending, the NCLC never gave up. Throughout their struggle they worked with a variety of groups, looked at the problem from different perspectives, or approached it in new ways. Federal laws prohibiting child labor were twice struck down by the Supreme Court in Hammer v. Dagenhart in 1918 and Bailey v. Drexel Furniture Company in 1922. After the Triangle factory fire, many states adopted minimum age laws for

> I have learned to accept the fact that we risk disappointment, disillusionment, even despair, every time we act...and that there might be years during which our grief is equal to, or even greater than, our hope.
>
> –Alice Walker

employment, but they were ineffective and not enforced (Meltzer, 1994).

Finally, in 1938 the Fair Labor Standards Act (FLSA) was passed. This was a national law that limited the employment of children who are under sixteen years old, established a minimum wage that made it less profitable for employers to hire children, and set forty hours as the acceptable number of work hours within one week. In 1949 a more inclusive law covered the businesses of manufacturing, transportation, and communications. Finally, legislation was in place that effectively protected vast numbers of children.

In 1954, its fiftieth anniversary, the NCLC celebrated the elimination of child labor as it had been known. But the NCLC has not considered its work complete. Members continue to combat violations of child labor laws, to make school more meaningful to children, and to support legislation that provides economic security for families (Trattner, 1970).

The NCLC had to try a variety of strategies to combat child labor. They worked to implement state laws to protect children, but they found these laws only protected a fraction of the children working. When state laws didn't adequately address the issue, they developed national labor laws that benefited both children and adults. It took almost fifty years to put these protections into place, but the reformers did not give up. Although our country has had these laws for sixty years, children continue to be misused in the labor market. The NCLA and other advocate groups for children continue to monitor conditions for children.

Children in Indian Boarding Schools

The history of education for Indians in the United States is a tragic chapter in American history. Through oppressive, insidious, and pernicious federal government policies and legislation, Indian people were deprived of their nomadic existence and were confined and geographically segregated on Indian reservations. The cultural warfare was supported by federally mandated boarding schools for Indian children, where the price of attaining literacy was the devastation and destruction of the children's tribal cultures, languages, and religions.

The indigenous population of the Americas was decimated by genocide, diseases, and warfare beginning with the first contact with European explorers in 1492. Estimates of the Native population in North America at that time ran from 1,500,000 to 5,000,000. By 1910 the native population in this country was at

220,000 people (Waters, 1993). Disease, skirmishes and wars, the massacres of buffaloes, massive relocations, and the establishment of reservations in 1854 had devastated American Indians and their life as they knew it.

By the 1800s, the policy of the U.S. government was to assimilate American Indian people. Education was viewed by policy makers as a primary way to implement this. In 1855 mission schools were funded by Congress to educate Indian children. In 1879 the Bureau of Indian Affairs established non-reservation Indian boarding schools in five states (Carlisle, Pennsylvania; Chemawa, Oregon; Lawrence, Kansas; Genoa, Nebraska; Chilocco, Oklahoma). Children were expected to learn the three Rs (reading, writing, and arithmetic) plus vocational skills. They marched to class and were timed by hourly bells. Children were severely punished for speaking in their native language or practicing their religion (Ballantine and Ballantine, 1993). This separation of children from their families and way of life caused great anguish and anger for both the children and their parents.

Traditionally, the education of American Indian children was done by the family. Parents, grandparents, and extended family members taught children what they needed to survive, to be responsible, and to be a part of the tribe. Children learned these skills through a healthy mix of watching, listening, and playing. They were taught with patience and gentle admonishments. For some offenses, some children were shunned or threatened with make-believe monsters. When a child was really misbehaving, he might hear, "The white man will come and take you to his home" (Riley, 1993). For thousands of Indian children, this became a reality.

As white settlers arrived, their attitude was one of cultural superiority. Indians were viewed as barbarians, incapable of leading a civilized existence. Many believed that American Indians should be taught the ways of European-Americans and assimilated into the American mainstream so they would no longer be distinct groups of people.

White leaders soon came to believe they could reach their goals more quickly if Indian children were taken far from their surroundings and immersed in what white people considered a more civilized society. In 1889 the Commissioner of Indian Affairs wrote, "The American Indian is to become the Indian American" (Strickland, 1982). The goal was to end the tribe as a separate political and cultural unit, to destroy the heritage of the American Indian people and replace it with white American's heritage (Strickland, 1982). Education was seen as the way to achieve this goal. In the beginning, government used the church to

Just as a tree without roots is dead, a people without history or cultural roots also becomes a dead people.

—Malcolm X

educate Indian children. The U.S. government would pay mission schools per Indian child. Later they built schools and gave land to the church (Deloria, 1992). They divided the country by denomination. Some of the denominations listed in a budget allocation document from those times were Presbyterian, Congregational, Episcopal, Friends, Mennonite, Lutheran, Unitarian, and Methodist, with the most money going to Catholic Missions (Washburn, 1973). In 1879 H. John Pratt founded the first federal off-reservation boarding school in Carlisle, Pennsylvania. It was located in an unused military base (Strickland, 1982). By the end of the nineteenth century, off-reservation boarding schools were educating thousands of American Indian children. At the height of their existence, thirty-five off-reservation boarding schools and numerous mission schools performing the same functions were in operation (Hirschfelder and de Montano, 1993).

The attitudes of Indian parents toward these far away schools differed. Many parents wanted their children to receive the education that was being offered, but they also wanted children close to home so they could learn the values and traditions of their own tribes. When this option wasn't allowed, many said that their children should go to school so they could help their tribe communicate with the outsiders. Other parents sent their children as a sign of bravery, or so their children could learn to adapt to the changes brought on by white people. Still others, suffering from the poverty that resulted from confinement and a loss of traditional sources of food and resources, sent their children because of the promise of food and clothing (Hoxie, 1996).

Some families resisted. They hid their children or refused to let them go. In response, the government passed the Appropriations Act of 1892, which required Indian children to attend school (Strickland, 1982). If parents did not cooperate, the federal agents were allowed to withhold rations from the parents. If this method of coercion was not enough to prompt compliance, children were forcibly removed from their homes.

In these military-type schools, children marched from dormitory and classroom and stood at attention until permission was granted to take their seats. Children were not allowed to speak their native languages. Infractions of the rules were met with strict discipline, such as shaving their heads, being whipped with belts, or being put alone into dark rooms (Lomawaima, 1994). Instruction consisted of a standard didactic curriculum, foreign to Indian children, and presented in English. Children studied in the morning, then were assigned household, carpentry, and farming chores in the afternoons. Schools would not have survived without the work of the children to support them.

While some children endured the changes that were thrust upon them, others defied them. They resisted as children might, dawdling at tasks, being uncooperative, and arranging pranks. Many physically participated in what was required but refused to embrace the new ways. In his life story, *Lame Deer: Seeker of Visions*, Lame Deer says, "I played the dumb Indian. They couldn't make me into an apple—red outside and white inside. From their point of view I was a complete failure" (qtd. in Riley, 1993).

Children held strong to the memories of families and traditions, and most returned to the reservation as soon as they were allowed. Some couldn't wait until their mandatory school years were completed. These children ran away. Officials went to great lengths to track runaway children and bring them back to the school. They were often severely punished for their attempts to return to their families.

Many children formed friendships with each other around their shared suffering. These relationships gave them courage and strength and helped them to remember their tribal and family life before the boarding school. These linkages strengthened political unity when, as adults, they entered the struggle to help their people (Ballantine and Ballantine, 1993).

Upon graduation from school, children found the education they received did not meet their needs on the reservation. Nor did their education sufficiently prepare them to find work and live in urban settings. They were often confused by the contrast between what they had been taught in school and their traditional upbringing. Some felt broken, as if they didn't belong in either world. No longer fluent in their languages, they felt like semi-strangers among their own people. Frequently they returned to learn that their loved ones had died while they were away (Ballantine and Ballantine, 1993).

Indian leaders had long been voicing their displeasure with the education their children were receiving, but their opinions were rarely publicized (Szasz, 1974). In 1928 a comprehensive study known as the Meriam Report revealed the inadequacies in education for Indian children and the abysmal conditions found in Indian boarding schools. It reported on overcrowded conditions that led to the spread of germs and disease, illnesses children suffered without adequate health care, and underestimated death rates. It told of insufficient amounts of food and of poor nutrition, leaving children near starvation. It exposed the conditions of broken-down buildings and the fire hazards they presented. In addition, it criticized the long and routinized hours required of the children (Wub-e-ke-niew, 1995).

The report recommended that the education of Indian children be closely tied to their communities and located in day schools that

Although the government saw boarding schools as a solution to the "Indian problem," the boarding school system itself became the problem. The true results were emotional damage…to our young children…the breakdown of tribal culture and language, and the alienation of Indian parents from the education of their children.

—Karen Gayton Swisher

could double as activity centers. It also recommended that Indian culture be introduced to the curriculum and that staff be better compensated and qualified.

According to Joe Kingbird (1997), "The Meriam Report was a catalyst for social change regarding Indian affairs. In response to this report, Congress passed the Indian Reorganization Act in 1934. This act ended the regimentation found in boarding school. Day schools were soon established on Indian reservations."

However, the boarding schools continued to operate as well. Another report, the Senate Subcommittee Report on Indian Education, was published in 1969, forty years later. It found little progress had been made at the boarding schools since the writing of the Meriam Report. The recommendations made in this second report echoed the first. In addition, it advised that Indian parents be involved in making decisions regarding their children's education. As the Handbook of Federal Indian Law reports, "Increasingly the goal of federal policy has been to achieve greater control and involvement by Indian parents, whether education is provided by the state or by the tribe" (Strickland, 1982).

Tribal leaders spoke up and fought for control over education, tribal restoration, self-government, culture renewal, and self-sufficiency. Finally, in the mid-1970s the general public recognized the importance of culture in the lives of the tribes. Two pieces of legislation, the Indian Education Act (1972) and the Indian Self-Determination and Education Assistance Act (1975), were passed by Congress that funded bilingual and bicultural education and gave responsibility to tribes for making educational policies.

The following three factors came together to change the way American Indians were educated:

> Public opinion began to shift from beliefs about assimilation to recognition of the importance of culture

> Indian leaders took control of educating Indian children

> Laws were passed allowing changes within the infrastructure of the system

Boarding schools still operate today. Through the efforts of Indian parents, tribal leaders, and reformers, the schools that once existed to assimilate Indians into the Eurocentric mainstream now successfully teach Indian culture. They help children recapture a sense of their heritage and keep tradition alive, and educate them to survive in the dominant culture as well.

Children in Slavery

Since European explorers landed on the shores of this continent, vast numbers of children have been affected by racism and prejudice. This racism in attitudes and practices formed the foundation for laws that codified discrimination in our society. Certainly, all of us have experienced prejudice due to personal characteristics such as weight, immigrant status, hair color, or gender. However, only some children have experienced the societal discrimination that was based on race or cultural identity and restricted opportunities, dismantled cultural traditions and beliefs, and enforced a permanent underclass status by law. This history has been particularly destructive for children.

European slave trade began in 1444 and continued for more than 400 years. It is estimated that Africa lost 40 million people, 15 million to 20 million of whom were brought to the New World (Bennett, 1969). However, these numbers are difficult to substantiate because of little or no documentation. Some estimates run much higher. The first slaves to arrive in the English colonies, about twenty in number, came ashore at Jamestown, Virginia, in 1619. However, decades passed before significant numbers of African people were brought to the colonies.

Although the northern colonies practiced slavery to some extent, it flourished in the South, where large plantations required a large labor force to cultivate crops of tobacco, rice, and sugar cane. After the invention of the cotton gin in 1793, cotton could be prepared for marketing so rapidly that the demand for cotton increased and, consequently, so did the demand for field hands to raise and pick cotton. The number of Africans forced into slavery hit a peak of 6 million in the eighteenth century.

The triangular slave trade was a highly profitable business. Ships would leave England with trade goods and land first at the west coast of Africa, where they exchanged their merchandise for African people. The slaves were usually captives taken in raids and wars and sold by tribal chiefs. More than likely, the tribal chiefs had little understanding or knowledge of what faced the captives as they were loaded on the ships. The journey from West Africa to the New World has been labeled the "Middle Passage." This Middle Passage was harrowing, with many Africans jammed into the hull, chained to prevent revolts or suicides. As many as 20 to 50 percent of the African slaves died on the journey. The ships would stop in either the West Indies or the English colonies, where the slaves were exchanged for agricultural products such as sugar. Then the ship would return to England. As Grolier states, "The point on which the triangular trade precariously balanced was the African slave, who was a source of wealth to tribal chiefs, to the shipping business, to plantation owners in the South, and to merchants and shipbuilders in the North" (Grolier, 1993).

The millions of people affected by the institution of slavery are staggering. The numbers involved can so overwhelm us that we forget the individual tragedies for families and children. Certainly, children raised in a family enslaved by others were affected in every part of their lives.

Slaves were owned as property and could be sold, punished, or abused at the will of their owners. The life of the slave, then, depended heavily on the owner. If the owner died, the slaves' situations could change very quickly depending on the whims of the new owners. Some slaves worked in cities as domestics, skilled artisans, and factory hands (Bennett, 1969). Others worked on small farms where the slaves numbered from two to thirty. Some Africans had been freed and found their living as they could. Africans in the above situations fared somewhat better than their counterparts on big plantations numbering a thousand or more slaves. Almost half of the slaves lived, worked, and died on plantations where treatment by an overseer was often brutal (Bennett, 1969).

The torment of enslaved African people began with the Middle Passage, the route between West Africa and the New World. Initially every slave on board the ship was branded with a hot iron. Women were lashed severely for crying. The slave traders used torture and brutality to "tame or break in Africans" so white colonizers would approve of the "docile" slaves. To achieve this, the slave traders took away people's names and tribal status, mixed up the tribal groups so there was no common language, took away clothes and possessions from Africa, forbade any religious ceremonies, and used torture to instill fear in the Africans (hooks, 1981).

Women represented one-third of the human cargo and were subject to rape and subsequent pregnancies. The numbers of black women who died during childbirth and the numbers of stillborn children will never be known. Slave traders would also torture children to break the will of the women. Ruth and Jacob Weldon, an African couple who experienced the horrors of the Middle Passage, told of an incident they had witnessed. A slave trader flogged a child continuously for hours when he refused to eat. When the flogging didn't work, the captain ordered the child be placed feet first into a pot of boiling water. When the child still did not eat, the captain dropped the child, causing its death, and ordered the mother to throw the body overboard (hooks, 1981).

Some white people who saw Africans leave the ships upon arrival noted they were happy and joyful. The whites assumed they were happy to be arriving in a Christian land. Instead, they were only expressing relief at leaving the horrific slave ships (hooks, 1981).

Once the Africans came ashore, they were sold. Conditions at various farms and plantations varied greatly. Some owners were more or less humane and less inclined to punish. Still, the slaves were treated condescendingly, as ignorant children, even when they weren't treated brutally. Other owners used methods of domination, torture, and intimidation to control slaves. The punishments were often arbitrary and difficult for slaves to predict. For example, Sojourner Truth was sold when she was nine years old to a couple who spoke English. She had grown up speaking Dutch. When she didn't do what her mistress requested because she didn't understand the words, she was punished. One time she was beaten until blood streamed from her body with rods heated in embers (Washington, 1993). Floggings were used on a regular basis to punish slaves who did not comply with rules, tried to escape, or questioned authority.

Whether the master was humane or brutal, the fact remained that the enslaved Africans were regarded as property to be sold, hired out, or controlled how and when the owner decided. This fact changed African families under slavery and how they raised their children.

Legally, slave families did not exist. Although marriage was sometimes performed by a minister and respected by slaves themselves, it was not protected by law. This meant the union could be dissolved by the sale of one of the spouses or by any of a number of arbitrary decisions by the master (Bremner, 1970). Masters often arranged marriages or would use African women to breed children to be used as slaves (hooks, 1981). Even young adolescent African girls were at risk for sexual assault by overseers and white masters (hooks, 1981). How did this power that white owners had over the lives of African slaves affect children?

Accounts told by freed slaves are filled with stories of separation from their families. Frederick Douglass, a prominent black abolitionist, was separated from his mother before he was a year old. She was hired out to a farm a long distance away. Before she died she visited him four times. She walked the twelve miles at night and then returned by sunrise to escape a beating (Bremner, 1970).

In traditional African societies, women keep their children close to them, only weaning them when they are almost three years old.

Until the weaning, sexual intercourse is not allowed (hooks, 1981). On plantations, mothers were expected to return to work in a few weeks, breaking traditional child care patterns. They were also expected to have sexual intercourse as soon as possible to produce more offspring (hooks, 1981). The workday for adults often began at 4:00 a.m. and ended many hours later. If the moon was full, labor did not stop until the middle of the night. Only on Sunday and periodic holidays were families able to spend time together. While their parents were in the fields, young children were cared for in a plantation nursery. One account of these nurseries describes about twenty-seven young children, mostly infants, being cared for in one cabin by one older woman and a few older children. Few of the babies were held or played with (Bremner, 1970).

Frederick Douglass described his life as a child on a plantation in his autobiography. He was not given sufficient clothing, especially in the winter. He wore shoes and a linen shirt down to his knees—no trousers, no stockings, and no jacket. He didn't have a bed, so he used a bag that was used to carry corn to the mill. He crawled in and slept on the cold damp floor. Meat was only given to adult males, so children were fed boiled corn. On this plantation, a large wooden tray or trough was set down for all the children. They weren't given

William Brown, a slave and an assistant to a slave trader, escaped from slavery in 1834. He recounted how a mother was separated from her baby by the actions of a trader. Brown described his feeling of horror and wrote of the vivid image of loss that haunts him.

He was traveling with Mr. Walker, a slave trader, to St. Louis along the Missouri River with approximately twenty-five men and women who were going to be sold. Walker and William Brown were on horses, and the slaves were chained together. One woman had a child in her arms who was only a few weeks old. The journey was difficult and took a long time. The child was very cross and

cried most of the day. Mr. Walker reprimanded the mother, but she couldn't keep the child quiet.

They stayed that night at an acquaintance of Walker's. In the morning the child began to cry again. Walker took the child by one arm and presented it to the lady of the house where they were staying. The mother fell on her knees and clung to Walker's legs. She cried, "Oh, my child! My child! Master, do let me have my child…I will stop its crying."

Walker ordered her to return to the slaves. She was put in chains with the others because only women with children were allowed to walk without restraints.

spoons, so they used their hands, shingles, or oyster shells to eat. The person who ate the fastest got the most.

These bleak pictures of floggings, separations, and drudgery allow little hope to emerge. However, the human spirit of the African people did find ways to keep and renew their sense of family, their human dignity, and their hope that freedom would be gained. Slaves resisted in the ways available to them: passive day-to-day resistance (such as working no harder than they had to), deliberate slow-downs, strikes, breaking implements, and trampling crops. There were also repeated insurrections, which were put down with severe punishments and hangings. Slaves ran away to Canada, Mexico, and to the swamps of Florida and established independent "maroon" communities (Bennett, 1969). The word *maroon* is derived from the Spanish word *cimarron* which was used to describe a domestic animal that had escaped and gone back to the wild. Escaped slaves took the word to describe their communities. In the 1840s Harriet Tubman led the Underground Railroad. The Underground Railroad was a network of safe houses and routes that helped slaves escape to the North. The escapees were aided by fellow slaves and liberal whites who provided lodging and other kinds of assistance.

Africans kept their heritage and memories alive through stories, music, and dancing. Sojourner Truth tells of how her mother told stories about her twelve brothers and sisters who had been sold away from their family. Because her mother was so careful to talk about them, name them, and keep them alive in memory, Sojourner Truth spent time after she was freed looking for them and was able to find several of her siblings (Washington, 1993).

One study of slave narratives described the games of enslaved children. Even their games communicated and taught values that helped a community survive. One very interesting characteristic is the absence of games that required the elimination of players. The rules of the games always include ways for the children to rejoin and start the game over. Hiner and Hawes (1985) speculated that this reflected the emphasis the slave community put on cooperation and community spirit. A sense of loyalty and group solidarity was essential for survival, especially when fathers, mothers, siblings, or any of the extended family could be sold or hired out at any time.

Some games reenacted events such as baptisms, funerals, and auctions. This play helped children deal with their anxieties and learn the values of cooperation and solidarity (Hiner and Hawes, 1985). Some rhyme and ring games would berate whites in songs, giving children a sense of empowerment:

> "My old mistress promised me,
> Before she dies she would set me free.

Slavery was meant to break our spirits and kill us, but the flip side went against that, because for some, it just made us stronger.

—Garlana Hill,
high school student

Now she's dead and gone to hell
I hope the devil will burn her well."
(Hiner and Hawes, 1985)

In the end, all the individual insurrections, escapes, or coping mechanisms did not change the institutional reality of slavery. It took a larger effort, enormous risk, and loss. The first organized opposition to slavery was started by the Quakers in 1724. Individual states banned slavery, beginning with Rhode Island in 1774. However, slavery was still protected by law in the Southern states. In the 1800s significant opposition to slavery gained ground both in Europe and the United States. The American Anti-Slavery Society held its first convention in Philadelphia in 1833. Many participants shared accounts about the dehumanization and brutality of slavery. In 1831 William Lloyd Garrison published the Liberator, an abolitionist newspaper, to build public sentiment against slavery. By 1840 the Underground Railroad was helping slaves escape to the North. Harriet Beecher Stowe wrote *Uncle Tom's Cabin*, which further stimulated anti-slavery feelings in the North. Abolitionist speakers who had lived under slavery's oppression, such as Sojourner Truth and Frederick Douglass, went around the country speaking to groups. Sojourner Truth was often harassed. In one town she was mauled by a mob, which caused her to walk with a cane for the rest of her life. In another town, she was told that the building she was to speak in would be burned if she attempted her address. Her answer clearly demonstrates the courage and resolve shared by many of those fighting against slavery. She answered, "Then I will speak to the ashes" (Washington, 1993).

Abolition of slavery became a major issue during Lincoln's presidential campaign. The nation could not survive half-slave, half-free. Consequently, the Civil War was fought partly over the issue of slavery. Approximately 900,000 soldiers lost their lives in this war.

In 1863 Lincoln signed the Emancipation Proclamation that declared all slaves free. Over 200 years of legal slavery ended when the United States passed the 13th Amendment in 1865. This amendment constitutionally abolished all slavery.

The legacies of slavery and the Indian boarding schools, with their attendant racism, live on today, even if the legalized institution of slavery and the harsh practices in federal boarding schools have ended. As a country, we still face complex issues in working to end the painful aspects of these legacies. Other cultural and racial groups also have legacies of oppression that remain unhealed. For example, the history of migrant workers in this country, many of whom are people of color, is one of abuse and exploitation. Pay is low, work hours are long and unpredictable, housing and education have been inadequate, and frequent moves are required to find work. Another example is the story of Japanese Americans who were forced to relinquish their property and reside in camps during the Second World War, although they had committed no crimes and many of them were American citizens.

But ending slavery and changing the methods of Indian education were victories. These victories were not won easily. Thousands of people risked and lost their lives. Many others were trampled before they could be rescued. Their examples help us understand why we need to be actively involved in the lives of our children and what can be at risk if we aren't.

Learning from History

The four historical situations we have presented are dramatic and sweeping. History helps us:

> Understand current problems and how they developed

> Learn strategies that worked for significant change

> Learn individual coping strategies that worked

> Understand the urgency of our problems and what we risk if we do not act

> Receive inspiration and hope

> Heal from our shared histories

As we researched past events we noted that many of the strategies for change were similar or had common threads running through them. In all the examples, those working for change did the following:

1. Researched the problem
   They observed, gathered stories, took pictures, and collected hard statistical data to define the problem.

2. Publicized the problem
   Activists used books, newspapers, speakers, political networks, and all available avenues they could to reach the general public and create alliances.

3. Built a consensus for change
   They used organizations, research, religious and cultural traditions, and their shared values to build a consensus for change.

4. Raised Funds
   They found creative ways, such as the March of Dimes, to raise funds to support research, speaking, and lobbying.

5. **Strengthened and supported individual children and groups of children**

   Groups worked to create legislation or national campaigns such as the polio vaccination push, the anti-slavery movement, or the Labor Act of 1934. Other groups worked with individual children. For example, treating those affected by polio or Indian parents who worked to keep cultural and religious traditions alive for their children.

6. **Conducted continual evaluation**

   All efforts required constant evaluation and reformulating to take into account emerging issues. And even though in each situation stated goals were met, we still need to work on new fronts. For example, we still want to end racism, fight for children's health, and end the exploitation of children.

7. **Kept hope alive**

   All examples demonstrate the power of hope and how it is a necessary ingredient in all efforts to create change. Without that vision and hope, the setbacks people experienced would have caused them to stop altogether.

The participants who changed the course of history for children addressed issues wherever it was needed—at the national level, the community level, and the individual level. They did not narrow their vision to only one kind of intervention. We too can and must address current issues on all fronts. We must start with an understanding of hope and how it nourishes us, as did those who came before us. We must visualize a future, hope for that future, and work to create that future.

Chapter Three

Starting with Hope

In our historical examples, we see hope intertwined with each attempt at change. In the fight against polio, hope kept the researchers searching for the most effective vaccine, the victims of polio's damage reaching toward recovery, and the public supporting all these efforts by holding Birthday Balls and saving dimes in March of Dimes folders. In the fight against child labor, hope continued even when laws protecting children were struck down by the Supreme Court, even when it took at least fifty years of constant work to pass a law that would limit child labor, and even when small children had to find some way to get through each day's toil. In the Indian boarding schools, children hoped for the time when they would return to the reservation, parents hoped that their children would return with more education and a continuing connection to family and tribe, and Indian leaders who spoke out hoped that they would be heard and that laws would be passed by Congress that protected the children and their heritage. During the years of slavery, African Americans hoped for freedom. Hope was in the hearts of those who attempted escape and in the hearts of those all over the United States who spoke out against the evils of slavery.

In these examples, resolution did not necessarily occur in the time or manner expected. Disappointments and setbacks plagued all those who struggled. But this fact does not alter the tremendous power and motivation hope brings us. When he was in prison, President Václav Havel of Czechoslovakia said that hope "is an ability to work for something because it is good, not just because it stands a chance to succeed...It is also this hope, above all, which gives us the strength to live and continually to try new things, even in conditions that seem as hopeless as ours do here and now" (qtd. in Edelman, 1992).

The historical examples we researched contain much pain and sorrow. The circumstances may seem extreme and removed from our own daily existence. However, all of us face difficult situations that test our resolve. Some of us experience divorce and dislocation. Others fight the effects of diseases such as cancer, heart disease, and AIDS. Some of us are afraid we will not be able to feed and house our children. Many parents have children with disabilities who require constant energy, advocacy, and sensitive decision making. Some of us are afraid our children will be injured or killed by police violence. Many of us fear violence in our children's schools. All of us face the deaths of loved ones, such as our parents, siblings, and even our children. Natural disasters like floods, hurricanes, earthquakes, and tornadoes often happen without warning. Events unfold that cannot be controlled or stopped. Hope is an integral part of the resolve to continue. Without hope each of us would give up or let events such as these take their course without trying to reach better solutions.

When we think about how we might impart hope to children, we are left with many questions:

- What exactly is hope?
- Do you just stumble onto hope?
- Are you born with hope?
- Does hope ebb and flow with life's changing circumstances?
- How do you hang onto hope when facing overwhelming odds?
- Can you teach hope?
- Do others give you hope, or is it internal?
- How do you pull hope from hopelessness?

We suspect that some individuals are born with a tendency to see hope around every corner and that others stumble onto it when encountering problems. Hope does recede when life is hard. Others do support and give hope, sometimes simply by listening. Yet hanging onto the hope of a better time must lie partly within an individual and a people. We believe that we can teach a more hopeful approach to life. We are part of an experiment to define how we consciously build hope in the hearts of our young children.

Elements of Hope

What do we learn about hope from historical examples and from our own experiences? What about hope do we emphasize? The elements of hope are difficult to separate from each other. Certainly there will always be an intangible quality that cannot be defined. However, if we are to instill hope in our children, we must understand the components of hope that will help teach the concept. What are the elements of hope that we pull out of the historical examples?

Elements of Hope

1. Ability to project a better future
2. Ability to suspend reality
3. Ability to reframe

4. A connection to greater meaning or purpose

5. Belief in oneself

6. Ability to see a plan

7. Ability to withstand failure

8. Ability to control aspects of a plan

9. Finding the support of others

10. Hearing the struggles of others

11. Finding inspiration

1. Ability to Project a Better Future

In each of the historical examples, participants could envision a future that would be better than the present. Without this vision propelling them forward, they could not have found the strength to overcome or even to survive.

This ability to see that things will get better is echoed in most people's description of how they maintain hope. Children cannot always envision the future, especially when they are very young and grounded in the present. Adults need to reassure them that things can get better.

The Toaster

Our old one was ancient,
had been in the family for dozens of years.
It spit the bread out
long before it was cooked enough.
We'd try to push it back in again,
it growled with angry electrical sounds.
One night, it turned into a ravaging dragon,
burned holes in the bottoms of paper plates
before I tossed it in the sink to douse it out.

The new toaster has extra wide slots.
I can toast four Eggo waffles at once if I want.
Its shining chrome stays cool to the touch.
Settings go as high as nine but I know five
makes the perfect piece of toast.
The children were so impressed.
Waffles tasted twice as nice and they saw
after so much sadness
our lives would be better again.

—Ronna Hammer

2. Ability to Suspend Reality

To endure stress and overcome it, it is necessary to escape from it for brief periods of time. When polio victims faced the fear of further paralysis or the inability to ever walk again, part of surviving was to get away from the pain, whether it was through conversation, humor, or meditation.

Sometimes children use play to perform this function. All is forgotten as they sing to their dolls, cook, or drive their toy trucks. Adults suspend reality in a variety of ways, including reading for pleasure, movies, theater, sports, and music.

Humor is a saving grace in the midst of life's problems. In the most sorrowful of times, humor gives us relief, brings a laugh, and builds a common connection. In the middle of funerals, families can smile or laugh as memories flood them. After a successful surgery, waiting relatives often express their relief with a joke. After we have found these brief escapes from reality, we can return renewed and ready to tackle even the thorniest issue.

Everyone, regardless of how naturally optimistic he or she is, has to work at remaining positive.

—Lenda Murray

3. Ability to Reframe

Changing our perspective when confronting problems is key to finding the best solution and fending off depression. We need the ability to reframe how we interpret problems, how we think about ourselves and our mistakes, and how we think about the actions of others.

When the reformers were working to find the best solution to the child labor problem, they highlighted the abysmal working conditions and developed state laws. However, these state laws did not adequately protect all children. The reformers had to reinterpret the problem in a broader way and focus on national legislation to achieve their goals. They used alliances they had built with labor unions to address working conditions and work hours for all. This produced a better solution for all.

Optimism and hope are built when we reframe how we see our own behavior. The child or adult who sees problems as the result of her personal unworthiness rather than just a human mistake, an illness, or the unfairness of a system will not be able to overcome adversity easily. For example, racism fosters this sense of personal unworthiness in people of color and undercuts natural abilities and confidence. Reframing can help people of color interpret a system that continues to discriminate unfairly by demonstrating that the system is at fault, not individuals or individual efforts.

How we see our personal mistakes, accidents, or failures can cause self-blame and denigration, or it can simply point to a change in behavior that will repair the mistake. If a child spills milk on the table, the child may think she is clumsy, awkward, and always spilling everything, or she may think "I am in a hurry, so I guess I need to slow down." The first interpretation will result in more self-recriminations, especially if reinforced by an adult. The second interpretation will result in a change of behavior. The adult can encourage this interpretation by treating the event calmly and suggesting that the child may have been in a hurry and that she can help clean up the spill.

Reframing also means taking another's perspective as problems occur. Looking at what others may be feeling about the same situation will bring a broadened view of the issue. For example, a child is playing quietly at the stove in the house corner. Another child steps next to her and pushes her a little. The first child gets mad and slaps the second child. By this time the incident is loud and disruptive with the children blaming each other. If the adult can help the first child understand that the second child wants to play, especially before the fight begins, the problem is reframed, the fight is avoided, and the children may actually choose to play together.

4. A Connection to Greater Meaning or Purpose

Spiritual connections, beliefs, and purpose can lift many from the immediate pain of a crisis and give them the strength to confront reality. For many Africans forced to work against their will as slaves in a strange country, spiritual faith was part of what kept them functioning on a daily basis. It gave their lives meaning and formed a foundation for shared values and ethical practice.

Faith can also provide a vision or purpose for the future. This purpose can find expression through the arts, a vocation, religious faith, a cause, or a spiritual quest. Nineteenth century and early twentieth century child labor reformers were dedicated to the cause of ending child labor. This purpose kept them searching for the right approach to publicizing the problems and changing the laws.

5. Belief in Oneself

Children and adults find more hope when they believe that others love them and believe in them. This belief can help carry them through immediate crises and through long-term illnesses or difficulties. Polio victims needed that belief as they confronted the pain and disability. They also found hope in their confidence that they could find the will to do the exercises, walk with a brace, or learn to use crutches.

Hopes are white stones shining up from the bottom of pools, and every clear day we reach in…, selecting a few and rearranging the others, drawing our arms smoothly back into the air, leaving no scar on the water.

—Natalie Kusz

6. Ability to See a Plan

A person who can see a plan has hope that things will change. After the Meriam Report outlined the terrible conditions in the Indian boarding schools, Indian leaders had official backing for their anger and outrage about the treatment of their children. They also could point to the recommendations made in the report. Equally important is the ability to generate more than one plan. Jonas Salk found an effective polio vaccine, but Albert Sabin kept experimenting and found an even more effective one. Solving problems requires constant evaluation. Even if the first plan doesn't work, the ability and resolve to find many alternatives keeps a child or adult ready to work on the problem again.

7. Ability to Withstand Failure

Part of the cornerstone of hope and its renewal is the ability to withstand failure, sometimes over and over. The issues we examined in history took decades or even centuries to address effectively. And even now we see lingering effects or damage caused by these historical practices. The racism that fueled the institution of slavery continues to plague our society today. But we continue our efforts to erase racism and its effects. Failure may temporarily stop progress toward a goal, but it should not derail our efforts permanently. Rather than failure being a signal to stop, it becomes a signal to reevaluate.

Failure and success must be redefined so that we see small successes as accomplishments, even if the larger issues remain. Short of that, we change our goal to more appropriately fit the problem. When doctors, nurses, and parents worked with polio victims, they may have accepted that a certain child could not walk without assistance, but they helped the child learn to walk with crutches.

8. Ability to Control Aspects of a Plan

Some control is vital to building and maintaining hope. Control can increase the feeling of competency and give a person a chance to experiment with her own uniqueness and creativity. It gives us power rather than leaving us with the feeling that something has been done *to* us.

Control was taken away from the slaves and the Indian children in the boarding schools. The authorities attempted to break the will of those they controlled by using methods like cutting the Indian children's hair and dressing them in regulation clothes and controlling the type of work, family arrangements, and severity of punishments slaves endured, among other things. As individuals and groups of people, both Indian and African people found ways to take back some control over their lives. Some Indian children continued to practice their traditional religion in secret, and American Indian leaders demanded a change in laws to support their traditional culture. Slaves found ways to sabotage their work by slowing down or breaking equipment, and African Americans like Frederick Douglass and Sojourner Truth were at the forefront of the movement to abolish the institution of slavery.

9. Finding the Support of Others

The support of others echoes again and again in the stories of survivors. Support may involve only one person or many. It can be a parent, a minister, a spouse, a teacher, a friend, or a neighbor. This support can take many forms, such as financial support, guidance, listening, or simply expressing confidence in a person's abilities and motives. In every historical example we read about, the support of others is a primary theme. For polio victims, parents and extended family were essential to recovery. Without the support of adults addressing the issues of child labor, children would not have been given the opportunities of education. Indian children clung to one another and to memories of their families and tribes while residing at the schools. Enslaved Africans desperately needed one another to survive the painful existence of slavery, and they also needed allies to achieve freedom. Without the support of others, it is difficult to maintain hope and resolve.

Someday I will have a friend all my own. One I can tell my secrets to. One who will understand my jokes without my having to explain them.

—Sandra Cisneros, from *House on Mango Street*

10. Hearing the Struggles of Others

Hearing about and understanding how those who came before us overcame their struggles is paramount to the development of hope. These stories can be about famous heroes, family members, or a cultural heritage. Marian Wright Edelman tells us, "Remember your roots, your history, and the forebears' shoulders on which you stand…Young people who do not know where they come from and the struggle it took to get them where they are now will not know where they are going or what to do for anyone besides themselves if and when they finally get somewhere" (Edelman, 1992). These stories about overcoming struggles inspire us, teach us, and sometimes, in those darkest moments, keep us going. The stories need to focus on the struggles as well as the victories so children know that they may fail initially, but they can keep trying and eventually achieve their goals.

11. Finding Inspiration

While some find inspiration by hearing the struggles of other, many find the inspiration to keep going by other means as well. For instance, one can find inspiration in nature, animals and pets, friends, music, books, history, movies, faith, poetry, and human fellowship. Children often use play, music, and their delight in life to find inspiration. Each person is inspired in unique ways.

Finding Hope for Ourselves

As caregivers and people concerned about the welfare of young children, we instill hope everyday, whether it is by caring directly for children or by drawing the circles of support around them. By doing this, we are communicating optimism and hope for their future.

To do all of this, we must pay attention to one indisputable fact. It is hard work to design those circles of support. It is hard work to care for children. Many times it is thankless work. The children and their families often cannot give us enough support when we are discouraged. We see much to discourage us. We have too many children to care for. Government policies are inadequate. Systems such as child protective services don't protect all children. Colleagues leave the field in frustration. People who work with children are almost always underpaid and overworked. We do not see enough change. We also have to work to build our own hope for the future. How do we do this? If we return to our list of the elements of hope, we see how it applies directly to our profession.

Ability to Project a Better Future. We can see that even though it may be slow, things will improve for children as a result of our efforts. Even if we do not see the fruits of our labor, we have confidence that eventually the seeds will sprout.

Ability to Suspend Reality. We can take care of ourselves. As we do this stressful work, we can recognize when we need to escape for a while, perhaps through physical exercise, relaxation, reading, music, or laughter.

Ability to Reframe. We understand that true change takes time and consistent effort. We do not take setbacks personally but understand them as the result of mistakes, lack of information, or systemic difficulties. We look at the opinions and feelings of others to help us find better ways to form solutions.

A Connection to Greater Meaning or Purpose. We believe in what we are doing and that what we do makes a difference. Our purpose can come in a number of ways: faith, a love of children, a belief in families, or a vision for the future.

Belief in Ourselves. We believe in ourselves. We know that we have the skills to help children and families, or we know where to get them. We know that we take care of children because we want to and we are good at it.

Ability to See a Plan. When we encounter problems, we are able to formulate plans to solve them. When the first plan does not work, we think of other options. We welcome the opinions of others when we are overcoming difficulties.

Ability to Withstand Failure. We may get discouraged, but we see failure as a way to find a solution. We do not let failure stop us. We reevaluate when our plan fails and then try another option. We redefine success. We recognize when we have changed the life of one child in one way, even if others still suffer.

Ability to Control Aspects of a Plan. We do not let ourselves give in to helplessness. We see where we have control of a situation, even if it is not total control, and we find a way to use that control constructively.

Finding the Support of Others. We recognize that we are not alone in our concern and anguish over children and their families. We find support in professional organizations, with friends, with family, and with colleagues. We create our own network of support. We take hope from providing support to others, as well.

Hearing the Struggles of Others. We find heroes and heroines both from within and from outside of our profession. We draw strength from their resolve and successes. We recognize the many fine people who work in our field with great dedication.

Finding Inspiration. We find inspiration from many things, whether from a hike in the mountains, a new piece of music, a new activity that the children love, or our faith.

Hope is a powerful motivator. We can use it to help children and to help ourselves. Sometimes we can feel as though having hope, especially in a hopeless situation, is foolish and simple-minded. Once a friend of ours expressed this thought after hospitalizing her young daughter for the second time due to an ongoing chronic illness. This was after her daughter had struggled an entire year with life-threatening medical conditions and attendant depression and rage.

Every pearl is the result of an oyster's victory over an irritation.

—Juliet V. Allen

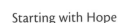

I get knocked down

But I get up again

You're never going to

Keep me down

— Chumbawamba

Our friend wanted to hope that her daughter would find help and some measure of peace and that life would again have moments of shared joy. But she felt like a fool who couldn't or wouldn't read all the signals. The signals were telling her that this child would not recover and that things were only going to continue to slide downward. After a long and heart-wrenching conversation, her pastor wisely told her that it was true that everything they were trying might not work and that her hope might not come to fruition. But what would her life be without that hope? By giving up hope, she would not only lose the powerful motivator hope gave her and her daughter, she would also diminish herself. Hope transforms us from feeling the cynicism to feeling the optimism, from feeling the despair to feeling the promise.

Hope motivates organized groups as well as individuals. One example of this is Mothers Against Drunk Driving (MADD). This organization was started by a group of mothers who had suffered the loss of their children in accidents caused by drunk drivers. They decided the laws were too lenient and favored those who carelessly drove when they were drunk. They have lobbied for and succeeded in passing numerous laws to reduce the amount of alcohol needed in the blood to be legally drunk, to raise the legal age of driving, and to stiffen sentences given to those convicted of drunk driving. All of this was done in the hope that no one will have to suffer their kind of loss again.

We must continually renew our hope as we create circles of support around children, whether in the classroom, in the community, or through policy. Just as those whose stories we have read, we can make positive changes for children. We wrote this book to explore concrete strategies that can work. We can focus on the national level, in the community, in the family, or in our care for children to impact the future of children in this country. We explore effective ways to move along the political and social agenda for children. We explore techniques and activities that teach children the strengths to sustain them in their personal journey. We begin this exploration with hope and a strong resolve to succeed.

Chapter Four

Rising to the Challenge

Building external supports for children can take place on a number of levels: on national and state levels, on the community level, in schools and child care programs, and in families.

We can advocate for children's issues with national or state policy makers. We can support families as they struggle to balance their commitments to work and home. We can analyze and design strategies that address problems for groups of children (for example, taking action to reduce smoking among teens). We can sit on committees and task forces that look to implement safety regulations in child care settings. We can start after-school programs for schoolagers.

The First Step: Recognize That Problems Exist

The first step in taking action toward improving conditions for our children, however, is recognizing that problems exist. The range of issues affecting children in our country is daunting. We briefly discuss five examples to illustrate that range: child care, divorce, poverty, violence, and media influence.

Child Care

As more children live with single parents and in homes where both parents work outside the home, the issue of who cares for the children has become a common one. Parents are often caught between conflicting demands, desires, and loyalties. While their parents are at work, children have less time with and less access to their parents. When children become sick, parents feel the conflict between their work and the genuine concern for their children. More children spend large blocks of time alone after school. Many are afraid to enter their empty houses. Some children care for their younger siblings. Summers become a stressful time for families as a combination of child care, summer camps, and daily activities has to be pieced together for school-age children.

Divorce

Many children also live through the separation and divorce of their parents. Currently, one out of two marriages ends in divorce. The changes that result from divorce can be significant, for a child may have to move, be less well-off financially, experience the loss of a loved one, or face the possibility of the remarriage of either or both parents. Particularly problematic are on-going custody battles. The effects of divorce last far beyond the one-time event. Researcher Judith Wallerstein and her team have published several books chronicling her longitudinal study of children of divorced parents. She says, "Divorce is a wrenching experience for many adults and almost all children. It is almost always more devastating for children than for their parents" (Wallerstein and Blakeslee, 1989).

Poverty

Although overall our country enjoys great wealth and a booming economy, many children today live in poverty, and 300,000 U.S. children are homeless (Children's Defense Fund, 1996). Almost one out of every five children in the United States does not have enough to eat on a daily basis or lives in inadequate housing. The poverty rate among children of color is high in proportion to white children. Nearly 40 percent of African American children live below the poverty line. Hispanic children are the poorest racial/ethnic group in the United States, with 40.3 percent living in poverty. The effects of the Welfare Reform Acts of 1996 have yet to be researched. However, the difficulties of problematic transportation, low wages, insufficient training, inadequate child care, and the lack of medical insurance will continue to plague poor families.

Violence

Too many children experience violence today. Some see it too easily on television, others see it too easily in their neighborhoods or homes. Many have witnessed anger, tantrums, and violent attacks in their schools and child care settings. Children living in our cities have watched drive-by shootings from their front windows. Mothers have described putting their children in interior hallways to protect them from the shooting outside of their homes. Domestic violence occurs in every socioeconomic class and exposes children to fear, anger, and sometimes physical injury. In rural areas, families are even more isolated. Children continue to suffer abuse and neglect as stresses increase for families.

Recurring violence in our inner city neighborhood had set the preschool staff at Southside Family Nurturing Center on edge. Teachers had seen youth with guns on the street and had heard gunshots in the middle of the day. Several staff had encountered youth with guns shooting at one another. Police had driven with their guns drawn through the local park in pursuit of suspects while our young children played out in the open on the swings and slides.

Teachers felt uneasy and feared for themselves, but were most concerned about the safety of our children. They knew that once shots were fired or police entered the park with guns drawn, they might have a difficult time gathering the children quickly and safely.

Southside has instituted two procedures. First, when drug raids or violent events are reported or increased numbers of squad cars are sighted in the neighborhood, teachers keep the children inside on that day and delay the arrival and departure of vans, if necessary.

Second, staff members teach the children gunfire drills. They tell the children that teachers want to keep them safe both indoors and outside, and that their teachers may sometimes sense danger when they are playing outside. The teacher will then blow the whistle and they need to get on the ground very fast.

The staff practice this with the children about twice a year. They do not mention guns or police or suspects because they do not want to scare them. Yet they wonder if they should mention these things. Many of the children live with the reality of violence in their neighborhoods every day.

Southside has not had to use our gunfire drill in real life, but staff are constantly sobered by the need to have one. The preschool practices drills for fires and tornadoes, and now guns—all dangers that menace the children we love.

—Sandy Heidemann,
Southside Family Nurturing Center

Media Influence

Many children today have access to more technology, which can provide wonderful learning opportunities. However, this same technology exposes children to sexual material, violent images, and emotional content that is beyond their years. Questions raised by educational experts about how television viewing affects reading ability and whether computer games improve visual-motor skills cannot be answered without further research. At the same time, teachers complain that they need to entertain their students to keep their attention.

Television advertisers target children with their products. Cereal, toys, movies, dolls, music, computer games, virtual pets, and bicycles are marketed to children. As a result, children want more and more and are satisfied with less and less. Movies and cartoons have tie-in products that draw children in. Parents don't always know where to draw the line and don't know where to look for guidance.

What Do We Want for Our Children?

The number one thing I got was the crucial importance of never letting ourselves become so immobilized with fear that we develop a state of apathy toward what is going on around us.

—Gerald Jampolsky, author of *One Person Can Make a Difference,* after viewing several films on the Holocaust

These problems have been well publicized. So well that at times we become apathetic or feel that nothing we can do can stem the tide. But if we start small, think big, and encourage one another, we can have an impact on how children experience their world. When we consider what we want for our children, we find a lengthy list:

- We want children to be physically fit and to spend time out of doors.
- We want children to be healthy and to attend school regularly.
- We want children to experience satisfying relationships with children of their own age and with caring adults.
- We want children to live in economic security so they have places to live and enough to eat.
- We want children to feel connected to their heritage.
- We want children to have access to opportunities.
- We want children to be free to go anywhere without fearing racist attacks.
- We want children to feel valued by their elders and, in turn, to value those older than them.
- We want children to feel loved and to love others. We want them to be interested and successful learners.
- We want children to experience joy, excitement, and pride.
- We want children to know how to respond to challenges, to be prepared to cope with disappointments, and to persist in the face of difficulties.
- We want children to be fair, honest, and caring.
- We want children to believe that life has meaning, that there is reason to go on, and that they have something to contribute.

"Children are more physically fit and spend more time out of doors in clean, safe environments than ever before."

"Black teenagers safe on the streets."

"All children receive culturally-relevant education."

"Record numbers of children receive vaccinations for preventable childhood illnesses."

"Caregivers receive salaries comparable to public school teachers—children benefit."

"Children are among the first priorities for national spending."

—Newspaper headlines we would read after having made progress toward our goals for children.

What You Can Do

You might ask yourself, "What can I do?" You might think, "I'm only one caregiver and these problems seem so big." You might wonder, "How can I do any more when Jamal is crying and pulling on his ears and I can't get through to his parents, Sarah is toilet training, and I still haven't filed last month's Food Program forms." You might feel that caring for children is enough. Or that your single efforts won't make a difference. But time and time again, others teach us that we can influence problems that seem too big for us to tackle.

When we know what we want for children we can take steps to make it happen. You wouldn't think a thirteen-year-old boy from Los Angeles could do much for homeless people, but Segura Williams is one person who has made a difference. He and other children have collected donations of food, clothing, and money for people without homes. His group, called Kids Helping Each Other, even organized a breakfast for the people whose temporary homes were tents pitched

> *For we can do nothing*
> *substantial toward*
> *changing our course on*
> *the planet, a destructive*
> *one, without rousing*
> *ourselves, individual by*
> *individual, and bringing*
> *our small, imperfect*
> *stones to the pile.*
>
> —Alice Walker

in a special campground for the homeless of Los Angeles. Segura first decided to do something to help others when he lived in this campground with his mother and nine brothers and sisters.

Segura Williams provides us with inspiration. We too can make a difference. We can play an important role at a number of different levels. We can become knowledgeable about what is taking place on a national level and voice our concerns for children. We can influence what goes on in our communities. We can affect the lives of the children we care for on a daily basis in positive ways. We can help support families.

Listed below you will find strategies to provide external supports on national and state levels, ideas to build stronger communities for children, ways to help children in our programs, and steps you can take to support families. Some ways to become involved require more time and effort than others. Perhaps one of them will match your interest, your time, and your passion. However, these suggestions are meant to start the discussion about how we help our children. Go beyond our strategies to address your community's needs. If each one of us chooses to do just one of these things, children will be better off than before.

Making a Difference on a National Level

Many of us think of ourselves as people who care for children but have little interest in politics. We need to extend our view of ourselves and believe in our ability to impact the lives of children. We can provide high-quality care for young children and be advocates for them. Children aren't able to vote or speak out for themselves against policies that impact their lives. They need us to be their voices and to cast votes that will better their lives.

Here are some ways that we can all contribute on a national level:

> Recognize that everyone has a collective responsibility for the welfare of the children in this nation. Government, individuals, parents, religious and civic organizations, foundations, businesses, and private institutions and agencies all need to be active in coming up with solutions that will improve the conditions in which children grow up. It will take the time, energy, creativity, resources, and the dedication of all. Thinking that it is the problem of parents or schools alone is short sighted.

> Listen to the research and experiences of advocacy groups. For example, children of color need culturally relevant programs available. The same answers don't work for all children, all families, or all communities.

> Become informed about what is taking place politically. Read magazines and newspapers, watch national and local newscasts. Carefully consider how proposals will affect the lives of children. You will understand how the children will be affected because you spend so much time with them. Let your concerns be known. Call or write your legislators and representatives. Write letters to the editor of national and local publications. Testify at public hearings. Your opinion matters.

> Keep parents informed about upcoming legislation that will affect children. Have voter registration cards on site. If you have E-mail, let parents use it to keep in touch with politicians.

Marcy Whitebook worked as a child care worker after graduating from college. But her commitment to the field led her in a different direction after 1977. She became more and more disturbed with the low wages and poor working conditions that led to the high turnover of her colleagues. To address compensation issues in the field of child care, she founded the National Center for the Early Childhood Work Force and the Child Care Employee Project (now known as the Center for the Child Care Workforce).

The center has initiated a number of national campaigns and studies to push the issue of adequate compensation. They began the Worthy Wage Campaign in 1991, a multi-year effort to support public education about the current conditions for child care workers. They also established the Compensation Initiative Project, a national effort to develop public policies that support a skilled and stable child care work force. Dr. Whitebook has been the project director for several studies of employment issues in the early childhood field: National Child Care Staffing Study (1988-1992), NAEYC's Accreditation as a Strategy for Improving Child Care Quality (1997), Salary Improvement in Head Start: Lessons for the Early Care and Education Field (1998).

In collaboration with Chabot College in Hayward, California, Dr. Whitebook developed a mentor program that operates in sixty-eight colleges throughout the state. This program is one of the first and largest programs to link increased training with improved salaries and benefits.

Dr. Whitebook believes that the child care worker is the key person in improving the quality of care for children. All her work is directed at making child care a viable profession for adults, a profession where child care workers are paid a living wage with accompanying benefits. When this happens, child care workers will benefit and so will the children.

In our way of life, in our government, with every decision we make, we always keep in mind the Seventh Generation to come. It's our job to see that the people coming ahead, the generations still unborn, have a world no worse than ours and hopefully better.

**—Chief Owen Lyons,
Onondaga Nation**

> Demand that legislation and program proposals carry a family impact statement prepared by an advocacy organization such as the Children's Defense Fund. The outcomes and consequences for families should be clearly communicated. People need information to make educated decisions about what they will support.

> Vote on behalf of children. Children cannot vote and their issues often are not heard by decision and policy makers unless we raise them. When you vote on issues affecting children, you help to protect those vulnerable individuals who cannot vote for themselves. Inform the parents of children in your program and encourage them to vote.

> Work for and support legislation that provides economic security for children. Families need a decent income to provide adequately for their children. Security might come through a variety of efforts: increasing the minimum wage, providing job training, increasing child support efforts, federal safety-net programs, tax breaks for parents, child care subsidies, and more.

> Encourage employers to develop benefit packages that meet the needs of a variety of families. Pretax dollars for child care and medical expenses, family and medical leave policies, elder care, and adoption assistance might be among the options. At the minimum, advocate for benefits that assist families, such as health benefits or child care assistance.

> Fight for family-friendly workplaces that encourage part-time work, flextime, job-sharing, telecommuting, four day work weeks, and annual hours contracts. Employers offering these options often see a reduction in absenteeism and an increase in loyalty to the company. They can use these attractive benefits as methods of recruiting and retaining employees. Families benefit when parents are able to be home with children when needed.

> Become an activist for policies and programs that support families. Families have strengths and strong ties that keep them connected even when they are in crisis. Programs need to look for and build upon these strengths.

> Assure that children have a healthy start by supporting programs that provide prenatal care. Good care increases the chances for healthy babies and decreases the chances for risk factors. Encourage parents to get prenatal care and plan for a healthy pregnancy.

> Advocate for medical care to be accessible and affordable. All children need preventative medical care as well as treatment for existing health problems. Healthy children attend school more regularly and have a better chance for success.

- Support programs aimed at preventing the spread of HIV and finding a cure for AIDS. If you haven't already, chances are good you will care for a child with HIV or AIDS as this devastating disease spreads. Most children with HIV contract the virus in the womb or as sexually active teens.

- Champion anti-violence and violence prevention programs. Children need to learn to solve conflicts with one another in peaceful ways. Programs that focus on problem solving and peer mediation begin teaching these skills at very early ages. Advocate that they be introduced in schools and programs throughout the country.

- Support sensible gun control laws and programs. Every day fifteen children are killed by firearms in the United States (Children's Defense Fund, 1996). The Brady Bill and programs like Premiums for Guns can help to reduce the risk children face from hand guns.

- Voice your objections to media violence. Call or write television executives about programs that glamorize violence. Children watch an extraordinary amount of television. When this consists primarily of violent images, they can become desensitized to violent acts and may begin to believe that violence is a commonplace or acceptable method of resolving problems. Limit television viewing and use the television rating system. Support public television.

- Join a professional organization that works toward solutions to problems that concern you. Organizations often work to keep their membership informed about important legislation that is being proposed. The National Association for the Education of Young Children (NAEYC) is one professional organization available to early childhood educators.

- Participate in national discussions and organized groups that are fighting racism. Groups such as study circles, national forums on race relations, and churches have opportunities to discuss issues, teach anti-bias workshops, and lobby for anti-racist policies. Join child care initiatives on implementing anti-bias curricula that are available nationwide.

Making a Difference in Your Community

For many of us, the idea of community has taken on new meaning. Traditionally, community has meant the neighborhood in which we live. Now the meaning has been extended to include more than just a geographic area. Community means people to which we have ties, obligations, and loyalty. This can include family, friends, ethnic

If you have a voice, you must use it for the world you live in, and if you are alive you should demonstrate it by using the space you occupy. You must help shape the world.

—Bernice Johnson Reagon

groups, and people with whom we work, socialize, or worship. For some, the people in their community may live across town or across many miles. For others it may be the people next door. A special bond develops between the people in a community, one of caring support for each other.

Being a part of a community offers some of the benefits extended families offered in the past. Communities provide advice, support, encouragement, needed breaks from the routines of daily life, and help. Children benefit from the feelings of community when they know there are adults outside their family who care about them and want them to succeed.

Become a vital part of your community. As an educator, you have many resources and skills to offer. Here are ways to develop community support for children and families:

Marian Wright Edelman, founder and president of the Children's Defense Fund, is a strong voice for children and families. Their mission is to educate the nation about the needs of children and encourage preventive investment before they get into trouble, get sick, or suffer too early pregnancies, or family breakdowns. Mrs. Edelman was born and raised in South Carolina in a family that emphasized service. She remembers cooking, serving, and cleaning in the Black home for the aged that her father, a Baptist pastor, started. She knew that as a young Black girl she "could be and do anything" and that "character, self-discipline, determination, attitude, and service are the substance of life" (Edelman, 1992). Her dedication sprang directly from those around her. Edelman states in her book, The Measure of Our Success (1992), "I have always believed that I could help change the world because I have been lucky to have adults around me who did—in small and large ways."

Marian Wright Edelman has realized many achievements in her lifetime. She is a graduate of Spelman College and Yale Law School. She was counsel for the Poor People's March in 1968. For two years she served as the Director of the Center for Law and Education at Harvard University, and in 1973 began the Children's Defense Fund. She has received the Albert Schweitzer Humanitarian Prize, the Heinz Award, and was a MacArthur Foundation Prize Fellow.

The children are her motivation to continue this crucial work—her own children and other people's children. They are the passion of her personal and professional life, "for it is they who are God's presence, promise, and hope for humankind" (Edelman, 1992).

- Become knowledgeable about what is taking place in your state and local government and the impact it has on families. Let politicians known about this impact by your vote and voice. Again, notify parents of legislation or regulations affecting children.

- Fight childhood hunger in your community by organizing a food drive, volunteering your time at a soup kitchen, or donating items from your own kitchen. Millions of American children go hungry. Being hungry makes it difficult for children to do well in school and can cause malnutrition and health problems. Push for breakfast programs in schools that do not already have them.

- Help homeless families by organizing games or activities for the children in a shelter, putting together a basket of things the families will need when they set up housekeeping again, donating furnishings, or volunteering your time to organizations such as Habitat for Humanity. Struggling families find it impossible to locate affordable housing. When they are forced to live on the streets, children are likely to miss school and fall behind in their education. The costs involved in reestablishing a household equipped with the basic necessities that we take for granted can be overwhelming. Sometimes homeless families are split up and the children placed in foster care.

- Provide clothing for a child who needs it by donating clothes that your infant or child has outgrown, buying an outfit for a child, or giving a jacket and warm clothing. Children often miss school because they have nothing to wear or are embarrassed by their clothing. They might also have poor school attendance because they are unable to dress for the weather.

- Support funding for schools and extra youth programs. Campaign and vote for school referendums and funding for preschool programs. The opportunities these programs provide help children reach their full potential.

- Make play areas clean and safe for children. Organize a neighborhood watch effort and work with others to clean up or revamp a playground. Children need safe areas where they can engage in physical activity.

- Give children a chance to remain healthy. Help to prevent childhood diseases by providing information about affordable immunization clinics, offering a family a ride to the clinic, arranging for the clinic to visit your child care, or offering parent workshops about ways to prevent the spread of communicable diseases. When children are healthy, they attend school more regularly and are better able to focus on the material being presented.

Communities are not built of friends, or of groups of people with similar styles, and tastes, or even of people who like and understand each other. They are built of people who feel they are part of something that is bigger than themselves.

—Suzanne Goldsmith

> Volunteer your expertise as a "warmline" consultant. Many communities have a phone number that offers parents information and advice on a variety of child rearing topics. You can share your knowledge and expertise about child development, guidance, age appropriate expectations, and more. If your community doesn't have a "warmline," start one.

> Share your talent. Offer to teach a class at a shelter or organization for children. Teach art, calligraphy, music, dance, gardening, or anything you enjoy. Organize a field trip, a game, sporting event, or tournament. Staffing can be tight for some of these organizations. Often their staff time is consumed with basic programming. If you offer an additional class or special program, you enrich the lives of the children involved.

> Become a mentor. Volunteer at a school or at a local boys' or girls' club. Children need relationships with many different adults. A caring relationship is vital to the well-being of young children. Be willing to commit at least six to twelve months to build the relationship.

> Give parents who really need it a break from parenting. Offer to care for their child while they get an important errand done or take time out for themselves. Parenting can be so demanding that sometimes it is difficult to take care of the necessities. Families who don't live near extended family especially need to rely on the help of others for the breaks that grandparents, aunts, and uncles might have otherwise provided. Help them out for an hour or two. They'll be better ready to parent when they are refreshed or have accomplished an important task.

Making a Difference in Programs for Children

New information is available on good beginnings for young children and what is needed for quality child care. Yet an alarming number of child care programs fall short of offering the best care possible. In order to give children what they need, child care providers need to learn from the most current research and apply it to their work with children. Some of this information is presented in this book. A great deal more exists and requires continuous study.

These strategies help to create programs that nurture children and families:

> Learn what high-quality care is and how you can provide it in your setting. As research is conducted and innovative programs are found effective, put the findings into practice. Develop programs and teaching strategies based on current knowledge of the field.

A bill that would fund sliding fee subsidies and generate resources to compensate providers for the cost of offering high-quality services was before the Minnesota state legislature. It included money for training to attract and maintain competent caregivers. Child Care Works—an advocacy group comprised of directors, teachers, and advocates—lobbied in an innovative manner. They decided to show legislators what it was like to care for children. They brought teachers and their classes to the capitol and played. To demonstrate the current state licensing ratios, they arranged to have four infants, seven toddlers, ten preschoolers, and fifteen school-age children and one teacher for each group. Teachers brought toys, blankets, art projects, and much enthusiasm. While the children played, another adult spoke about the developmental needs of the children.

A particularly poignant moment occurred when one of the toddlers approached a senator in the audience. The senator began to sing "The Itsy-Bitsy Spider." Soon the whole chamber joined in, delighting adults and toddlers alike.

One of the directors, Nedra Robinson, offers her description of the event:

"On Friday, March 7, 1997, I testified before the Senate to help pass some early childhood legislation. Seven toddlers from my center, Melvenia Williams (one of my lead teachers), and my father (whom the children know and love) accompanied me. I was so glad they were with me, because I was scared to death.

"I felt that this was an important adventure for us because it was an opportunity to advocate for child care and to make a positive change for children. It was a way to let parents know what was going on politically regarding children, to teach and prove to them that being involved matters and can change things for themselves and their children. They were very proud of their children, as I was. The children were proud of themselves! Even at their young age, they knew they were doing something very important, although they had no idea what!"

> Support standards that provide for the safety of young children. Children have the right to be protected from hazards. Regulations ensure that spaces for children are inspected. Adhere to basic safety standards. Exceed expectations in any way necessary to keep your environment free from risks. Pursue accreditation from NAEYC and commit yourself to excellence.

> Commit yourself to seeing the good within each child. Believe that each child has unique characteristics and qualities. Nurture the development of each child to his fullest. When you see the good in each child, you help encourage him to develop his potential.

> Build a climate of acceptance in your setting. Children have the right to be accepted by their peers and their caregivers. Value each child's race, culture, and economic status. Recognize each child's unique learning style and behaviors.

> Implement anti-bias curriculum with the children in your care. Do activities that recognize differences and teach children to value them. Join a discussion group, do extra research, or attend workshops to examine your own attitudes. As a result of your willingness to listen to others' experiences, you will be more able to form authentic relationships with the children and families you serve. It will also give you tools as you struggle to form answers to children's questions and comments.

> Monitor school curriculum and its teaching of history and current events. Are the lessons complete and accurate? Are they fair? From whose perspective are history and current events taught?

> Develop meaningful and lasting relationships with children. A child who has this type of relationship with a caregiver is more likely to explore actively, take reasonable risks in learning, and get along with others. This provides a child with a foundation for learning in the future.

> Offer learning opportunities that foster children's ability to solve problems, get along with others, and learn successfully. The environment you arrange and the attitude you convey about the child's emerging abilities will do much to support confidence and competence.

> Foster skills that help children learn to interact respectfully with others and to resolve conflicts in a peaceful way. Gaining control of emotions and learning to get along with others are important areas of growth and development. The interpersonal skills children practice at this young age will be helpful to them throughout their lifetimes.

> Teach the skills that help children overcome obstacles, cope with adversities, and face life with optimism and hope.

> Offer a multicultural curriculum every day. Children have the right to be proud of who they are and fare better when they understand and appreciate differences.

Making a Difference in the Lives of Families

Most parents want what is best for their children. They do the best they can, given the pressures they are experiencing. Children sometimes exhibit difficulties when families become distressed. It is easy to decide that parents are responsible for the problems we see. We might say, "If only her parents would discipline her more at home," or "His parents baby him too much." When we blame parents, we oversimplify a complex situation and may inadvertently make the parents feel guilty and under more stress.

Parents need the support of others. They deserve to be paid enough to provide a decent living for their families. They need to be allowed to take time off from work to care for sick children and meet with their caregivers. They need programs and policies that help to make their families stronger.

Each family is unique. What works for one family may not be appropriate for another. We must recognize each family's strengths and build upon them. Educators can do much to make a difference in the lives of families. Honig (1986) concludes from her research review that child care workers "not only built secure positive relationships with young children, but in addition, they provided a buffering social support for families."

Use these strategies to help make a difference in the lives of families:

➤ Include parents at all levels of planning for programs and policies that affect them. What we believe to be helpful might not be what parents find most useful. With parent influence, programs are more likely to be culturally relevant.

➤ Know the resources operating within your community. Most families will need outside support at some time. Be prepared with names and phone numbers of organizations or agencies that can provide the level of support needed. In some cases, you might offer additional support like caring for a child or sitting with a family member while they make the call.

➤ Be aware of the financial pressure additional program costs may cause families. It can be difficult for families who are struggling financially to afford even a small amount for a field trip or to provide a snack for the group. Consider how unexpected costs can be avoided, fees waived, or scholarships made available for families who need them.

➤ Build strong relationships with families. Assume you will work out problems together. Recognize that there are a variety of parenting styles and that no one way is the right way to parent. When you respect the diversity of parenting styles and respect the opinions of others, you are more likely to come to agreement about ways to solve problems.

➤ Help families develop a list of alternative care options when their children become sick. This inevitability is difficult to deal with unless you are prepared. Suggestions might include grandparents or other relatives, a trusted neighbor, a child care center or service that specializes in caring for moderately ill children, and substitute caregivers who might care for a child at home. When parents bring children who are marginally ill to their caregivers, understand the guilt they feel from not having adequate time off to care for their children.

➤ Find ways to make communication easy. Parents and providers need to communicate regularly. Some do better with written information, others with verbal. All do best when information is presented in their native language. New methods of communicating exist through the technology available. Make use of voice mail, E-mail, and fax machines. Create a computer web page, write newsletters, make bulletin boards, and talk with parents. Use a combination of communication techniques so that you meet the needs of more parents. A video of a child while at child

As a mother of a child with special needs, Theresa struggles to find effective and accessible resources to help her son. Her son, Derek, was diagnosed with Attention Deficit Hyperactivity Disorder (ADHD) at three and a half years old. Since then he has received additional diagnoses of bipolar depression, language delay, anxiety disorder, oppositional defiant disorder, and obsessive-compulsive disorder. School, home life, friendships, and simple tasks in life are a challenge for Derek.

To help him be successful, Theresa needs to constantly find and monitor services to support Derek. Currently, he is in day treatment and in a therapeutic after-school program. He has a therapist and a child psychiatrist. Theresa has arranged respite care on appointed weekends and gets support for herself from a county social worker. Her extended family helps out with child care and emotional support when they are able. At school her son has an individual educational plan (IEP) to address his academic needs. At particularly difficult times, Theresa has had to push for hospitalization and more intensive services.

Theresa interacts with doctors, therapists, teachers, psychiatrists, and respite caregivers when planning for Derek. She has to decide about medications, behavior plans, the correct school environment, and how to manage her home.

Juggling the advice, making the decisions, and maintaining her own job along with this is exhausting and time consuming. However, Theresa advocates for Derek relentlessly. She knows that when Derek receives positive external supports, he can bring out his sense of humor, his intelligence, and imagination—all strengths that help him succeed. As Theresa succinctly states, "There's a neat kid in there and it's my job to bring that out."

care can be educational, reassuring, and a joy to parents who cannot be there.

- Develop support materials that provide information about child development. Often parents don't have easy access to information that makes parenting more manageable. Offer a library of videos, written material, and audio tapes on a number of important parenting topics.

- Arrange for speakers and informational workshops that offer support to parents. The suggestions made can offer help to parents who are frustrated by challenging situations encountered when raising children. In addition, parents receive support from others who attend. Both help to increase parents' ability to do their job well.

- Sponsor parent-child activities or informal family gatherings that give parents a chance to meet one another and form support networks. Activities that offer enjoyment for parents and children can also provide parents with an opportunity to observe other children of the same age.

- Help parents learn to monitor their children's television viewing. Describe ways parents can limit how much and what kind of television shows their children watch. Let them know about the importance of discussing what children will watch and processing what they see. Emphasize the importance of play and physical activities, as well as other alternative activities.

- Educate parents about ways to help children solve problems nonviolently. Most parents don't want their children to resolve conflicts aggressively, yet they may not know any other way to do it. Teach parents and the children the steps in problem solving.

- Put together a toy, book, or activity library for parents to use at the time they drop off or pick up their child. This can save parents time and offer alternatives to the toys and materials that they have at home. It makes it easy to recommend specific activities that will enhance skill development too.

- Find out what will make it easier and more enjoyable for parents to attend school functions. Do you need to offer supper along with activities, offer activities for older school-age children, arrange child care for siblings not enrolled in your program, or limit the number of activities offered? Parents in each community may need slightly different things.

- Pair families for mentor relationships. Give families that are new to your setting the name of another family to call for support and advice.

All families are embedded in a culture that informs their parenting. This culture or heritage is often a source of pride and strength. Giving the child a consistent culture between home and school increases self-esteem, confidence, and a sense of belonging. Think of ways you can explore this with the parents and children.

> Send home a questionnaire that asks parents what they value about their culture. With permission from the parents, put up a parent bulletin board with their comments.

> Ask parents to share with the children the practices, art objects, or special talents that represent their heritage.

> Host a "culture night" where parents bring food representative of their heritage and share cultural objects or practices with other parents.

> On holidays, ask parents how they celebrate. Incorporate those ideas in your discussion of the holiday with the children.

> Explore with parents how they care for their child. Talk about bedtimes, mealtimes, and special caregiving routines. Try to incorporate these into your routines with the child.

> Reflect the home language of the children in your care. Even if you cannot speak it fluently, learn a few words to greet and comfort a child. Consider adding children's home languages to the labels in your classroom.

Moving Forward

All of the suggestions in this chapter help to build external supports around children that will contribute to their success. The external supports range from national and state legislation to the community, the family, and to the child care setting. External supports can be put in place for children as a whole, a group of children, or individual children. It requires the ability to analyze effective solutions, to lobby, to consult with others, to listen to what children and families need to function well, and to advocate.

Start with this list and build more suggestions of your own. If you are just starting to do advocacy work for children, start small. Choose one issue that you care about deeply and work on it. When you experience success on that issue, it will be easier to broaden your work. We have compiled a list of resources you can use and organizations you can contact to find out more information about ways to advocate for children's issues (see the appendices for this). Many of us aren't sure that our phone calls, committee work, or writing will change outcomes. However, legislators and other policy makers continually emphasize the influence constituents' letters and phone calls have on their decisions.

As we move our discussion in the next chapter to the internal skills that children learn to help them surmount difficulties, we want to emphasize again that children need both the internal strengths and the external supports to successfully overcome the hurdles they encounter. Internal strengths will help a child cope with adversity and rise above it, but the adverse external conditions will still exist. We run the risk of losing those children who cannot overcome these conditions by sheer will. For instance, in our historical examples we discussed the institution of slavery and how children grew up within its cruelties. Even if an individual child could withstand those cruelties, that child would still be a slave. It was imperative that slavery be abolished so that children and their families could attain freedom.

Adults can establish the best conditions for children to thrive. We can use these suggestions and other strategies to create a framework of support for children. We can also help children build a repertoire of internal strengths. The next chapters discuss how you can encourage the acquisition of these strengths by incorporating them into your curriculum, your environment, your interactions, and your activities.

Chapter Five

Standing Strong

We have explored the outer circles of support surrounding children. We are now at the center of the circle: the child herself. What are the child's strengths? What capabilities does the child bring? What qualities can we help the child develop?

In the first chapter we discussed Werner's (1989) three factors that protect a child from adversity: 1) Strengths in the internal make-up of the child, such as sociability, intelligence, and competence in language and reading, 2) Emotional support within the family, whether from parent or sibling, and 3) External support systems such as school, child care programs, or church.

We have explored ways to strengthen emotional support in the family, build strong external support systems, and lobby for laws and policies. Now we ask, "What do children need internally to overcome the difficulties life presents?" To answer this, we looked at various studies on resiliency.

Resiliency research is a body of work that looks at children who seem to do well in spite of the stresses in their lives. Garmezy gives us two definitions for resiliency: 1) a "healthy child in the unhealthy setting," and 2) "coping and adapting well in the face of the major, enduring life stress" (qtd. in Cowen et al., 1990).

Werner and Smith (1982) describe a resilient child as one who "works well, loves well, and expects well, notwithstanding profound life adversity." Masten, Best, and Garmezy (1991) define resiliency as a "process of, capacity for, or outcome of successful adaptation despite challenging or threatening circumstances." All of these definitions present a picture of children who are able to function well in spite of overwhelming difficulties.

Observations about resiliency emerged from research on children at risk because of environmental conditions such as poverty, mental illness in the family, or abuse and neglect. The studies have covered a wide variety of cultures and ethnicities. As researchers analyzed the effects of discouraging environmental conditions on children, they consistently saw a proportion of their research group doing quite well, in spite of the problems surrounding them. They decided to study these children as a group. This subset of children often shared certain characteristics which remained more or less consistent throughout varying research locations and designs. To understand these conclusions further, we looked at a few studies in more depth.

One of the most extensive studies is by Professor Emmy Werner. She has studied all the babies born on one Hawaiian island in 1955 for over thirty years. This study involves 700 children from different ethnic backgrounds. Many of the families live in chronic poverty or in persistently disorganized family environments. Within this group of 700 children, she found 72 who were highly resilient despite poverty and stressed families (Werner and Smith, 1992). Some of the external supports the children had include the following:

> Small families with more than two years spacing between the children

> Other caretakers they were attached to

> A strong support system (for example, ministers, friends, and teachers)

> Success in school

However, equally important were the following internal qualities the children brought to the equation:

> An active and vigorous approach to solving life's problems

> A tendency to perceive their experiences constructively, even if they involved pain or suffering

> The ability, from infancy on, to gain positive attention from other people

> A strong ability to maintain a positive vision of a meaningful life

These children had the ability to thrive even when one would predict serious learning and behavior problems. One of the subgroups of children Werner analyzed carefully was children of parents with mental illness. Some of these children were able to thrive with both the internal and external supports available to them. Perhaps because of the other adult supports in their lives, they were able to detach from the stress of their parents' mental illness and see it as a problem of their parents, not something for which they were to blame.

On the other hand, children from unstable families who developed serious learning and behavior problems also had risk factors such as prematurity, low birth weight, or obstetrical problems. In other words, infants with difficult temperaments who interacted with distressed caretakers had a greater chance of developing serious problems. These children suffered a breakdown of both external and internal supports.

Other resiliency research has focused on the presence of risk factors and determining which protective factors can minimize or cushion their effects. For instance, research done by Masten, Best, and Garmezy (1991) shows that the following factors are associated with lower academic achievement, more emotional or behavioral problems, lower work achievement, and trouble with the law:

1. Poverty

2. Low maternal education

3. Low socioeconomic status

4. Low birth weight

5. Family instability

6. Schizophrenia in biological mother

Protective factors can moderate the effects of individual vulnerability or environmental hazards. With these protective factors in place, the child may have a more positive outcome.

When children suffer acute trauma, such as a death in the family, severe accident, or a natural disaster, resiliency refers to the ability to recover from the trauma. No one is invulnerable to extreme pain, but some children are better able to recover. The children who are able to recover more quickly often have a number of protective factors in place, such as a favorable temperament and extensive supports.

Project Competence, one of the studies on resilience done by Garmezy and Masten (1986) at the University of Minnesota, studied 200 eight- to thirteen-year-old children in an urban area of Minneapolis. They looked at the cumulative effects of life stressors on various aspects of competence, and they focused on "stress-resistant children"—children who maintained competence despite exposure to stressful events. Although the balance between risk and protective factors proved to be complex, stress-resistant children consistently shared three protective factors:

- Connection to a supportive competent adult

- Good problem-solving skills

- Stress-tolerant disposition

Michael Rutter found similar protective factors or processes operating when he studied the incidence of psychiatric disorders in ten-year-old children in two different areas in England (1987). He found six risk factors associated with children's mental illness:

- Severe marital discord between the parents

- Father's criminality

- Psychiatric disorder of mother

- Low social status or poverty

- Overcrowding or large family size
- Secondary care through local authority (for example, foster care)

The presence of two of these risk factors increased the children's risk for psychiatric disorder four-fold, while the presence of four risk factors and above raised the risk for psychiatric disorder ten-fold. However, even in the very high-risk groups, children with a warm and loving relationship with one of the parents could lower their risk (Honig, 1986).

Mrazek and Mrazek (1987) researched children growing up in abusive and violent homes or environments. Abuse and neglect can severely impair a child's ability to function, sometimes for a long period of time. Such experiences, especially if chronic and long-term, can actually affect the neurological development of the brain (Shapiro et al., 1996). Yet many abused and neglected children do not grow up to be abusers. Children who do well despite these severe conditions have the following characteristics in common:

- Recognizing and reacting to dangerous situations
- Seeking information about the hazards in one's environment
- Forming and using relationships for survival
- Decisive risk-taking
- Believing they are loved
- Reframing experiences to emphasize positive
- Optimism and hope

In study after study, researchers emphasize two things that resilient children share: a close loving relationship with an adult, and internal strengths that helped them to cope with the challenges. Rutter especially emphasized that children can have a measure of protection when they believe in their own worth and have a conviction that they can cope successfully with life's challenges. Rutter notes that the two types of experiences that form a protection for the child are a secure and harmonious loving relationship and a successful accomplishment of tasks important to the child (qtd. in Honig, 1986)

We have talked about the necessity of a close loving relationship when we discussed the importance of family and the relationship of adults in children's lives. We are still left with two main questions: What exactly are the internal strengths that protect children, and can they be taught?

What Are the Internal Strengths?

We found that ten internal strengths kept surfacing throughout the literature on resiliency. Although other individual talents and skills can help in overcoming adversity, these ten strengths were consistent, both in the research and in our experiences. They seemed to form an inner core that allowed children to withstand or at least survive difficult tests.

We also found that some of these strengths came up as predictors of success in later life. Many careers require a high standard of literacy, quantitative skills, and scientific thinking. However, along with technical skills, our children need social skills, such as flexibility, adaptability, cross-cultural communication, problem solving, and perseverance (Hamburg, 1992). Listed below are the ten strengths:

1. Self-Esteem and Sense of Competence
2. Cultural Competence
3. Identification and Expression of Feelings
4. Empathy
5. Perseverance
6. Responsibility
7. Ability to Recognize Cause and Effect
8. Ability to Reframe
9. Problem-Solving Ability
10. Optimism and Hope

Description of the Ten Strengths

1. Self-Esteem and Sense of Competence

Children with self-esteem feel valued and secure. With this as a foundation, they work toward mastery in school or in other activities such as music and sports. They withstand setbacks by returning to the task again and again to get it right. One often sees pleasure in small children when they accomplish something new like tying their shoe or climbing the stairs. But it often disappears as children experience failure in their endeavors. Self-esteem is not a static quality but rises and falls according to the child's experiences. Self-esteem can be reinforced by encouraging children to overcome their obstacles. Accomplishment and mastery build confidence that then translates into self-esteem.

As a child matures into an adult, life's events can challenge this sense of worth. But if it is firmly in place, the previous accomplishments, proven competence in other areas, and self-esteem helps the adult meet the new dilemmas.

2. Cultural Competence

Children who are culturally competent are able to value and feel grounded in their own culture. They take advantage of opportunities to return to those family members, communities, and places that nurture them. They have the confidence to seek out new experiences, but they always know who they are. Culture in children's lives gives them competence, confidence, and connection (as reported in Far West's video, *Ten Ways to Culturally Sensitive Child Care*).

Children who are firmly grounded in their own culture are also better able to accept and value the culture of others. Babies as young as six months notice differences in people based on skin color, and children as young as three years have learned to make stereotyped characterizations of people based on skin color and race or ethnicity. A child who is culturally competent remains more open to differences and is less likely to offer stereotypes.

Children with cultural competence are able to move easily between groups of people and negotiate cultural conflicts. They are able to communicate with people from cultures other than their own. They have a beginning understanding of the unfairness of stereotypes and challenge them when they see them in books or on television.

This learning is a life-long undertaking. The adult who learns to negotiate these divisions will succeed both personally and in the workplace. Adults who can value, seek out, and manage cultural connections, both within their own culture and between cultures, will experience a richer world and be able to share these learnings with their own children. The racial, class, and cultural divisions in our society affect all children growing up today. Children see these divisions in our world, but they also see our efforts to bridge them.

3. Identification and Expression of Feelings

Children who can identify and express their feelings comprehend basic feelings such as anger, sadness, happiness, and fear. They accept these feelings in themselves and can express them appropriately.

The teacher should encounter the child— every child—with humanity and a little awe.

—Bill Ayers

In *Emotional Intelligence* (1995), Daniel Goleman states that children can be taught to understand, control, manage, and express their feelings. Goleman proposes that we address the awareness and management of emotions. Children need to be aware of their own feelings and name them. As they gain this understanding, they can begin to see the connection between the feelings and who or what causes them. Equally vital is the ability to discern the difference between feelings and actions. Teaching children to manage and control their feelings of anger, sadness, and fear results in more positive emotions about self, school, and family.

Being able to understand the feelings of others and express your feelings so that others can hear and understand your point of view leads adults to better relationships. Adults use these skills heavily in job settings where they must work with others in teams. Certainly these skills are essential in more intimate adult relationships such as marriage and friendships.

4. Empathy

Children who can empathize with others tend to reach out to help those who need it. They notice when others are distressed, crying, mad, or sad. Children may show empathy for other children, for example, by crying when another child cries or offering a hug or toy when a friend is upset. Empathy helps to build a feeling of belonging to a special friend or to a group of peers because children sense one another's emotions and recognize that they too have felt the same. Expressing this recognition can help heal divisions and solidify group identification.

The ability to understand what others are feeling and to offer assistance helps adults to be generous friends, welcome team members and colleagues, responsive spouses, and kind, loving parents. Empathy can also motivate adults to identify and challenge discrimination and unfair practices that others experience.

5. Perseverance

Children who can persevere at a task show determination to succeed, even when blocked from achieving their goal. When an obstacle is placed in their way, they find another way to go at it rather than giving up. A child learning to build a tower may not build the tower very high the first time. It may fall with a large bang. But after repeated attempts, the child learns to put large blocks on the bottom and stack them evenly. Rather than thinking she is not good at blocks or building, she discovers that repeated attempts can lead to success. Because our society puts a high value on success, children often feel that they are either good at something or they are not. They think they are good at art but bad at sports. Or they are good at music but bad at schoolwork. Learning to persevere means giving up that mode of thinking and instead focusing on goals and how to achieve them. Natural abilities in specific areas can guide choices but should not block attempts.

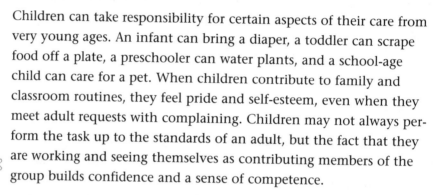

Endurance pierces marble.

—Berber proverb

Perseverance will aid children throughout their lives. No matter how much ability people have, they will not accomplish their goals without the drive to continue trying even after repeated failures.

6. Responsibility

Children can take responsibility for certain aspects of their care from very young ages. An infant can bring a diaper, a toddler can scrape food off a plate, a preschooler can water plants, and a school-age child can care for a pet. When children contribute to family and classroom routines, they feel pride and self-esteem, even when they meet adult requests with complaining. Children may not always perform the task up to the standards of an adult, but the fact that they are working and seeing themselves as contributing members of the group builds confidence and a sense of competence.

Adults have to take responsibility in many areas of their lives. In their work and in their family life, others depend on them to follow through and take initiative. A commitment to responsibility leads to high achievement and consistent performance. Responsible adults become responsible citizens who participate in the political process and community initiatives. Responsible parents are committed to their children and thoughtfully plan how best to solve problems.

7. Ability to Recognize Cause and Effect

When children can see danger coming and see its cause, they may be able to avoid it to some extent. They understand how a certain event causes what follows. If children understand the natural consequences of an action, they can make a choice about their actions. This is really a skill of prediction. But it involves more than just being able to understand physical properties, such as observing that food falls when they drop it from their high chair or the wind blows objects out of their reach. Children must learn to predict danger so they can keep themselves safe. They must also learn to trust their instincts and follow them. Learning this puts more control in the hands of the children. Learning this skill is key to being able to build optimism. When children understand cause and effect, they can anticipate possible consequences and influence the outcome. When children believe that they can change the course of events, they have more hope that they can solve problems.

Adults need to understand cause and effect in all areas of their lives. They predict consequences of actions as they make decisions about job changes, where to live, who to marry, and how to avoid dangerous situations. These predictions give them the power to influence events.

8. Ability to Reframe

Children who understand a problem from another perspective often do not blame themselves or internalize the problem. They may be bothered by it, upset or angry, but they do not necessarily think that they are bad or the cause of the problem. When an alcoholic parent yells and throws dishes, a child who reframes the problem understands that it is the alcohol and the parent's abuse of alcohol that is the issue, not the child's misbehavior. The child's original question—"What have I done to make my parent angry?"—becomes, "How do I handle it when my parent is drunk?" Being able to reframe helps children to see the problem in a new light and perhaps make it possible to come up with new options. For example, when two children are fighting over a toy, they may say the problem is caused by the other child because she is hitting, when in reality both children are fighting over the toy. If you help the two children see that the problem is between the two of them, they are better able to come up with a successful solution.

Another part of reframing is understanding that no matter how bad you feel, it probably is not the end of the world as you know it. When a friend disappoints a child, she may state, "I'm not going to invite you to my party." The other child needs to understand that this threat probably doesn't mean the end of their friendship. Instead it means, "You hurt my feelings." If the offending child can recognize and state the reframed problem as "I hurt your feelings and I'm sorry," the two children could begin to explore how to be better friends. Seligman (1995) has listed several ways children and adults can reframe their negative experiences:

> Thought-Catching
"I need to catch my negative thoughts."

> Evaluating Automatic Thoughts
"If I stop for a minute to listen to my thoughts, I can evaluate what I am doing."

> Throwing Out Negative Thoughts
"Once I have evaluated these thoughts, I can stop or throw out the ones that blame myself or the overly negative thoughts about the situation."

> Different Explanations
> "I can replace explanations with ones that are more accurate. The adversity becomes a solvable problem, not an indictment of myself."

> Decatastrophizing
> "I can put the problem in perspective by understanding that what has happened is not the worst thing in the world."

Adults who use the skill of reframing are not as quick to blame themselves or others when trouble appears. This leads to quicker, more positive, and more effective problem solving, which in turn helps prevent depression and self-blame.

9. Problem-Solving Ability

Children's ability to successfully solve problems is closely related to self-esteem and perseverance. In order to solve problems, children need to feel that they can do it and to try and try again. In a circular fashion, when children are able to solve a problem, they feel more confidence and the willingness to try and try again.

In order to solve problems, children have to learn a subset of skills: anger management, impulse control, flexibility, generating alternatives, seeking information, and making choices. Problem-solving skills can be used to resolve conflict, solve a physical dilemma such as putting a puzzle together, or building a relationship by thinking about how to be a friend.

Key to problem solving is children's internal locus of control. This means that children will be motivated by factors inside of them, such as pride and wanting to succeed. Children with an external locus of control are more motivated by the control and approval of others. They may need limits, reminders, and coaching from others to stop negative behavior and often are unable to solve a problem independently.

Being able to solve problems is also closely related to learning to identify and express feelings. If a child reacts explosively when a problem occurs, it is impossible to find solutions. However, when that same child can control her anger and express her frustration with words, more options can be generated.

Most folks just don't know what can be done with a little will and their hands.

—Gloria Naylor,
from *Mama Day*

Steps in Problem Solving

1. Identify the problem.
2. Gather information.
3. Generate solutions.
4. Choose the best one.
5. Implement the plan.
6. Evaluate how the plan is working.
7. Revise the plan as needed.

(Hewitt, 1995)

Adults also use the subset of skills we listed to solve problems. Adults who are effective problem-solvers often feel less helpless. They are chosen for difficult assignments because they use creativity and energy to get through difficulty. They use these skills to resolve conflicts with others or among a work team. Feeling ineffective at problem solving leads to passivity, negativity, and for some, depression.

10. Optimism and Hope

This strength influences all of the other strengths. If children maintain a feeling of hope, even the most persistent difficulties will not hold sway over their futures. Optimism becomes an approach to life. Feeling hope means that children can see ahead to a time when it won't feel this bad. It also means that children can see a way to solve their difficulties and believe that they have some influence in solving them. Children can bring a sense of hope to things both large and small. They hope for cookies, toys, or some time with their parents. Escape and enjoyment are additional ways to maintain optimism. Some activities that help children do this are dramatic play, hobbies, relaxation, reading for pleasure, and sports.

Caregivers and parents can teach optimism or pessimism. Seligman (1995) outlines four ways children gain a pessimistic attitude:

1. Genetics
2. Parental pessimism
3. Pessimistic criticism from parents, teachers, or coaches
4. Having experiences of helplessness rather than mastery

However, if learned early in life, optimism or hopefulness can become a way to look at and experience life. It supports effective problem solving, perseverance, and self-esteem. It also attracts others to be supports and confidants. The ability to see a better future motivates all who can envision it.

Can We Teach These Strengths?

Resiliency is not a childhood given, but is the capacity that develops over time in the context of person-environment interactions.

—Maxine Weinreb

Although we have a firm belief in humans' capacity to change and learn new skills, we were concerned that the research could be saying that children just naturally had these strengths, or that they were born with them. Did that mean that those who weren't born with them couldn't develop them?

There does seem to be some evidence that genetics plays a part in the development of resiliency. In the Werner study (1992), the resilient children were active, affectionate, and easy to manage as babies. As they got older, they were self-sufficient and very sociable. They had good self-help skills even as toddlers. When they were frustrated, they were able to ask for help. Optimism seemed to be a temperamental quality early on. Kyrios and Prior (1990) studied the influence of temperament, stress, and family factors in the behavioral adjustment of three- to five-year-old children. They found that individual temperamental qualities did seem to be consistent over time and that temperamental characteristics were causally related to children's overall behavioral adjustment. Temperamental characteristics, particularly of low reactivity and high manageability, appeared to lessen the influence of adverse family factors on the children's adjustment.

Martin E. Seligman (1995) lists genetics as a way that children gain pessimism. However, he also has designed a program to counter this pessimism and to teach the child to think in an optimistic and hopeful way. Just learning that it is possible to find ways around barriers can help build optimism. This teaches children to see adversity not as a character flaw, but as a problem that can be solved.

Goleman (1995) also believes that we can and must teach children to manage and understand their emotions. He advises parents to include this awareness in their interactions with their children and argues that schools should teach emotional intelligence.

Michael Rutter (1987) states that "self-concepts are not set in early (or even late) childhood. There is much evidence that they continue throughout life to be modified by life experiences." Rutter lists four factors that can help children find resources to counter adversity:

1. Reduction of Risk Impact
   Putting protective factors in place that cushion the impact of the risk factors.

2. Reduction of Negative Chain Reaction
   Finding ways to interrupt the negative cycles that begin to operate. For example, if a child is beginning to seek attention in nega-

tive ways, interrupt her attempts and find ways to give her positive attention.

3. Establishment and Maintenance of Self-Esteem and Self-Efficacy
   Provide ways for the child to find and continue building self-esteem and confidence.

4. Opening Up of Opportunities
   Continually finding new ways for the child to learn these skills and take measured risks that can succeed.

Even if some children are born with more favorable temperaments, we can help all children develop these qualities. We assume all children will face challenges and that it is our job to prepare them to face one challenge at a time. The challenges can be small, like children not getting the meal they want or losing a valued toy, or they can be large, like experiencing the death of a grandparent or being in a car accident. Children need to develop the resolve to move on after a disappointment. Not playing the position you want on the team or not getting invited to a birthday party are life lessons. They are opportunities to foster the perseverance and reframing that is needed during crises and trauma.

As providers and parents, we want to protect our children from harm. Certainly, children need to be protected from threats that are beyond their capacity to handle. We want children to explore their environment, but not at the risk of climbing too high or going too far from home. However, small challenges can teach very big lessons. Although genetics initially plays a strong role in the development of the abilities needed to meet challenges, all children can be taught to successfully engage in life through thoughtful planning and guidance. This book includes many activities to teach these strengths, both formally and informally.

Providers help children develop these inner strengths in two main ways. First, we can model how to solve problems, how to show empathy, and how to maintain a positive attitude. We all have days when everything seems to go wrong. We run out of bread for sandwiches, toys break, children get sick, and our food inspector shows up. Children watch us as we handle our frustration, keep our sense of humor, and continue on with our routine.

Secondly, we can teach the strengths in a more formal way. We can plan activities that address attitudes, we can expect children to contribute to the environment, and we can teach problem-solving behaviors to all of the children in our care. We can balance the challenges and protections in our environment and curriculum so that children can succeed when they take risks. More important, we can demonstrate patience as children try over and over again to acquire these strengths.

Protection resides not in the evasion of risk, but in successful engagement in it.

—Michael Rutter

Ten Strengths to Build Resiliency: A Summary

My job is to be resilient.

That's why I call life a

dance.

—Bill T. Jones

1. **Self-Esteem and Sense of Competence.** Works toward mastery in at least one area. Has a positive self-esteem that can withstand setbacks.

2. **Cultural Competence.** Identifies with own culture while accepting the culture of others.

3. **Identification and Expression of Feelings.** Can recognize others' feelings and constructively express own feelings.

4. **Empathy.** Can be oriented to others' feelings and needs.

5. **Perseverance.** Will try to overcome obstacles over and over again.

6. **Responsibility.** Receives and accepts responsibility that is appropriate to age.

7. **Ability to Recognize Cause and Effect.** Can predict what consequences will result from actions.

8. **Ability to Reframe.** Can look at the same situation from differing perspectives.

9. **Problem-Solving Ability.** Demonstrates ability to control impulses, define the problem, generate alternatives, and make positive choices.

10. **Optimism and Hope.** Can see a future that is better than the present, has an ability to solve problems, and finds enjoyment in play, hobbies (for older children), relaxation, reading for pleasure, and school experiences.

Chapter Six

Right Here, Right Now

When you enter an early childhood setting where the provider focuses on the ten strengths, you will see a lot of learning taking place. For example, you might see two children in the housekeeping area arguing about who should be the baker. In the library corner, a small group of children may be gathered around a parent reading a book about a child who uses a wheelchair. Another child might stand in front of a low shelf looking at the puzzles and manipulatives before deciding which to play with. There might be a child squirting warm salt water on a huge block of ice and watching the results. In the block area, the provider could be playing with the children who have built a hospital and are busy attending to figurines which have been injured in one way or another. Imagine them rushing the people to the hospital they have created as the sirens blare.

In this busy room, children have the opportunity to practice a number of the internal strengths. Those arguing are working on problem-solving skills. Children in the book area are learning about the life of someone who uses a wheelchair. The child by the shelf is practicing making choices, and the child in the science area is investigating cause and effect. As the teacher plays, she is modeling how to care for others, helping children to express their feelings, and teaching children to negotiate.

This caregiver has done many things to support the development of the ten strengths. She has structured the environment and made materials available for children to make choices, set out books about children overcoming barriers, and created hands-on activities. She uses teachable moments to teach problem solving, and she uses temporary snags in her plans to demonstrate optimism. In this way, she models the internal strengths for the children to emulate. These interactional methods she uses are vital in teaching the strengths. In addition to the environmental and interactional methods, she can offer structured activities that teach these essential lessons. All the children she cares for will benefit from her efforts.

How to Use This Chapter

This chapter is divided into ten sections that correspond to the internal strengths. To begin, determine what strength you want to focus on and read the material presented. For example, if you are working with a child or a group of children who are not yet skilled in talking about their feelings, turn to the section on identification and expression of feelings. Or if you recognize that a child is giving up easily, look at the section on perseverance.

Each section begins with an explanation of things you can do in the classroom to lay a foundation of support. This foundation enhances the development of the strength highlighted and offers ideas about good early childhood practice. There are five building blocks you can put into place to support the development of the internal strengths:

1. Structure the environment.

2. Use teachable moments to communicate the lessons.

3. Model the inner strengths.

4. Read stories that reinforce the ten strengths.

5. Plan activities that teach the ten strengths.

A number of children in Bobbie's care were having difficulty remembering all the steps that are involved in completing an art project. After some thought about the different strategies she could use to help the children, she decided to post a pictorial checklist near the art area.

First Bobbie took photographs of a child doing each step. Then she used the pictures to make her checklist. She included a picture showing a child putting on a paint shirt, writing her name, sitting and working at the table, *putting her work on the drying rack, and putting her paint shirt away. Children who needed help could go to the checklist and see the steps. Many of the children referred to the checklist only once or twice, while others needed to check it more often. Eventually everyone was able to internalize the routine Bobbie had so carefully helped them learn. They had also learned an important lesson about being responsible for themselves during this activity.*

1. Structure the Environment

There are many things that can be done throughout your environment to support the development of the internal strengths. Providing a safe place for children to explore, to be independent, and to practice the skills they are learning leads to feelings of self-esteem. Offering an exciting, fun place that children look forward to attending gives them a sense of optimism. Structuring the environment so children will learn to take care of themselves and the materials they use can help them learn to be responsible. Posting pictures of people caring for one another fosters empathy. Displaying pictures of people with different facial expressions helps children identify feelings. And putting up signs reminding children to stop, relax, and think can reinforce problem-solving skills. Letting children play with the props used in a story or a puppet play you have done allows the children to make sense of the information presented while they retell it in a personal way. Included in each section are specific suggestions of ways to structure the environment to support the strength discussed.

2. Use Teachable Moments to Communicate the Lessons

The second way to help children develop resiliency is by using teachable moments that occur in your setting. Early childhood settings offer a myriad of chances to emphasize the ten strengths. Catching these moments requires your close attention and observation. The moments present themselves quickly, so you will have to be alert to the opportunities and clear about what you are trying to teach.

Teachable moments may occur when you least expect them. A provider had been emphasizing the importance of persistence with her group of children. After about a week of discussions, she was working with a child on a difficult floor puzzle and said, "We're having trouble with this. Should we just give up?" A child nearby promptly chimed in, "Don't quit. Try again!"

Be ready to help a child reframe a situation, to encourage perseverance, to problem solve with children, and to help them express their feelings. Coach children as they attempt to put learning into action. Watch for the ways that children use the ideas you have presented, and comment on the connections you see. For instance, you might tell a child, "I heard you say that cleaning the doll house is your responsibility. We've been talking about being responsible, haven't we?" Specific examples of teachable moments that may occur appear at the beginning of each section of this chapter that corresponds to the ten strengths.

3. Model the Inner Strengths

Modeling the inner strengths is a third way you can teach resiliency. Children are keen observers. They watch how you interact with others, how you overcome adversity, and how you handle frustrations. Then they try it for themselves. Nurture the strengths within yourself so you can provide children with a picture of what each strength looks like.

Roz recognized that things were escalating. The noise level had risen so that people needed to talk very loudly in order to be heard, some children were beginning to have arguments, and some were crashing their toys into one another. She knew she was nearing her tolerance level and was concerned that many of the children would soon lose control.

Roz turned off half the lights to get the attention of the children. She identified the problem as she saw it by saying, "It seems like some of us are getting overexcited. I want to take a minute for everyone to calm down." As she spoke she again noticed how tense she was.

She took a deep breath and then continued, "I can tell my heart is pounding fast. Put your hand on your heart and see if it is pounding fast. I'm breathing really fast too, are you? I've been using a loud voice so you could hear me. Now I want to use a quieter one. Let's all take some deep breaths and try to calm down. Okay, let's go back to our play, but remember, you can use a quiet voice and move slowly and still have fun."

By taking this short break from play, Roz modeled a way to identify and express feelings and give the children an example of how they might calm down.

One way providers model is to use self-talk. When you use this technique, you describe what you are doing, feeling, or thinking. For example, you might say out loud, "I wonder what will happen when I mix this pink and yellow playdough. Oh cool, it turned orange." Self-talk can be an effective way to model many of the strengths. You can provide children with an example of how you might handle frustration, how to talk about your feelings, how you wonder about cause and effect, and how you look at a situation optimistically. Self-talk is particularly helpful with toddlers and young preschoolers. You might find it useful with preschoolers and schoolagers, although you probably won't have to rely on it as much. Be careful to find a balance between talking enough to model a concept and talking so much that the children begin to tune you out.

Model these concepts throughout the day as well as during play. Demonstrate how to handle frustration, express your feelings in an appropriate way, and recognize how others are feeling. Let children see how you solve problems with others. Show children how you might have to look at a problem in a new way in order to solve it. Model comfort and acceptance of people from different backgrounds. Show how you care for others as you play with dolls. Pretend to take stuffed animals to the veterinarian, or notice and comfort a crying child.

4. Read Stories That Reinforce the Ten Strengths

Children's books are an ideal way to teach the ten strengths. They provide a place to begin discussion or they teach a lesson about a strength. Having the strength highlighted in the books motivates children to emulate it. In the well-known story "The Little Red Hen," the other animals learn about responsibility. In the story "The Runaway Bunny," a bunny's self-esteem is bolstered when he learns that his mother will go to great lengths to be with him and to protect him. Through books, children can also learn about people from different cultural backgrounds to which they don't have much exposure.

Examples of children's books that focus on each strength are included in the sections. The lists are not exhaustive but give you several stories which may be used to teach resiliency. You may know many of them. As you begin to recognize resiliency themes, you will be able to add many more books to the list.

After reading the story "The Tortoise and the Hare," the provider asked, "What lesson does this story teach?" One child answered, "Not to be sassy. Don't think you are going to win unless you really try." Another child added, "Yeah, and not to give up. Be like the turtle." A third child jumped into the conversation with, "My mom says, 'Slow and steady wins the race.'" The provider prompted the child, "Can you tell the other children what your mom means by that?" "If we keep walking we'll make it to the park, but if I lie down, we'll never get there!"

5. Plan Activities That Teach the Ten Strengths

Each section contains a collection of activities from which to choose. All children will find the lessons beneficial. Children experiencing difficulty will find the activities especially helpful.

The compilation of activities is not intended to be a sequential curriculum. Curricula taught in a prescribed order can be out of sync with the daily experiences of children. Instead, this collection offers a resource from which to choose activities that best fit your situation. Consider which internal strengths you want to focus on, turn to the appropriate section, and choose an activity that reinforces the specific concept you are trying to teach.

Activities found here are geared toward preschoolers, but you will need to think about how you will simplify or extend them to meet the needs of individuals. Specific suggestions for toddlers and schoolagers have been included in each lesson plan. Older preschoolers may be ready for some of the suggestions made for schoolagers, and preschoolers may enjoy the adaptations for toddlers. You will have to gauge what level of difficulty is right for the children in your group. In addition, we have organized the activities in each section from basic to more complex in order to help you judge the level of difficulty.

To reinforce the learning, periodically repeat an activity or develop one that is similar to it. These activities are a place to begin. We encourage you to develop your own ways to promote the ten strengths.

Activities will work best when you work with small groups of eight to ten children, or fewer. Consider how you can break large groups into smaller groups throughout the day. Smaller groups allow for greater participation and learning. If it is not possible to meet with small groups of children, activities can be adapted for large groups. In addition, you may find it most appropriate to do an activity with an individual.

Be creative about the time of day you introduce an activity. For example, activities involving discussions are presented as group activities. However, many could be used as a basis for informal conversation with an individual or as mealtime conversation.

Recently Jolene had heard a number of children say that others couldn't play because they were a girl or a boy. She had talked with the children about this when it came up, but she felt she needed to do something more. She decided she would plan a group activity to help children think about whether it is fair or unfair to leave someone out based on their gender.

Jolene brought beads and strings to group time the next day. When everyone had gathered, she counted the strings loudly enough so all could hear. Then she counted the children. She exclaimed, "Humph, six strings and ten children. Oh well, I'll only give them to the girls. The boys can just watch." As she started to pass them out, one of the boys said, "What about me?" Jolene answered, "Well, I'm sorry, but there just aren't enough."

Jolene watched as the girls started to string the beads and the boys looked on. She didn't want to let any of the children become anxious, so before long she stated, "I feel funny about this. Let's stop and think about it. How do the chil-dren who got the strings feel about doing beads today?" Responses included, "Happy," "Good," and "Lucky." Then Jolene asked, "How do the children who did not get strings feel?" Many of the boys said, "Bad" or "It's not fair."

Next Jolene asked, "How do you think it feels if someone says you can't play because you are a boy or because you're a girl?" All the children said that it would feel bad and that they wouldn't like it. Some remembered a time when someone had said they couldn't play. Then Jolene asked, "What do you think we should do about including boys and girls in our play?" The children answered, "Not say they can't play," "Say it's okay for everyone to play," and "Tell them it's not fair."

The activity didn't solve all the rejection problems right away, but it seemed to raise the awareness of many of the children. They came to Jolene for help when they couldn't work out their problems and seemed more willing to add children to their play when she talked with them about it.

Format of Activities

Goals: Each activity has as its primary focus one of the ten strengths. Because the strengths are interrelated, more than one strength may be enhanced through an activity. Each activity lists the primary focus first, then the other strengths that the activity also helps to support. The activities will also help to reinforce a child's skills in other areas of development that are not the focus of this book. For example, language, fine motor, gross motor, and mathematical thinking may be part of the activities.

Materials: A list of the things you will need to complete each activity has been provided. Most items are readily available. If you don't have the exact item, think of a substitute. Use items that make activities more relevant to the children in your care. Additional materials may be needed for schoolage and toddler variations.

Procedure: An outline of the steps to take in preparing for and presenting each activity to the children is provided. When appropriate, example questions are included to help you lead discussions or prompt further thought. End an activity before the children lose focus.

Because children learn in different ways, the activities have been designed to allow children to create, take part in discussion, become involved in stories, and practice skills through play or role-play. Examples of this range of teaching strategies have been included. Specific ideas about how to implement each teaching strategy follow. We encourage you to go on to create your own ways to present the content.

Activities will be most meaningful to children when they are relevant to their experiences. Adapt the activities to reflect your community and the varying cultural practices of the families you serve. Make the activities that involve characters more recognizable by changing their names, their behavior, or the setting. Be careful not to change the activity to the extent that you alter the intended goal. With this caution in mind, we encourage you to adapt.

Variations for Toddlers and Schoolagers: You must decide if the level of difficulty suggested in an activity is appropriate for your group of children. Adaptations for school-age children and toddlers have been included. You may need to further simplify an activity or make it more complex. If an activity seems too complex to work with your group right now, consider it again in a few months. Activities that are clearly inappropriate for a specific age group are noted.

Adapting Activities for Children with Special Needs

Many providers care for children with special needs or disabilities. As with all children, it is essential that children with special needs develop the ten strengths that support their resiliency. It is crucial that children not be excluded from an activity because of a disability. Depending on the child and the disability, you may have to adapt some of the activities or choose alternatives to make them accessible to all the children in your group.

For example, if you are working with a child who is Deaf or hearing-impaired and you want to have a class discussion or tell a story, you will need to think about the adaptations that will be needed. Some ideas include making sure the discussion or story is interpreted into American Sign Language, having the child sit close enough to the caregiver so that she hears, or telling the other children to talk one at a time and speak very clearly. Which solution you choose will depend on the needs of the child and what works best for her communication style. Likewise, you may need to rethink physical activities to make sure that children with mobility impairments are able to take part actively and don't end up as observers. Children with developmental delays may need activities broken down into parts and presented one step at a time. Children with receptive language delays may need visual prompts, physical gestures, or an individual practice session prior to the group experience with an activity.

Any child with a disability is eligible by federal law for support from the public school system. If you are working with a child who has a disability, you may be able to get help choosing and adapting activities from an early interventionist, a physical therapist, or an occupational therapist. Often a child's parents are the best resource. They know the child's abilities and what kinds of adaptations work best.

Teaching Strategies

A number of different teaching strategies have been used in the activities. Discussion, storytelling, puppet plays, role-plays, and the arts are among the suggestions. Some lessons use a combination of teaching techniques. Keep the following general guidelines in mind as you use these strategies.

Free-Play Activities

Children can explore many of the activities included in this collection independently. Put the materials out and let a child follow his interest. When he is exploring the activity, expand his understanding of it by asking questions, making suggestions, or offering additional information or materials when requested.

Group Discussions

Discussions provide children with many opportunities to learn. As children share their ideas, they learn to communicate with one another and practice language skills. Listening to the ideas of others exposes children to other ways of thinking and can lead to respect. The flexible thinking children need to successfully solve problems develops when children brainstorm.

Children need to feel comfortable with one another before they risk sharing their ideas. Make sure they know one another and have built trusting relationships within the group before trying activities that involve discussion.

To get the discussion going, use the suggestions in each activity. Ask the children for their ideas about the topic. Probe for additional thoughts by saying, "That's one idea. What's another?" or "Is there a different way to do it?" Encourage and respect a variety of answers. Avoid appearing as if you are looking for one "right" answer. Offer your ideas as one of the members of the group, but be careful not to overpower.

Be ready for the unexpected! Some children will offer ideas you haven't thought about. Others may make comments that seem unrelated. Give children a chance to explain their ideas. You can sometimes follow their train of thought. Other children may become distracted and offer comments that are clearly off task. Help a child refocus by rephrasing the question at hand.

Be prepared to make on-the-spot decisions throughout any discussion. For example, you may need to decide how to respond to a child's comment that is in direct contrast to a concept you are trying to teach. More specifically, what will you do if a child suggests hitting as a solution to a problem? You could take note of it at this point and evaluate its consequences later, or you could address it by asking questions that help clarify the child's thinking. If you immediately point out that this child's suggestion won't keep everyone safe, you risk inhibiting further participation by this child. However, if you include the suggestion, other children may view it as an indication of approval. Use what you know about the individuals in your group and the social context from which they come to make an appropriate decision about how to handle this. For a more detailed discussion of group conversations, see Diane Levin's book *Teaching Young Children in Violent Times*.

Christine led a morning and an afternoon preschool class that were very different from one another. In her morning class many of the children were able to work out their difficulties. When they couldn't, they usually came to the teacher for help. Many children in the afternoon class became aggressive or dissolved into tears when they were faced with conflict. She led discussions in each class where the children tried to think of things they could do when they wanted a turn with a toy.

The children in the morning class thought of many things they could do. Their suggestions included asking for a turn, waiting, making a trade, and getting a teacher to help. Then one child said, "You could hit 'em. Then they would give it to you." Christine had to decide if she should include the suggestion or if she should make sure that everyone knew that hitting was not okay. Christine decided that since many of the children were able to problem solve successfully, she would write the suggestion down and evaluate it with the children at a later time. To help children decide which idea to try first, she asked the same questions about each one of their suggestions: "What might happen if you tried that idea? What would that person feel like?" When they reached "Hit 'em," the children were able to point out that someone would get hurt, you might get into trouble, and you might not get the toy anyway. Christine felt satisfied that the children had pointed out the consequences of hitting.

In her more aggressive afternoon class, hitting was the first suggestion they made. Christine felt she needed to respond differently than she had in the morning since there were so many children in this group who did not clearly understand that this was not an acceptable solution. In this case she asked right away, "What might happen if you tried that idea? Would that person feel safe?" Then she said, "Hitting hurts. It's not okay to hurt people." She continued the discussion about more acceptable responses by asking, "What's another thing you might do?"

When possible, write down the ideas the children give during discussion or draw simple pictures that represent the ideas. This assists visual learners, helps children feel their input is important, and can be useful when it is time to summarize what you have been talking about.

The Arts

Art, music, and drama are important ways in which children express themselves. Through these experiences, they can sometimes communicate thoughts and dreams that are difficult to voice in other ways. When possible, activities have been included that allow this type of expression. Be creative in your use of the arts to teach or allow an individual's expression of internal strengths. Ask open-ended questions and use encouraging statements to invite participation.

Role-Plays

Some of the activities presented include role-plays for the group. Do the role-play, then discuss what took place. Role-plays can be a great way for children to see the behavior or the skill modeled. Do a role-play with another adult, a child, or a puppet. When you do this with another person, rehearse enough to get the outcome you expect. If you plan to role-play with a child, ask for a volunteer to help. Some children might be uncomfortable if forced to "perform" in front of others. Avoid demonstrating or exaggerating the inappropriate during role-plays. This can become silly and may leave a lasting impression for some children instead of the lesson you want to emphasize.

Other activities suggest that pairs or small groups of children do role-plays. This practice is helpful to children as they try to use the concepts. Even after a role-play has been demonstrated, some children may need your help to find words to use as they try it on their own.

Puppet Plays

When you really want to draw the attention of most children, get out the puppets. They can be used to begin a discussion, demonstrate a concept, and model skills. Do the brief puppet play suggested in the activity. Then help the children understand the events depicted by asking questions about what took place. For example, ask:

- "What happened first?"
- "What did the puppet do next?"
- "What problem did the puppets have?"
- "How did they work it out?"

Help the children apply the story in the puppet play to their lives. Encourage them to talk about an experience they had that was similar to that of the puppets. Let the children use the puppets to retell the story during free play. Watch for the children to demonstrate the strength modeled in the puppet play. When you see them use it, comment on it. This helps children connect their behavior to the lesson taught.

Stories

Many cultures use stories to entertain, teach a lesson, illustrate a point, or emphasize a value. In addition to the books listed, original stories have been included to demonstrate how you might tell a story of your own. As you tell a story, change the inflection in your voice and use gestures and facial expressions to add interest. Accompany this auditory learning experience with visual learning. Illustrate a story with pictures cut from magazines, plastic or wooden figurines, simple line drawings, or flannel board pieces.

After telling a story, set out the necessary props for the children to retell the story. Put the props in the block area, housekeeping area, or in the doll house. Or you could act out the story by assigning different children to be the characters. If the story doesn't have enough characters for all the children who want to be involved, make up some extras. You can easily add trees or a pet to most stories. Narrate the story as the children perform the actions described. Whenever possible, let children say phrases from the story for themselves, such as, "Who's that tramping over my bridge?" Be ready to tell a story over and over again because this tends to be a favorite activity for many children. Develop your own stories to fit your circumstances.

Charts

Charts are useful in a number of ways. They provide a way to visualize information that might be difficult to understand when just talking about it. They allow children to draw conclusions about the information presented. Children can "read" them when simple pictures are used.

A few charts have been included in this compilation of activities. When first introducing this teaching strategy, make the charts easier for children to understand by having the children physically involved in making them. For example, on a chart asking "How Do You Like Your Apples?" have those who like applesauce best stand together. Those who like apple juice make up another group, and those who like whole apples are in a third group. After experience with physical groupings, you can use photographs or name cards to represent each child on a poster board chart.

Transition Activities

Even during transitions from one activity to the next, you may be able to work on some of the ten strengths. A few transitional ideas are included in this compilation. Generally, these activities are short, can be done anywhere, and require few props, if any. Many of the transition activities suggested here provide a break from exciting play. Most focus on helping children who are getting overstimulated and excited learn to relax. These activities also enhance the children's ability to control their impulses.

Parent Involvement

Educators recognize the importance of involving parents in the education of their children. Parent involvement and input help build relationships and consistency between home and the early childhood program. Parents and caregivers also build opportunities to learn from one another. Parents can give their perspective on topics you discuss and help children practice a skill in other settings.

Build respectful and cooperative partnerships with parents that help you learn about the individuals within your group and the families you serve. This understanding is essential as you strive to build each child's strengths and make activities meaningful. Ask questions about cultural practices that may differ from your own. For example, you might say, "I'd like to do an activity on family celebrations. Do you celebrate events with your family? What do you do?" Use the information to modify lessons so they are inclusive and meaningful to all participants.

Parents teach the internal strengths from the beginning and will continue the lessons after your involvement. They do this by nurturing, supporting, and modeling skills for their child. While parental involvement in your program is important, so is having time to be a parent. Overburdening parents with things to read or homework assignments may take away from the time they have to spend enjoying their child and for other positive family interactions. Requiring parents to be highly involved can place additional stress on already busy families. Keep your expectations realistic. Respect differences in the amount of time, talents, and abilities parents have by offering a wide variety of ways to be involved. Make it clear they don't have to "do it all."

Many parents will want to know what they can do to develop the important internal strengths presented here. Several simple ways to share what has been taught and involve parents in the activities follow. Add your own ideas.

- Post a paragraph on your parent bulletin board that describes the importance of the internal strength that you are focusing on and doing activities to build.

- Write a letter to parents explaining the goals you are currently addressing. Provide example phrases of words you are using to teach a concept. Suggest they use the same words.

- Set up a voice mail system where you can leave a brief message for parents recapping an activity and what it teaches. Summarize why you are doing that activity.

- At a parent meeting, describe a game you played or a simple activity you did and what it taught.

- Post signs that describe the process of various activities and what is learned from them. Post the signs where the activities usually occur and where parents can see them. For example, above learning centers, near displays of children's projects, or on charts.

- Display an example activity or lesson plan on your bulletin board and tell the internal strength it builds.

- Suggest ways parents can modify an activity so they can play it in the car as they travel to and from child care.

- Post the lists you develop when brainstorming or doing problem-solving activities next to the entrance or on a bulletin board so parents can see them.

- Post charts you create in an area where parents can glance at them as they drop off or pick up their child.

- Send home children's work. When it's appropriate, label or write captions that help to explain an activity or drawing.

- Ask parents to work with their child to cut out magazine and newspaper pictures to be used in murals or other projects once in a while. Or ask them to donate magazines for you to use.

- Ask parents to discuss with their child a concept that will be used in an activity during the upcoming week. For example, to prepare for an activity on lullabies, you might ask parents to talk with their child about the songs they sang to their child when they were a baby or the songs they sing now.

- When children make a booklet or a picture as part of an activity, ask parents to review it with their child.

- Make a point of personally talking to the parents of children who are working to develop a specific strength. Describe how you are addressing the strength and ways you might work together to develop it.

Self-Esteem and Sense of Competence

Benjamin is developing a positive sense of self. On a typical day, Benjamin walks into child care and returns the greetings of a number of children who notice his arrival. He scans the room, looking where to play first. When he notices some of the other children playing in the block area, he walks over and compliments their work saying, "Hey, this is cool." He sits down next to them and continues to observe for a short time. Benjamin makes a suggestion to expand the race track the others have begun. When his suggestion is not accepted, he tries again. This time he offers to make the ticket stand where the fans come in and the others enthusiastically agree to the addition.

Benjamin approaches tasks and people with assurance. He feels a sense of belonging to this group. He persists when faced with challenges. He has learned to make positive statements about others and expects that he will be accepted. Benjamin believes that he can be successful at most things he tries and doesn't feel a great need to compete with others. When children like Benjamin possess a positive attitude about themselves and their capabilities, they believe they can tackle problems and cope with change.

Early childhood is the time when children begin to form beliefs about themselves and their abilities. You can help young children build their self-esteem by doing the following:

> Create a setting in which a child feels valued, accepted, and safe regardless of their behaviors or abilities.

> Respond to their needs in a predictable, respectful manner.

> Plan activities where children can succeed yet feel challenged.

> Encourage children to explore materials and draw their own conclusions.

Following are suggestions for your environment, examples of teachable moments, ideas about ways to model, and activities that support children's healthy self-esteem.

Environment

> Establish a consistent schedule that allows children to know what to expect next and to prepare for transitions. This consistency helps children feel comfortable and secure.

> Set up routines for daily events. For example, have a specific way to clean up the toys, wash hands, and get ready for nap.

> Concentrate daily on building and nurturing your relationship with each child. Notice what she enjoys, how long she plays with various toys, and who her friends are. Relationships with caring adults are the cornerstone of resiliency.

> Accept, acknowledge, and celebrate individual differences in interests, abilities, and cultural backgrounds. This unconditional relationship values children for who they are. Highlight the strengths of a child with physical challenges. Take interest in and learn about cultural events celebrated by the children in your group.

> Include plenty of time for self-directed play. Through play children practice social skills, develop language that helps to direct play, and learn to control the objects in their environment. The sense of competence and pleasure derived from play fosters a positive self-image.

> Offer choices to children in activities, materials, and directing their own behavior. Give them opportunities to influence decisions that affect them, such as what they might do at the next group celebration. In this way children learn that they have some control over what they do.

- Emphasize cooperation and minimize competition. Fostering cooperation helps everyone feel like they have something to offer and they are an important part of the group. For instance, instead of playing a competitive game like musical chairs, change it to a cooperative game of musical mats. In this game, you use small throw rugs or large mats and instead of eliminating children you eliminate rugs. When the music stops, children find ways to make room for everyone to touch a part of a rug until all the children huddle together on the only rug left.

- Display photos of the children in the group and pictures they have drawn. Let them decide which ones should be posted. You might ask them to choose a drawing they worked on for a long time, the one they worked the hardest on, or one in which they tried something for the first time.

Teachable Moments

- Focus your attention on each child every day. Warmly greet each one as they arrive. Listen when a child shares her ideas. Get down on the floor and play with a child to demonstrate you value them and what they are doing.

- Demonstrate to a child that you are really listening to her by reflecting back what she is saying. Paraphrase what she is telling you by repeating her comments in your own words. For example, if a child is telling you about a fishing trip with Grandpa, you might say, "It sounds like you and your grandpa had a wonderful time fishing even if you didn't catch anything."

- Recognize when children master a skill they have been working on. Give specific praise describing what the child is now capable of doing. For example, "It used to be hard for you to find your name on the chart. Now you spot it right away."

- Offer activities at a developmentally appropriate level. Activities that are open-ended and focus on the process rather than the product are ones in which children have opportunities to be creative and successful.

- Keep your expectations realistic and convey your confidence by saying, "I think you can do it" or "I know you will make it."

- Find something you like about every child, especially those who are sometimes difficult to like. Be careful not to blame one child for the things that go wrong.

Modeling

> Provide an example of self-acceptance by giving yourself credit for your strengths and working on your weaknesses. For example, you might say, "I've been working hard to solve this problem. I think it's going to work out. I'm glad I stuck with it."

> Make statements about your own feelings of competence. You might say out loud, "I might be able to help with that. It worked for me one other time I tried it."

Children's Books

Carlson, Nancy. *I Like Me!* New York: Scholastic, 1988.

Corey, Dorothy. *Will There Be a Lap for Me?* Morton Grove, IL: Whitman, 1992.

Henkes, Kevin. *Sheila Rae, the Brave.* New York: Greenwillow, 1987.

Hutchins, Pat. *My Best Friend.* New York: Greenwillow, 1993.

Moose, Barbara. *Mama, Do You Love Me?* San Francisco: Chronicle, 1991.

Morris, Ann. *Loving.* New York: Lothrop, 1990.

A child care consultant shared the following story about a situation in which scapegoating was clearly an issue.

"I had been asked by a director of a child care cooperative to observe three children having difficulty in one of their classrooms. My job was to watch what was taking place and then talk with the staff about ways to work with these children.

"On the day I visited, I noticed that when there was a loud noise or a problem, many of the children stopped what they were doing and looked around to find out what was happening. This is not out of the ordinary. However, what caught my attention were the two or three small groups of children who kept playing without much disruption. I wasn't sure how to explain this until later when I heard the children say to one another, 'Jonathan did it' or 'There goes Jonathan again.' I still wasn't sure of the dynamics until one more incident took place.

"A child was getting a little rambunctious and bumped into a shelf, knocking over the rack of puzzles. In an effort to conceal her own responsibility, she quickly blamed Jonathan. I had now heard Jonathan was to blame for three things that had taken place that morning. What made this even more disturbing was the fact that Jonathan wasn't even in attendance that day. Clearly Jonathan had become a scapegoat."

A Really Big Puzzle

Goal:

Develop self-esteem and sense of competence; support cultural competence

Materials:

- group photograph enlarged to 12 by 16 inches or larger
- glue
- poster board
- craft knife or scissors

Procedure:

1. Show that all the children in your group are valued by taking a group photograph. It can be one in which the children are posed or at play.

2. Have the photograph enlarged to at least 12 by 16 inches. Mount it on heavy poster board. Then cut it into simple puzzle pieces.

3. Put out the photo puzzle for the children to put together. Encourage them to name the people pictured. When they know the children well, they might also be encouraged to say something they know the child in the picture likes to do. For example, "This is Rhona. She likes to build with blocks."

4. Talk with the children about how everyone in the group is important. Take out one puzzle piece and talk about how the group wouldn't be the same if one of the children in the picture was missing.

Variations for Toddlers:

Prepare the photo puzzle as described, making sure the puzzle pieces are very simple. Before presenting the puzzle, do a name chant so each child remembers the names of others. Say, "Katy's here today, Katy's here today, Katy's here today. Yea! Katy!" Work on putting the puzzle together with the children. Encourage children to point to each child in the picture and say their names.

Variations for Schoolagers:

This activity will work for schoolagers in its present form.

Showing Love

Goal:

Develop self-esteem and sense of competence; support cultural competence

Materials:

- large paper for mural
- scissors
- glue
- magazines

Procedure:

1. Enhance feelings of self-worth by helping children recognize ways people express love. Brainstorm all the different ways people show love. Include activities such as:

- hugs
- kisses
- smiles
- gifts
- cooking and eating good food
- reading together
- playing together
- sending cards
- listening to one another

Note: A child may say something about punishment being a way that people show love. If this comes up in your discussion, you might say something like, "Some people think that's a way to show love, but there are many other ways too. Can you think of another way?"

2. Ask the children to help you make a mural showing as many of the different ways people show love as possible.

3. Provide the materials. Let the children page through the magazines and find pictures of people showing love to one another. Have children cut out the ones they find. If you don't see the connection, ask the child to explain. Include any picture that the children can defend; the child may have good reason for it. If they can't describe how a picture fits, save it for another day or let them take it home.

4. Glue the pictures on the large paper. Write a title for it and display it somewhere the children and their parents can enjoy it.

Variations for Toddlers:

Provide precut pictures for toddlers to choose from and paste. Model words that describe the way each picture shows love.

Variations for Schoolagers:

Prepare booklets with five or six blank pages. Ask schoolagers to paste pictures in their book that show ways they feel loved. Or ask each schoolager to draw one way that they feel loved and then compile all of their pictures into a group book.

I Feel Loved

3

Goal:
Develop self-esteem and sense of competence; support cultural competence

Materials:
- chart paper
- markers
- *Loving* by Ann Morris

Procedure:

1. Bolster feelings of self-worth by helping children recognize ways people show love for them. Write at the top of the chart paper in bold letters "I feel loved when…"

2. Read the book *Loving* by Ann Morris.

3. Ask each child to tell you when she feels loved. Write down what they say. You may choose to write down the name of the child who said it as well.

Note: A child may connect punishment and love. If this comes up in your discussion, you might say something like, "Some people think that's a way to show love, but there are many other ways too. Can you think of another way?"

4. Summarize by saying something like, "People feel loved in many different ways." Reread the list.

Variations for Toddlers:
This activity is not developmentally appropriate for most toddlers.

Variations for Schoolagers:
Have familiar words (like *love, mom, dad, hug,* and *kiss*) written before the group meets. After writing their responses, see if they can find and match any of the sight words.

> **Children's responses when asked, "When do you feel loved?"**
> *When I go to my grandma and grandpa's.*
> *When we go fishing.*
> *When my mommy kisses me.*
> *When my mom and dad tuck me in.*
> *When my mom and dad take me to the fair.*

Let's Tell the Teacher What To Do

Goal:

Develop self-esteem and sense of competence; support perseverance and problem solving

Materials:

- whiteboard or chalkboard
- dry erase markers or chalk
- eraser
- simple figures drawn on 3 by 5 inch slips of paper
- a hat or a bowl

Procedure:

1. Build feelings of self-esteem by giving children a chance to control what takes place. Begin by drawing simple figures on each slip of paper. Draw such things as a circle, square, line, animals, flower pot, and person. Place them in a bowl or a hat.

2. Tell the children that they are to give you instructions and you will draw a picture for them. (Doing this in a small group might help shy children participate more fully.)

3. Have one child pull a picture from the hat. Ask the child to give you specific directions about how to draw what he sees without telling you the name of it. For example, "Start at the top of the paper, then go to the side, then down and around." Draw the outlines of the shapes or objects as they describe them.

4. Ask questions to help clarify their suggestions, such as, "Where do I start?" "How big?" and "Then where do I go?" You may be erasing a lot! Be clear that the children are not to criticize your work, but they can redirect you if you don't draw what they intended.

5. When you are finished drawing the outlines, let the children color the picture. Put their names on it and display.

Variations for Toddlers:

This is not developmentally appropriate for most toddlers.

Variations for Schoolagers:

After the children have done this activity with an adult, have them try it with one another. Divide the group into pairs. Give each person a chance to experience giving and getting directions.

Look What I Can Do Now

5

Goal:
Develop self-esteem and sense of competence; support optimism and hope

Materials:
- booklets with empty pages
- pencils
- crayons
- markers
- colored pencils
- stapler

Procedure:

1. Give children an opportunity to identify their strengths. Prepare a booklet for each child by stapling 5 to 6 blank sheets of paper together in a book form.

2. Tell the children that they are going to make a book over several weeks. Focus on the skills children are mastering as a way to show growth and competence. One day each week (or more, if they choose), talk about what the children are learning to do. It could be all kinds of things, such as being a friend, riding a tricycle, petting their dog, or doing the dishes.

3. Ask each child to identify something they have learned. Write it in their book. Have the children illustrate that page of their book.

4. Each week ask the children to make a new page. Be sure to observe the children and note the things they are learning while you are together. Share your observations with the children, especially if someone is having a difficult time thinking of what they have learned.

Variations for Toddlers:
Precut pictures from magazines for toddlers to choose from and paste in a group collage. Find pictures of things the toddlers in your group are learning. Label each picture with the name of each toddler. Include things like dressing, eating, sharing, picking up toys, sitting in a car seat cheerfully, toilet training, arriving and departing from child care, making friends, talking, and showing affection.

Variations for Schoolagers:
About once a week, ask children to reflect on something they learned during the past few days. Have them journal about it with pictures or words. Date each entry and have the students periodically review their accomplishments. Share these journals with parents.

Things I'm Good At

6

Goal:

Develop self-esteem and sense of competence

Materials:

- pictures of activities found on the next page
- booklets with 5 to 6 empty pages
- paste or glue sticks
- markers or crayons
- stapler

Procedure:

1. Give children an opportunity to identify their strengths. Prepare a booklet for each child by stapling five to six blank sheets of paper together in a book form. For those who aren't yet writing, make a cover page that reads, "I am good at…."

2. Determine if the children are capable of drawing their own pictures. If the children in your group become easily frustrated when drawing, make copies of the pictures provided on the next page, set them out, and have the children choose from those available. They can make their booklets by pasting the pictures of activities they are good at on each page. Children who are capable of drawing their own pictures can be given empty booklets to illustrate. Write captions for their pictures.

3. Talk with the children about things you are good at and those you have some trouble with. Say, "I'm good at…but I have to work hard at…." Then ask the children what they are good at and what is hard for them. If they are having difficulty thinking of things, offer suggestions. Have the children draw or paste a picture of something that they are good at on each page of their books.

- blocks
- paints or markers
- numbers
- dress up
- friends
- cleaning up
- books
- running
- ball
- dolls
- action figures
- tying shoes

4. If the children who are choosing from predrawn pictures name things that they are good at which are not pictured, have the children dictate words for you to write.

5. Have each child read their book to you or dictate captions for the pictures.

Variations for Toddlers:

For toddlers, focus on "Things I like to do all by myself" instead of "Things I am good at." Paste the pictures in a book. Expect that they will include many pictures in their book just because they are having fun gluing. Take time with each child to look at the pictures in their book.

Variations for Schoolagers:

After discussing types of activities, schoolagers can make their own books. Have the children draw their own pictures of things they are good at doing.

Cultural Competence

Louis is in the housekeeping area pretending to cook. He sets the table then stirs a pot on the stove. When he brings the pot to the table he says, "Here are the beans and rice. Get a tortilla and let's eat." Elijah hears the menu and says, "I've never had rice and beans, but I'll try them."

Culturally competent children are proud of their own traditions and backgrounds. They notice differences in people, what they eat, what they look like, and how they celebrate. They accept differences without rejecting or putting others down. They are able to play with children whose experiences are different from their own. As children grow up in this diverse society, it is essential that they be culturally competent.

Children learn attitudes about diversity through their observations, by noticing what is valued and respected, and by listening to what is said as well as what is not said. At very young ages, children notice how they are similar to and different from those around them. Our similarities mean that we share human characteristics. Our differences make us interesting and unique. However, in our society, some differences are assigned negative characteristics which children absorb.

In her book *Big As Life,* Stacey York offers four goals for teaching children about diversity:

1. Foster each child's positive, knowledgeable, and confident self-identity within a cultural context.

2. Foster each child's comfortable, empathetic interaction with diversity among people.

3. Foster each child's critical thinking about bias.

4. Foster each child's ability to stand up for himself or herself and others in the face of bias.

There are many things you can do to promote these goals. You can help children learn to be proud of who they are and appreciate the differences they notice (Chang, Muckelroy, and Pulido-Tobiassen, 1996). You can help them explore similarities and differences they recognize, address questions they have, and learn to recognize and confront bias they encounter.

We encourage you to continue your study about anti-bias education and cultural competence by reading, listening to others, viewing parents as resources, and seeking out community resources. Some resources that explore this topic in more depth are *Big As Life* by Stacey York, *Anti-Bias Curriculum* by Louise Derman-Sparks, and *Multicultural Issues in Child Care* by Janet Gonzalez-Mena. There are many others.

Listed below are a few examples of things you can do in your environment, ways you can respond to children's questions, things you can do as you interact with children, and activities you can offer.

Environment

❥ Create an atmosphere of acceptance where all people feel welcome and valued. For example, if a child in your setting speaks another language, make an effort to learn how to say some words in his home language. Be sure you know how to correctly pronounce and spell names of family members.

❥ Display posters and pictures that are positive reflections of children in your care. Every child should see that they are represented. Go beyond those in your group to include people of other ethnic groups as well.

❥ Display pictures of different kinds of families, including foster families, adoptive or blended families, grandparents, single parents, families with gay or lesbian parents, extended families, and interracial families.

❥ Decorate with materials from other cultures, such as wall hangings, rugs, baskets, and artwork.

- Make sure the books you read, the materials you put out, and the foods you serve are varied and reflective of all cultures. Access materials through libraries, museums, cultural resource centers, ethnic stores and restaurants, and parents and early childhood catalogues (Chang, Muckelroy and Pulido-Tobiassen, 1996).

- Include a spectrum of flesh tone colors in your art supplies. Crayons, markers, paints, and playdough need to reflect the diversity of the children you serve. This allows children to accurately depict themselves and helps them feel valued.

- Place a number of different materials in your sensory tub that might be familiar to children of various cultures. Each week you might use something different, like coffee beans, rice, and dried corn. Talk with parents about their feelings regarding the use of food items as play materials before offering these. Some parents feel strongly that children should not play with costly food.

- Place materials in the dramatic play area that are familiar to the children in your care. Depending on the cultural backgrounds of the children, items such as a tortilla press, rice steamer, or lefse turner might be included. Clothing items should also reflect the backgrounds of the children. Additional items to include might be kimonos, parkas, turbans, veils, ribbon shirts, moccasins, and serapes (Chang, Muckelroy and Pulido-Tobiassen, 1996). Ask parents what would reflect their cultures respectfully.

- Have toys that include people with disabilities. Plastic figurines in wheelchairs, dolls fitted with hearing aids, and books written in braille help children become familiar with adaptive equipment.

- Play music with a variety of sounds and tempos as background music, for children to dance to, and for all to relax to. Collect instruments that offer sounds that are familiar to children as well as those that are new to them. Wooden recorders, finger pianos, drums, and stringed instruments introduce children to the variety of sounds heard in music in different cultures.

Teachable Moments

- Respond to a child's questions about differences with matter-of-fact, simple information. For example, when a child asks, "Why doesn't he have any fingernails?" the provider responds, "He didn't have any fingernails when he was born. He has three fingers that are shorter on that hand too. It is a little harder for him to catch a ball, but he has figured out a way to do it. Would you two like to play ball for a while?"

➤ Challenge the thinking of children who describe stereotypes. When Asha met a woman who was a pastor, she said, "You can't be a pastor, only men." To ignore this comment would leave her with incorrect information and may lead to more narrow views of the roles women can take. Say something like, "Have all the pastors you've known been men? Now you know a women who is a pastor. What other jobs do both men and woman do?"

➤ Intervene when children reject others because of race, gender, ethnicity, or disability. Respond as you might when one child physically hurts another. Stop the behavior, comfort the child whose feelings have been hurt, and then problem solve (Neugebauer, 1992).

➤ Tell a child who rejects others that it is not okay to say you won't play because of skin color, gender, ability, or language (Derman-Sparks, 1989). Say something like, "It's not fair to say you won't play because his skin is brown. It hurts his feelings and you're missing out on a great friend" (Derman-Sparks, 1989).

➤ Learn and use words from a child's home language. Find out how to say common words like those used to show appreciation, to greet others, to ask for help, and to ask how the child is feeling. Be sure you know what words the child will use to let you know that he has to use the bathroom or to ask for something to eat or drink.

➤ Listen for, take an interest in, and learn about cultural events children in your care talk about. For example, a provider heard a child talk about her jingle dress. The provider asked her supervisor what it was and found out it was a ceremonial dress the child wore, at powwows. The provider was then able to ask more questions about the dress as well as the child's participation in powwows. She also took the time to talk with the child's mother to learn more about how the dress was made.

➤ Use words to describe what you are doing, the play taking place, and to label common objects for children who are learning English as a second language. They need opportunities to hear it spoken and then to try it on their own. Do not correct pronunciation errors but repeat the word back to them using the correct articulation.

➤ Periodically observe to see if there is a mixture of both boys and girls using the block area and the housekeeping area as well as all the learning activities in your setting. Encourage children to participate in each activity.

- Talk about and celebrate the family traditions of the children in your care. Invite families to come and talk about their traditions. Be careful to balance the attention paid to celebrations with an equal amount of attention paid to real, everyday living. Ignoring celebrations gives the message they are not important, while planning your curriculum around celebration after celebration gives the impression that this is how families live. *Celebrate!* by Julie Bisson contains further information on celebrating holidays in culturally responsive and respectful ways.

Modeling

- Model comfort in talking about differences. If you are unwilling to talk about something a child notices, you may convey the message that there is something embarrassing or shameful about differences.

- Show children how you work out cultural differences with coworkers and parents. Let them hear you talk respectfully with others who have different child rearing practices or have differences of opinion. Work with the other person to come to a common understanding.

- Demonstrate for the children how important it is to continually learn about your own culture and the culture of others. Attend workshops, read books, talk with people who have a culture that is different from your own, attend ethnic celebrations, and visit ethnic shops to learn about others.

- Model respect and patience with people who speak a language that is different from your own. Children need to see that you are willing to take the time to communicate with all people.

Children's Books

Ashley, Bernard. *Cleversticks*. New York: Crown, 1991.

Carlson, Nancy. *Arnie and the New Kid*. New York: Puffin, 1990.

Kissinger, Katie. *All the Colors We Are*. St. Paul: Redleaf, 1994.

Martin, Bill, Jr. *White Dynamite and Curly Kidd*. New York: Holt, 1986.

Morris, Ann. *Shoes, Shoes, Shoes*. New York: Lothrop, 1995.

Pellegrini, Nina. *Families Are Different*. New York: Holiday House, 1991.

Surat, Michele Maria. *Angel Child, Dragon Child*. New York: Scholastic, 1983.

Finger Paint Mix-Up

Goal:

Develop sense of cultural competence; support self-esteem

Materials:

- finger paint paper
- powdered tempera paints (black, brown, red, yellow, and white)
- liquid starch

Procedure:

1. Help children explore skin color through finger painting. Put a small amount of black, brown, red, yellow, and white powdered tempera onto finger paint paper.

2. Pour about 3 tablespoons of liquid starch on the paper. Invite children to mix the powdered tempera and starch by finger painting.

3. Encourage them to make skin colors. They could even try to make the color of their own skin.

Variation for Toddlers:

Let toddlers paint with a variety of premixed skin colors. Notice the tone that is closest to their own. Say something like, "This is a beautiful cinnamon color, just like your skin."

Variation for Schoolagers:

Schoolagers can paint their skin tone. After it dries, they can cut the paper into the shapes of their faces and then add facial features with markers or cut outs to make self-portraits.

From *Big As Life* (1998), by Stacey York. Published by Redleaf Press, St. Paul, Minnesota, 800-423-8309. Used with permission.

High Stepping

Goal:

Develop sense of cultural competence; support self-esteem

Materials:

- skin tone shades of liquid tempera paint
- pie plates
- plastic dishpan filled with water
- towel
- large sheet of butcher paper
- drop cloth
- tape

Procedure:

1. Help children explore the shade of their own skin color by making a mural of footprints. You may want to do this activity outside. If you choose to stay inside, start by spreading a large drop cloth on the floor. Tape down a large sheet of butcher paper for the children to walk on.

2. Have one child at a time find the flesh tone paint that is closest to their own skin color. In the pie plate, mix a small amount of one or more colors to lighten it or darken it for a better match. Spread the paint over the bottom of the pan.

3. Take the child's shoes and socks off. Have the child step into the pan with one foot, then the other, and then walk across the butcher paper.

4. Have the dishpan of water and towel waiting on the other side. When the child reaches the end of the paper, he steps into the water to wash his feet. Dry them with the towel before putting on shoes and socks.

5. Write all the names of the children who contribute to the mural. Display the mural where the children can see it.

Variations for Toddlers:

It is essential to have two adults working with the children when you do this with toddlers. One to work with the child who is painting, the other to work with the rest of the children. Perhaps a coworker or parent volunteer would be able to help.

Variations for Schoolagers:

This activity will work for schoolagers in its present form.

We All Celebrate

9

Goal:

Develop sense of cultural competence;
support self-esteem, optimism, and hope

Materials:

- three-ring binder or folder
- paper that fits the binder (three-hole punched)
- note explaining the project to parents (optional)

Procedure:

1. Explore the variety of things people do when they celebrate by asking parents to help create a page for a classroom book. Do this activity at a special parent-child event or send the materials home with each child to do and then return to you.

2. Explain to parents or send a note home explaining that you are making a book to have in your classroom showing how different families celebrate special events.

3. Suggest that they talk with their child about the different celebrations they have throughout the year. Perhaps they have been to a family wedding, celebrated a birthday, or enjoyed a special religious ceremony they would like to share with their classmates.

4. Provide paper that will fit in the folder or notebook where the pages will be compiled. Have each family decorate the sheet by drawing a picture, writing a brief story about their celebration, or attaching family photographs.

5. Ask them to write a caption that tells what celebration is depicted.

6. When all of the children have completed their pages put them together into a three-ring binder or a folder. Make a cover for the book. Look at it with small groups of children or let each child tell the group about the page they contributed.

Variations for Toddlers:

Ask parents to contribute a photograph of their family as they celebrate a special event. Be sure to label each photo with the name of the family and the celebration pictured. Make a bulletin board with all the pictures at the children's eye level. Cover it with clear vinyl so the children can see it but can't touch the photographs.

Variations for Schoolagers:

Schoolagers may be able to complete this activity without parental help. Ask children to draw a picture and below it write a paragraph about their celebration.

What Language Is That?

10

Goal:

Develop sense of cultural competence

Materials:

- audiotape of people speaking or singing in different languages
- tape recorder

Procedure:

1. Explore how languages are similar to and different from one another. Make a cassette tape of adults and children speaking different languages. If you don't know many people who speak a different language, contact an English as a Second Language program in your community.

2. Play the tape and ask the children if they know what language the people are speaking. Can they tell when the language changes? Can they recognize when someone is speaking English? How do they know when someone is speaking a different language?

3. Expand the discussion by talking about the languages spoken in your community. Ask the children, "What are some of the languages you've heard people use?"

Variations for Toddlers:

While the children play or at naptime, play songs that are sung in different languages.

Variations for Schoolagers:

Expand this activity for schoolagers by exploring how people's voices are similar to and different from one another. Discuss how people can change their voices and talk in different ways.

From *Big As Life* (1998), by Stacey York. Published by Redleaf Press, St. Paul, Minnesota, 800-423-8309. Used with permission.

Tasting Bread

11

Goal:

Develop sense of cultural competence

Materials:

- pictures of different types of breads eaten around the world
- *Bread, Bread, Bread* by Ann Morris
- plastic bread sets
- variety of breads
- butter
- knives
- toppings (optional)

Procedure:

1. Buy or ask parents to donate a variety of breads such as pita bread, French bread, naan, chapatti, whole wheat bread, flat bread, and others. Cut into sample pieces.

2. Talk with the children about the name of each bread pictured, or read the book *Bread, Bread, Bread*. Discuss the fact that many people eat bread and that bread comes in different shapes and sizes.

3. Provide butter and knives for spreading. If you want, set out a variety of toppings too. You might include cinnamon sugar, marmalades, or hummus.

4. Let the children taste each bread.

Variations for Toddlers:

Toddlers might enjoy tasting a smaller number of breads.

Variations for Schoolagers:

Cook food that complements the breads from two to three other cultures. For instance, make hummus to go with pita bread or a lentil soup to go with Arabian breads.

12

We All Have Drums

Goal:

Develop sense of cultural competence

Materials:

- drums or pictures of drums from varied cultures (snare drums, African drums, American Indian drums)
- audiotapes of drumming
- an empty oatmeal or coffee container cover for each child
- a small dowel for each child
- masking tape
- construction paper cut to the length of the container

Procedure:

1. Study drums and their uses in different cultures by demonstrating the drums you have collected. Talk about the pictures and listen to the audiotapes. Talk about the function of drums in varied cultures. For example, to warn of enemies, to communicate information, to dance, to entertain, and to use in spiritual ceremonies.

2. Follow up your discussion with an art project during free play. Ask the children each to make a drum. Each child can cover a container with paper of their choosing. Decorate it with markers or collage materials.

3. Make a stick for drumming by wrapping masking tape around one end of a wooden dowel.

4. Ask children to demonstrate how their drum sounds.

5. Later that day or the next, have a drum group where all the children play their instruments.

Variations for Toddlers:

Demonstrate the drums you have collected. Let them try the drums. Let them each decorate a drum. Prepare by having containers covered for them.

Variations for Schoolagers:

Let the children research drums. For example, they could research the names of different drums and their uses. Have them label the drum that they make. Have the children play their drums with tapes of different kinds of music so they need to listen carefully to the beat.

Gender Stereotypes

13

Goal:

Develop sense of cultural competence

Materials:

- chart with two columns
- marker
- plain chart paper
- 8 to 10 books about children

Procedure:

1. Help children recognize how messages from books and materials can be unfair. Make a two-column chart. Label one column "girls," the other "boys." Gather eight to ten books about children with which the children in your group are familiar.

2. Look at each one and talk about who the story is mostly about. Is it a girl or a boy?

3. Make a tally on the column of your chart for each book about a girl and for each book about a boy.

4. Count and compare how many books are about girls and how many are about boys. Is it fair? How does it make people feel if there aren't many books about them? How do people feel if there are books about them?

5. Continue the activity by listing on a plain sheet of chart paper the things that the main characters do. Help the children decide if these are fair or unfair stories of what boys and girls can do.

6. You could expand this activity by having the children count how many books are about children of different races or children with disabilities. Talk about what it would feel like to someone who didn't have many books that reflected them.

Variations for Toddlers:

This activity is not developmentally appropriate for most toddlers.

Variations for Schoolagers:

Expand this activity by talking about the activities of the main characters shown in the children's favorite movies or television programs.

From *Big As Life* (1998), by Stacey York. Published by Redleaf Press, St. Paul, Minnesota, 800-423-8309. Used with permission.

Identification and Expression of Feelings

Samuel walked into his dining room and noticed there were a number of relatives gathered around the table looking at something. As he moved further into the room, he recognized that they were looking at photographs and talking about one of the pictures in particular. When he focused on his mother, he noticed her big, toothy smile and the little wrinkle lines around her eyes. He heard her laugh and decided she was happy.

Samuel was able to identify how his mother was feeling. To be able to do this, children must become keen observers. They need to recognize visual, auditory, and contextual clues as they make judgments about how another person might be feeling.

Along with reading the emotions of others, children need to be able to recognize and express their own emotions. Children need to learn many words with which to label their feelings and the intensity of them. Learning that there is a difference between being upset and really angry and knowing how to match the intensity to the circumstances are important. For example, Tina was able to express the intensity of her feelings when she told her provider, "I was so sad when Bambi's mother was shot that I didn't want to watch the end of the movie."

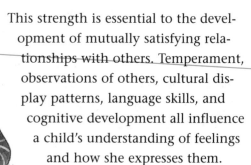

This strength is essential to the development of mutually satisfying relationships with others. Temperament, observations of others, cultural display patterns, language skills, and cognitive development all influence a child's understanding of feelings and how she expresses them. You can support learning about feelings by creating a secure environment, naming feelings for children, helping them read the cues of others, helping children learn to control their emotions, and helping children understand the reasons people feel the way they do.

Arranging the environment, using teachable moments, and modeling are essential in teaching about feelings. Activities can be helpful, but they will be only one part of your overall approach to helping a child learn about emotions. Use the ideas below to support children's learning of this strength.

Environment

> Provide plenty of opportunity for pretend play. Play offers children a chance to enact and verbalize a wide range of emotions. Play sometimes includes learning to recognize and react to the emotions of others. At other times, play allows children to understand their own emotions as they replay them and act them out.

> Display posters of people expressing various emotions. This helps children learn to read visual clues and lets them know that all feelings are acceptable.

> Place mirrors at children's eye level so they can observe their own reflections as they demonstrate emotions. When this is available, you will often see children watching themselves cry, laugh, or act surprised.

> Expect that children will display emotions in different ways. Children learn ways to express emotions within their cultures. Learn from the child's parents and other members of the cultural group how to understand and appreciate differences in the way children express feelings (Katz and McClellan, 1997).

> Include an area for sensorimotor play that involves such things as water, sand, playdough, and oobleck. This type of play attracts every child but can be especially helpful for a child who needs help to calm down.

> Label feelings you see depicted in books or expressed in songs and games.

Teachable Moments:

> Validate feelings. Be careful not to say, "Don't be angry," but rather "I see you are very angry." Then think with the child about ways she could handle her anger that would not hurt herself or others. She might scribble or draw a picture showing how she feels. She might talk about her feelings. Or maybe take time to be alone for a while.

> Notice how children are feeling. If a child is having difficulty expressing herself, make a statement about what her feelings might be. You might say, "You look so mad. Maybe you are angry about Jerry taking your toy." By doing this you give the child feedback about what she is doing and what you think she might be feeling. This can help a child feel understood or give her the opportunity to correct you.

> Draw attention to feelings others are displaying. Say, "Amanda looks sad. Let's go talk to her and see if she's unhappy."

Modeling

> Express your own feelings. When children are avoiding clean-up, you can state, "I am getting frustrated because you are not cleaning up like I asked. Now we will have less time for snack."

> Show your interest, surprise, pleasure, frustration, and disappointment. Young children need many opportunities to understand appropriate expression of feelings.

Children's Books

Berry, Joy. *Let's Talk About Feeling Angry.* New York: Scholastic, 1995.

Carlson, Nancy. *Harriet and the Roller Coaster.* New York: Puffin, 1982.

Crary, Elizabeth, and Shari Steelsmith. *When You're Happy and You Know It.* Seattle: Parenting Press, 1996.

Hazen, Barbara Shook. *Fang.* New York: Atheneum, 1987.

Lewin, Hugh. *Jafta.* Minneapolis: Carolrhoda, 1983.

Mayer, Mercer. *I Was So Mad.* New York: Western, 1983.

A Feelings Guessing Game

Goal:

Develop ability to identify and express feelings

Materials:

- simple pictures of emotions
- 2 1-inch loose-leaf rings
- 2 8 ½ by 11 inch pieces of cardboard
- 6-inch piece of string or ribbon
- tape or glue

Procedure:

1. Let children practice imitating and reading the facial expressions of others. Make an easel using these directions. Punch two holes at the top of each of the two pieces of cardboard. Attach the pieces of cardboard by putting each ring through a set of corresponding holes. At the bottom of the cardboard, glue or tape one end of the ribbon. Run the opposite end of ribbon to the other piece of cardboard and tape it to the bottom. (When you stand the easel up, the ribbon keeps it from sliding apart.)

2. Find magazine pictures depicting various emotions, such as happy, sad, mad, disgusted, scared, or surprised. Punch holes in the top of the pictures so they can be placed in the rings for the easel. Place the easel on a table.

3. Explain to the children that it takes two people to play this game. One person sits in the front and looks at the pictures. She imitates the expression shown. The other person sits across from her and guesses how she is feeling.

Variations for Toddlers:

Prepare the easel and pictures as described. Tell toddlers that each child on the card is telling them something with their face. Ask the children, "Tell me what you see. What is this person telling us?"

Variations for Schoolagers:

This activity will work for schoolagers in its present form. Expect that some children will try to peek at the picture on the other side of the easel.

From *The Peaceful Classroom: 162 Easy Activities to Teach Preschoolers Compassion and Cooperation* (1993), by Charles Smith. Published by Gryphon House, 1-800-638-0928. Used with permission.

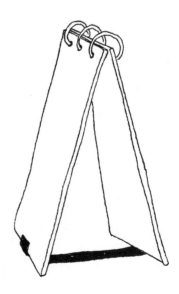

Name the Feeling

Goal:

Develop ability to identify and express feelings

Materials:

- tagboard
- round head paper fastener
- markers
- scissors

Procedure:

1. Use this simple game to practice naming feelings. Make a spinner by cutting a piece of tagboard into a circle. Draw spokes from the center to divide the circle into six even spaces. Cut an arrow from tagboard. Fasten this to the center of the circle with a round head paper fastener. Draw simple pictures of faces showing different emotions in the sections of the spinner. Some feelings to include might be:

- happy
- sad
- angry
- surprised
- scared
- disgusted

2. Demonstrate for the children how to use the spinner. Explain that they can take turns spinning, naming the feeling shown, and showing how they look when they feel the same way.

Variations for Toddlers:

Use only four segments on the spinner. Delete *disgusted* and *surprised*. Let toddlers have a turn to spin the spinner. Read the feeling that the spinner lands on. Say something like, "It landed on *mad*. This is what I look like when I'm mad. Show me what you look like when you are mad."

Variations for Schoolagers:

This activity is not developmentally appropriate for most schoolagers.

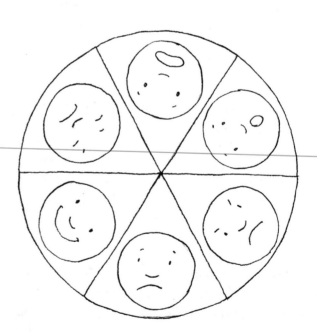

Looking for Clues

16

Goal:

Develop ability to identify and express feelings

Materials:

- stiff construction paper
- scissors
- posters or pictures of individuals with a variety of facial expressions (magazine pictures will work too)

Procedure:

1. Help children learn to "read" how people are feeling. Make a template with three or four pages bound together. In the center of each page cut a hole, each one increasing in size. The smallest one should be in the front.

2. Look at the pictures. Talk about how each person is feeling. Ask, "How can you tell?" "What are the clues?" Answers might include: "She's smiling and her eyes are crinkled." Or "She has her arms crossed. Her teeth are clenched." Draw attention to the eyes, mouth, body language, and context shown.

3. Explain that you need to look for all the clues to know how someone is feeling.

4. On another day, place the emotion pictures behind the templates. Say, "See if you can guess how this person is feeling."

5. Turn one page at a time to reveal more of the picture. If the children guess before all the clues are revealed, say, "Let's see if you're right." Continue to reveal more of the picture.

Variations for Toddlers:

Introduce this activity to toddlers by looking at large pictures or posters of faces of such common animals as dogs, cats, and birds. On another day, use the templates to slowly reveal more of the animals' faces. On a third day, show pictures or posters of faces showing emotion. Finally, use the emotions pictures with the templates.

Variations for Schoolagers:

This activity will work for schoolagers in its present form.

Feelings Word Book

Goal:

Develop ability to identify and express feelings; support the understanding of cause and effect

Materials:

- large index cards with holes punched out so they can be fastened together
- crayons
- colored pencils
- pencils
- markers
- loose-leaf rings

Procedure:

1. Give children an opportunity to express their feelings with this word book. Introduce a word by acting out or talking about the word. Plan to do about one word a week. For example, if you are talking about feeling frustrated, relate a time when you got really frustrated. Then ask the children when they have been frustrated. Following are some words you may want to include in your book:

- angry
- sad
- happy
- disgusted
- scared
- surprised
- frustrated
- confused
- amused
- enraged
- embarrassed

2. Working with individuals or with small groups of children, ask each child to talk about when they were frustrated (or the word of the week). Have them draw a picture of the situation or decorate the card in some way. Write the feeling word on the card.

3. Bind each child's index cards together with a ring to make a flip book. Each week add another page. Review those feelings discussed in the past.

Variations for Toddlers:

Make a poster with four parts. In each part paste a picture of someone showing the emotions sad, angry, happy, and scared. One day each week introduce each emotion with a short puppet play. Use the poster to have children point to one of the emotions. Say, "Show me _____."

Variations for Schoolagers:

Include schoolagers in making the list of words that they will include in their books.

I Was So Mad

18

Goal:

Develop ability to identify and express feelings; support problem solving

Materials:

- chart paper
- markers
- tape

Procedure:

1. Build children's awareness of their physical responses to anger and what to do when they feel angry. Talk with an individual child or small group of children who are having difficulty refraining from hitting. Describe a time that you felt mad. Perhaps it was when you were trying to read a story and everyone was talking or when it was time to pick up toys and the children were still playing. Say, "I got so mad that I looked like this." Demonstrate how your face and body might look (clenched jaw, tight fists, frown, wrinkled forehead).

2. Ask the children to show you what they look like when they are angry. Ask, "What does it feel like?" "What parts of your body change?" Possible answers to these questions include hands and tummy getting tight, crossing arms, and stamping your feet. Draw simple pictures of each thing the children list.

3. Tell the children that you want them to pay attention to what it feels like when they get angry. Have them practice angry expressions two or three times. Encourage the children to relax between each attempt.

4. Explain that there are three things the children need to do when they feel angry:

    1. *Stop what you are doing and take a deep breath.*

    2. *Don't hit.*

    3. *Do something different to solve the problem.*

5. Depending on the interest level of the children, you may want to stop here and continue another day. If the children are capable of further discussion, continue by asking, "What could you do differently to solve the problem?" List and draw their ideas. Post them in your room when you are done.

6. During play, watch for the signals that a child is becoming upset. Help her recognize them. You might say, "Your fists are getting tight. I wonder if you are feeling mad." Then review the steps by saying, "Stop, don't hit, and do something different." Ask the child what she could do instead. If needed, take her over to the poster of other ways to express anger and solve problems.

Variations for Toddlers:

This activity is not developmentally appropriate for most toddlers.

Variations for Schoolagers:

In addition to this activity, regularly talk about alternative behaviors. Act out common situations in which children become angry and can use alternative strategies for coping with anger.

**What kids said when asked,
"What could you do when you feel mad?"**

Stamp the floor.

Get help.

Punch a pillow.

Move away.

Tell the other child to stop.

Put hands on my hips.

Take a deep breath.

Count to ten.

I Might Explode

Goal:

Develop ability to identify and express feelings; support the understanding of cause and effect

Materials:

- balloon
- marker
- manual air pump (optional)

Procedure:

1. Draw a simple face on a balloon. Keep the expression fairly neutral with the mouth straight across. Inflate the balloon just a bit, either by blowing it up or by placing the stem of the balloon on the nozzle of the air pump.

2. Show the children how the balloon flies around out of control before all the air is out. Inflate the balloon again and slowly let the air out. Talk about how the air slowly goes out.

3. Inflate the balloon before you begin to tell the story on the next page. Shorten or lengthen the story to fit the attention span of the children in your group. Each time Harold gets upset and doesn't tell how he is feeling, inflate the balloon a little more.

4. Interrupt the story at strategic points to discuss how Harold is feeling. Talk about how Harold is keeping all these feelings inside. Ask "What might happen to Harold if he doesn't tell people how he feels and we keep pumping air into him?" Talk about how Harold might explode if he doesn't tell someone about his feelings. Ask what it might look like when someone explodes. Possible answers include that they yell, shake their fists, have a tantrum, or make an angry face. Ask the children, "Who could Harold tell

about how he is feeling?" Suggest that maybe Harold doesn't know how to tell people what he is feeling. Ask them what he could say.

5. When you have added as many disappointing incidents to Harold's story as the children's attention span will allow, tell the children you are going to change the story a little to see what might happen if Harold told people how he felt. Holding onto the stem of the balloon, let a little air out of the balloon each time Harold tells his feelings.

Variations for Toddlers:

This activity is not developmentally appropriate for most toddlers.

Variations for Schoolagers:

After telling the story, have the group pretend that they are balloons bottling up their feelings. Have them act out expanding and then gradually deflating.

This is Harold. He's a five year old at Kid's Rule Child Care. Harold has a problem. He has a tough time telling people how he feels. His child care provider and his mom and dad are worried about him. Can you guess why? Let's find out.

One day Harold came to Kid's Rule with a frown on his face. His teacher asked him if something was wrong, but all Harold said was "Aw, nothing." (Inflate the balloon a little bit.) He went to his cubby and sat down beside it.

At breakfast Harold was trying to reach for some cereal and he spilled his juice. It went all over his new outfit, the one he and his dad had picked out specially the night before. He had to change into some old clothes he kept in his back pack. Harold was very disappointed, but he didn't tell anyone. (Inflate the balloon a little more.)

During free play, Harold really wanted to build a huge building he had been thinking about. When he tried, the pieces kept falling down. Harold felt like throwing the blocks, but he didn't. He just clenched his fists and said nothing. (Inflate the balloon a little more.)

Harold saw that they were going to read his favorite book at story time. He felt a little better, until he found out it was his turn to set the table for snack. He would have to miss it. Harold stood up. He felt like stomping the ground, but he didn't. He just walked to the snack table with his head hanging down. (Inflate the balloon a little more, then pause for discussion.)

Harold decided to tell his teacher that they were reading his favorite book and he didn't want to miss it. She said to ask a friend if they wanted to set the table for him. Jeremy was excited to set the table for him and Harold felt better. (Let some air out of the balloon.)

At snack Harold told his friend about the great building he was thinking about but that he couldn't get it to stay up. His friend said he would help. Harold felt a little bit better. (Let some air out of the balloon.)

When Harold's mom picked him up, she noticed Harold was wearing the old clothes from his back pack. He told her how disappointed he was that he didn't get to wear his new outfit. She promised to wash it so he could wear it all day tomorrow. Harold felt a lot better. (Let the rest of the air out of the balloon.)

What About the Spider?

Goal:

Develop ability to identify and express feelings; support empathy and reframing

Materials:

- drawing paper
- markers

Procedure:

1. Use some common nursery rhymes to help children identify the feelings of others. Invite the children to say the nursery rhyme "Little Bo Peep."

> *Little Bo Peep*
> *Has lost her sheep*
> *And can't tell where to find them*
> *Leave them alone*
> *And they'll come home*
> *Wagging their tails behind them.*

2. Say, "Oh no, Bo Peep's sheep are lost!" Ask the children, "Have any of you ever been lost? How did you feel?" Then ask, "What do you think the lost sheep are feeling?"

3. Have someone act out the nursery rhyme "Little Miss Muffet."

> *Little Miss Muffet*
> *Sat on a tuffet,*
> *Eating her curds and whey;*
> *Along came a spider,*
> *Who sat down beside her*
> *And frightened Miss Muffet away.*

4. Ask the children how Miss Muffet felt.

5. Then ask, "Why do you think the spider came and sat beside her?" Children will probably say that the spider wanted to scare her. Ask for additional ideas by saying, "What's another reason?" Possible answers include that the spider wanted to be her friend, the spider wanted to get something to eat, or because she was sitting on the spider's web.

6. Ask the children to each decide how they think the spider felt. Have the children draw a picture of the spider. Encourage the children to include things that show how the spider is feeling. Write captions for their pictures, or have the children write captions.

Variations for Toddlers:

Use a doll to be Bo Peep and rubber sheep to act out the nursery rhyme "Little Bo Peep." Ask the children to think about how it feels to be lost. Have them show you how they look when they feel that way. Then ask how the sheep might be feeling.

Use the doll, a plastic spider, a pillow, a bowl, and a spoon to act out the nursery rhyme "Little Miss Muffet." Ask the children what *frightened* means. Ask what Little Miss Muffet did when she was frightened. Then have the children show you how they look when they are frightened.

Variations for Schoolagers:

Ask schoolagers to think of other nursery rhymes they know and identify the feelings expressed in them. Make a chart listing the titles of the nursery rhymes and the feelings portrayed.

Empathy

When Shabaz saw Tim sitting on the floor clutching his knee and grimacing, he quickly moved to his side. Shabaz watched as the teacher cared for the scraped knee and continued to show his concern after the knee was cleaned and bandaged. Shabaz stuck close to Tim for twenty minutes following the accident and was overheard asking, "Does it still hurt?"

Shabaz showed his ability to empathize with others when he recognized that Tim was hurt and offered friendship and concern during their play that followed. Empathy is the ability to feel what another person feels. This understanding often compels a person to help ease the distress or enjoy the pleasure of another. When children see others who are upset, comforting or helping them reduces their own feelings of discomfort and can lead them to feel proud of themselves. Children learn to understand the emotions of others and respond in an empathetic way through their own experiences with a supportive caregiver, through the modeling of those around them, through direct instruction and encouragement, and through everyday experiences helping others. Nurturing empathetic responses will go a long way in helping children grow up to be kind and caring adults.

To build empathy among children, you can create an emotion-centered environment, make use of teachable moments, model empathetic responses, and offer activities that focus on this strength.

Environment

- Point out the expressions of others in real-life situations and in stories. Guess how they might be feeling and why. Say something like, "Sarah looks sad. I wonder if she feels bad because her ear hurts."

- Set up dramatic play areas like a veterinarian's office or zoo to give children practice caring for animals.

- Display pictures and posters of people experiencing different emotions. Talk about how the people might be feeling and why.

- Talk about helping others in daily conversation.

Teachable Moments

- Suggest ways concerned children can offer support or comfort to those who are distressed. They could bring the child a favorite toy, a comfort object, or offer a hug.

- Talk with children about how they can help when someone has a spill, drops something, or when the tower they are building falls down. Prompt them to get a paper towel, a broom, or help to build the tower again. Encourage children to help one another tie shoes, carry heavy things, or put a hard puzzle together.

- Help children understand the feelings of others by connecting them to their own experiences. For example, "Meng misses his mom. Remember your first day at child care? How did you feel? Maybe he would feel better if you brought him a toy."

- Ask the children to consider the feelings of others as they make choices for themselves. "How might Jayvier feel if we decide to start reading the story while he is still washing his hands?" (Katz and McClellan, 1997).

- Point out how a child's behavior affects another. For example, you might say, "I feel frustrated when I'm talking and you interrupt," or "He feels sad when his blocks are knocked down." When you call a child's attention to the feelings of others, you encourage him to understand their perspective (Eisenberg, 1992).

- With the children, discuss problems that affect your community and think of ways they can help. Some ideas might be to collect cleaning supplies for people affected by a tornado or a flood, make cards to give to people who are shut in, or videotape a play the children put on and send it to a local children's hospital.

Modeling

➤ Demonstrate your caring attitude. Show children how to respond to a child who is upset. Move close, talk to, and comfort the child until he is feeling better. Verbalize what you are doing by saying, "Juan looks unhappy. I'm going to go see if he wants a hug."

➤ Show children appropriate responses when problems or illness touches one of the families of the children in your care. Offer comforting words, send a card, or support them in other appropriate ways.

Children's Books

Campbell, Alison, and Julia Barton. *Are You Asleep, Rabbit?*
    New York: Lothrop, 1990.

Cohen, Miriam. *Jim's Dog Muffins*. New York: Greenwillow, 1984.

de Paola, Tomie. *Now One Foot, Now the Other*. New York:
    Putnam, 1980.

Gackenbach, Dick. *What's Claude Doing?* New York: Clarion, 1984.

Joslin, Sesyle. *What Do You Say, Dear?* New York: Harper, 1986.

Mayer, Mercer. *Just For You*. New York: Western, 1975.

How Am I Feeling?

Goal:

Develop feelings of empathy; support reframing and the identification and expression of feelings

Materials:

- props to support any role-plays you develop

Procedure:

1. Help children understand how another person might be feeling. Act out some of the following situations. Use appropriate facial expressions to support your role-plays. Ask the children to guess how you might be feeling. Accept more than one answer.

- Twirl in a circle.
  Ask, "How am I feeling?"

- Bump into a chair.
  Ask, "How am I feeling?"

- Try to tie your shoe or zip your jacket, but fail.
  Ask, "How am I feeling?"

- Role-play searching for your favorite toy and being unable to find it.
  Ask, "How am I feeling?"

- Pretend to trip over something, fall, and hurt yourself.
  Ask, "How am I feeling?"

- Act as if you just received a present. Say something like, "What? A present for me! Thank you."
  Ask, "How am I feeling?"

- Explain, "I slept so late today that I missed breakfast."
  Ask, "How am I feeling?"

- Say, "I haven't seen my mom for a long, long time."
  Ask, "How am I feeling?"

- Pretend to answer the phone. Say, "Hello. Yes, I can come over to your house to play. I'll be there soon."
  Ask, "How am I feeling?"

Variations for Toddlers:

The first six ideas listed are the most appropriate for toddlers. Add situations that are common to the children in your care. Use exaggerated facial expressions and dramatic gestures as you act them out.

Variations for Schoolagers:

After several examples, have schoolagers act out their own role-plays and ask the rest of the students to guess how they are feeling.

Walk in Someone Else's Shoes

22

Goal:

Develop feelings of empathy;
support cultural competence

Materials:

- rope on floor
- rocking boat that is turned over to form steps
- variety of shoes (for example, sandals, high heels, hiking boots, clogs, ballet slippers)

Procedure:

1. Explore what it feels like to walk in someone else's shoes. Put a variety of shoes out for the children to try. Ask them to perform simple tasks like walking up the stairs, balancing as they walk along a rope on the floor pretending that it's a high wire, and walking on their tiptoes. Be safety conscious and lend a helping hand when a child needs it.

2. Have the children change shoes a number of times and try the activities.

3. Either as children experiment with the shoes during free play or as a large group demonstration, ask one child to walk in one of the more unusual pairs of shoes. Ask, "What does it feel like to walk in those shoes?"

Variations for Toddlers:

After trying on the shoes and activities, ask toddlers if it is "easy" or "hard" to walk in someone else's shoes.

Variations for Schoolagers:

Talk about how sometimes people misunderstand what it feels like to do something if they haven't tried it for themselves. Give examples of this, such as walking on the moon, living in another country, scuba diving, or living with another family. Ask schoolagers to think about a time they may have been misunderstood. Have them write a letter and explain how it feels to walk in their shoes.

Some Like It, Some Don't

Goal:

Develop feelings of empathy; support cultural competence and the identification and expression of feelings

Materials:

- construction paper
- tape

Procedure:

1. Help children recognize that people are similar to and different from one another. Give them the opportunity to experience accepting differences without rejecting or putting others down. Draw a picture of a happy face on construction paper and tape it up on one side of the room. Draw a picture of a sad face and tape it up on the other side of the room. Tell the children they are to decide if they like the activities and situations you are going to list for them. Have the children move to the picture that shows how they feel. The happy face designates where they should stand if they like the activity or situation you describe to them. The sad face designates where they should stand if they do not like what you describe.

2. Read each of the following activities and situations. Encourage the children to decide for themselves what they like and what they don't like. Provide the children with enough time to make a decision and move to either the happy face or the sad face.

- eating an ice cream cone
- eating green beans
- reading books
- going on a roller coaster

- hearing thunder
- finger painting
- shopping for groceries
- smelling onions
- playing in sand
- eating tuna

3. If all the children go to the same picture in the beginning, ask if anyone has a different feeling. Or you may need to talk out loud about something you don't like and demonstrate how you can have your own feelings about the item.

4. Talk about how some people like each thing and some people don't. Accept the feelings of every child without question or judgment.

Variations for Toddlers:

During informal conversation, ask one toddler if he likes one of the items. Recognize others who like the item too. Accept the feelings of those who indicate they don't like it. Go on to the next toddler and the next item on the list.

Variations for Schoolagers:

Have schoolagers conduct their own survey about who likes the things on the list and who doesn't. Or the children can develop their own questions, poll others in their group, tally the responses, and report the results.

Adapted from *Second Step: A Violence Prevention Curriculum* (1991), by the Committee for Children, Seattle, WA. Used with permission.

How I Helped

Goal:

Develop feelings of empathy; support reframing

Materials:

- heavy skin-tone construction paper
- crayons
- markers
- scissors
- *Helping* by James Levin and Jackie Carter

Procedure:

1. Introduce children to the many ways people help one another. Begin by reading a book like *Helping* by Levin and Carter or telling a story about a child who helps others.

2. Trace each child's hand; use a marker to make a thick line. Let the children cut out the hand shapes if they are able. If not, an adult can cut out the traced hands or leave the background intact. Invite the children to decorate the traced hands.

3. When the children have finished decorating their traced hands, ask each child whats he has done to help someone. Make suggestions if they can't think of any possibilities, or ask, "How could you help someone?" Write their ideas on their traced hands.

4. Display the decorated hands on a bulletin board titled "How We Help Others."

Variations for Toddlers:

Trace the toddlers' hands for them. Let the children decorate the shapes. Tell each toddler what you have seen her do to help others. Write it on his paper. Display the hands at the toddlers' eye level along with magazine pictures of people helping others.

Variations for Schoolagers:

This activity will work for schoolagers in its present form.

I'll Guide Your Hand

Goal:

Develop feelings of empathy; support perseverance, problem solving, and the understanding of cause and effect

Materials:

- blindfold (a scarf or child-sized sunglasses with lenses that are covered with tape)
- single form puzzles

Procedure:

1. Give children an opportunity to discover what it feels like to be without the sense of sight. Pair children together. Let them work at the puzzles to become familiar with them.

2. Blindfold one child. Ask the blindfolded child to relax and let his hand be guided.

3. The other child is to help complete the puzzle by guiding the hand of the blindfolded child. When the puzzle is finished, ask the child to take the blindfold off.

4. Children can trade places.

5. Recognize that some children may not be able to do this activity if they are tactilely defensive or very shy. If this is the case, let the child watch before trying and then decide for himself if he will participate.

Variations for Toddlers:

This activity is not developmentally appropriate for most toddlers.

Variations for Schoolagers:

Since this activity involves trust issues, schoolagers may be selective about who they are willing to have as their partners. Use more difficult puzzles, or try incorporating more difficult activities for this age group, like throwing beanbags into a container.

Hot Lava

Goal:

Develop feelings of empathy; support responsibility and problem solving

Materials:

- hula hoop or chalk circle
- rope
- squares of carpet or fabric

Procedure:

1. Give children a chance to help others by saving them from the imaginary lava. Put a hula hoop or chalk circle on one side of the room. Designate a place on the other side of the room that is safe. The rest of the area is hot lava.

2. Ask two or three of the children to be the rescuers. The rest of the group stands inside the chalk circle or hula hoop waiting to be rescued.

3. Give the rescuers a rope and some carpet squares or washcloth sized scraps of fabric. Explain that they can use these items to help them save the others. Make it clear that they are to work together to save all of the other people.

4. Give a number of children a chance to be the rescuers. Encourage rescuers to try new ways to rescue the children.

5. Be prepared to find other props (or something they can use as a substitute) if the children need them for their rescues.

Variations for Toddlers:

This activity is not developmentally appropriate for most toddlers.

Variations for Schoolagers:

Have schoolagers brainstorm lots of props that could be used in their rescue efforts.

27

What Could You Do to Help?

Goal:

Develop feelings of empathy; support the development of responsibility and problem solving

Materials:

- adhesive bandages
- blanket
- pillow
- play telephone
- stuffed toy dog

Procedure:

1. Help children explore ways to help others. Hide a toy dog before you begin. Explain to the children that there are many times that we might be the first to notice that a person needs help and then help. Act as if you are searching for something as you sing the nursery rhyme "Where Has My Little Dog Gone."

> *Oh where, oh where has my little dog gone?*
> *Oh where, oh where can he be?*
> *With his ears cut short and his tail cut long,*
> *Oh where, oh where can he be?*

2. Ask the children how they think you would feel if you lost your dog. Ask, "What could you do to help?" Encourage the children to search for the toy dog.

3. Ask for volunteers to act out the nursery rhyme "Jack and Jill."

> *Jack and Jill*
> *Went up the hill*
> *To fetch a pail of water;*
> *Jack fell down,*
> *And broke his crown,*
> *And Jill came tumbling after.*

4. Ask the children to think about how Jack is feeling.

5. Have the children pretend that they were standing nearby when Jack fell down. Ask, "What could you do to help?" Let each child act out their idea. Their ideas may include the following:

- Call 911!
- Put a Band-Aid on him.
- Get him a blanket.
- Give him a stuffed animal.
- Run and get his parents.

Note: You may want to gather the props before beginning and cover them with a towel. When the children can't think of any more ideas, uncover the props to spark another round of discussion.

Variations for Toddlers:

1. Gather a doll bed and blanket, paper cup, and transparent container. Use a puppet to say the nursery rhyme "Where Has My Little Dog Gone?" Have the children pretend to be sad like the puppet when he can't find his dog. Ask the children if the dog could be under a cup. No, it wouldn't fit. Ask the children if the dog could be in the transparent container. No, they would see it. Ask the children if the dog could be in the doll's bed. When they find it, the puppet and the children can show happy feelings.

2. Tell the nursery rhyme "Jack and Jill" using the following props: a ramp or the stair side of a rocking boat as the hill, a plastic bucket, and puppets for Jack and Jill. Talk about Jack's "owie." Ask the children how they feel when they have an "owie." Ask, "What do we do for bumps and cuts?" Put adhesive bandages on the puppets. Model and have the children use caring words like "sorry," "too bad," and "owie all better." Have the children use soothing and comforting touches, patting, rubbing, and hugging the puppet to help him feel better.

Variations for Schoolagers:

This activity will work for schoolagers in its present form.

What children said when asked, "How could you help Jack after he falls?"

Get him a drink.
Get them something to eat.
Get him a book.

28

Say Something Friendly

Goal:

Develop feelings of empathy

Materials:

- variety of play materials (for example, a pegboard and pegs, blocks, small plastic animals, a beanbag, markers)
- chart paper

Procedure:

1. Give the children an opportunity to practice verbally supporting others. Introduce the activity by saying something like, "Sometimes you can help a friend feel good by saying something friendly. Today, we're going to practice saying friendly things."

2. Write the heading "Say Something Friendly" on chart paper.

3. Demonstrate a role-play by asking one child to play with a toy, such as the pegs or the blocks. Comment on a specific aspect of the child's play. You might say, "I like the way you are stacking the blocks" or "You can build big buildings."

4. Ask two children at a time to do a role-play. One is to play, the other is to say something friendly. Encourage the second child to start her sentence with "I like…" or "I like the way…." If a child can't think of anything to say, ask the others in the group to help with ideas. Give those who are really stuck words to use.

5. Write down the friendly things they say.

6. Review by reading each statement. Remind them to say something friendly when they want to help another child feel good.

Variations for Toddlers:

Do a puppet play based on the book *What Do You Say, Dear?* by Sesyle Joslin, which provides humorous guidance to polite things to say in a variety of social situations. Then have two puppets do a role-play—one plays with materials, the other says something friendly. After each role-play, ask the children, "What did the puppet say that was friendly?"

Variations for Schoolagers:

Have schoolagers practice the role-plays with their partner. Then ask them to comment positively about what they have noticed about the talents and accomplishments of someone else in the group.

> **What children said when they participated in this activity:**
>
> *I like the way you lined them up.*
> *I like the rainbow colors you used.*
> *I like the way you stacked them up high.*

Perseverance

Amy sat bent over her shoe. The tip of her tongue stuck out the corner of her mouth as she concentrated. She slowly and carefully wrapped one shoelace and formed a loop, then held on tight as she looped the other. When she went to complete the knot, the laces loosened and fell to either side. Amy picked up the laces and started again.

What prompted Amy to try again instead of giving up in a huff? Amy was persistent. She tried over and over, knowing that with continued practice she would get it. Perseverance is the ability to keep trying when faced with a new skill, a difficult situation, or a problem. People who are persistent have an attainable goal in mind. They develop a plan for reaching it and keep working until they are successful or they find that they must modify their goal. Children who learn persistence grow into determined adults who realize it takes effort to succeed.

Some children are more naturally persistent. It is a matter of their temperament. At a very early age they continue with an activity despite obstacles. Children for whom persistence does not come naturally must learn to continue in spite of difficulties they encounter. Adults can help them focus when their attention wanders, learn to deal with frustration, break a task down into smaller steps, and encourage their continued efforts.

Use the following suggestions as you look at ways to encourage persistence through your environment, through teachable moments, through your own attitude, and through the activities you offer.

Environment

- Make your environment an interesting one in which materials are rotated or added periodically to keep children engaged. For instance, don't put all the props for a dramatic play theme out at one time. Add props as children become familiar with the first and need new challenges.

- Help children learn to stick with activities. Teach them to focus on their activity with gentle reminders (for example, "look right here") or reassurance that a disturbance across the room is being taken care of.

- Offer activities that match the developmental levels of the children in the group. Make them challenging without being so difficult that the children become frustrated. Find ways to individualize the activities so they are developmentally appropriate for each child.

- Provide low barriers between interest areas so children can better concentrate on their activities. Encourage children who are wandering around the room or changing activities frequently to make a plan and "settle in" to an activity or to find an activity and "stick with it."

- Promote "sticking with an activity" by offering sensory activities that tend to engage children for long periods of time.

- Create an environment where children are expected to try again and again. Encourage children not to give up or to try the activity just one more time.

Teachable Moments

- Encourage a child who is working on a new skill. Use reflective statements that describe what the child is doing. For example, "Oh, you are stretching your legs so far when you climb that ladder." Help her understand that when she continues to practice she will get it.

- Give unqualified support to each child. Communicate your belief that each child will learn increasingly difficult tasks. Express your confidence by using messages like, "I know you'll make it" or "I think you can do it—keep trying."

- Move close to a child who is trying something repeatedly. Your presence can offer support. Comment on how hard the child is trying.

- Offer the least amount of help that will allow a child to be successful. For example, simply hold the string in place while the child knots a necklace, or offer to put tape on the end of a piece of yarn so it won't unravel. Help the children without taking over.

- Teach a child to take a break if she is trying something new and becoming overly frustrated. Let her know that when she comes back to it, she might be more successful.

- Help a child see a slightly different way to perform a task. Ask, "Can you think of a different way to do it?" Or make a suggestion like, "Maybe if you try that puzzle piece down here it will work."

Modeling

- Show children that you also have to try things more than once. When something goes wrong, voice your frustration, then tell how you are going to try again or try another way.

- Communicate your positive perspective. When trying new activities say, "I think this will work."

Children's Books

Brown, Marc. *D.W. Flips!* Boston: Little Brown, 1987.

Carle, Eric. *The Very Busy Spider.* New York: Philomel, 1984.

Keats, Ezra Jack. *Whistle for Willie.* New York: Viking, 1964.

Piper, Watty. *The Little Engine That Could.* New York: Platt, 1976.

Schlichting, Mark. *The Tortoise and the Hare.* Novato, CA: Living Books, 1993

29

The Turnip

Goal:

Develop perseverance; support problem solving

Materials:

- flannel board (optional)
- flannel board pieces for story (optional)
- artificial leaves

Procedure:

1. Introduce the concept of perseverance by reading "The Turnip," a folktale found on the next page. Or tell the story using the flannel board. As you tell the story, ask the children if the old man gave up. In addition, identify the problem he had and what he did to solve it.

2. Retell the story and use volunteers to play each character. The children can gently pull on each other as they act out trying to get the turnip to come up. Stop throughout the reenactment and ask, "Should they give up?"

3. Repeat the reenactment as many times as children want to play the characters in this folktale.

4. Have props available during free play so children can reenact the story on their own.

Variations for Toddlers:

Tell the story using puppets or dolls and stuffed animals as props.

Variations for Schoolagers:

Tell about a time that you had to work hard to achieve something. For example, learning how to whistle, ride a bicycle, or jump rope. Have the children think of a time when they needed to try again and again or when they needed some help before they were successful. Ask each child to draw a picture or write a paragraph about it.

The Turnip

Once upon a time there was a grandpa who liked the taste of turnips. So he planted one in his garden. While it grew he watered it, weeded it, and took good care of it. It grew and grew and grew. When it was ready, the grandpa went to pull it up.

He pulled and pulled and pulled.
But he couldn't pull it up.

He called to Grandma.
"Graaaandmaaa!"

Grandma pulled Grandpa.
Grandpa pulled the turnip.
They pulled and pulled and pulled.
But they couldn't pull it up.

Grandma called to the girl.
"Girrrrrl!"

The girl pulled Grandma.
Grandma pulled Grandpa.
Grandpa pulled the turnip.
They pulled and pulled and pulled.
But they couldn't pull it up.

The girl called to the boy.
"Booooy!"

The boy pulled the girl.
The girl pulled Grandma.
Grandma pulled Grandpa.
Grandpa pulled the turnip.
They pulled and pulled and pulled.
But they couldn't pull it up.

The boy called to the dog.
"Dooooog!"

The dog pulled the boy.
The boy pulled the girl.
The girl pulled Grandma.
Grandma pulled Grandpa.
Grandpa pulled the turnip.
They pulled and pulled and pulled.
But they couldn't pull it up.

The dog called the cat.
"Bow-wow, bow-wow!"

The cat pulled the dog.
The dog pulled the boy.
The boy pulled the girl.
The girl pulled Grandma.
Grandma pulled Grandpa.
Grandpa pulled the turnip.
They pulled and pulled and pulled.
But they couldn't pull it up.

The cat called the mouse.
"Meeeeeow!"

The mouse pulled the cat.
The cat pulled the dog.
The dog pulled the boy.
The boy pulled the girl.
The girl pulled Grandma.
Grandma pulled Grandpa.
Grandpa pulled the turnip.
They pulled and pulled and pulled.

And finally they pulled it up!

30

Goal:

Develop perseverance

Materials:

- pom-poms or cotton balls
- tongs
- plastic jar

Procedure:

1. Put the materials out for children to explore. Suggest that they use the tongs to fill the jar with cotton balls. Encourage children to stick with the activity until the jar is filled.

2. Notice when children have persevered. Comment on how they worked until it was finished and they didn't give up.

3. Vary the activity by using beads and tweezers.

Variations for Toddlers:

Encourage toddlers to fill a cup with sand or cornmeal at the sensory table. Talk about working until it is all filled up. Clap for children who fill the container or comment on how they stuck with it until it was filled.

Variations for Schoolagers:

Schoolagers can be encouraged to keep working until they complete a board game, a mile walk or run, or a complex art project.

Where's My Bone?

Goal:

Develop perseverance

Materials:

- dog puppet or stuffed animal
- block for a bone or a dog treat
- small rubber ball
- a hand towel

Procedure:

1. Gather the children and tell the following puppet play to demonstrate the perseverance of the main character.

"This is my dog Maggie. She's a very smart dog and can do some tricks. Would you like to see one of her tricks?"

"Maggie sit." (The puppet sits.) *"Maggie shake."* (Shake hands with the puppet.) *"Maggie lie down."* (Lay down the puppet.)

"That's a good dog! Here is a treat for you." (Give the dog a bone. Have Maggie wag her tail and walk around happily.)

Next have Maggie pretend to dig a hole in the towel and bury her bone in it.

Have Maggie play with the rubber ball for a short time.

Then have her start sniffing all around as if searching for her bone. Ask the children what they think she is doing.

Have her start to dig near the bone but not find it.

Have Maggie whine and lie down as if to give up. Ask the children if she should give up. Have them encourage her to keep trying.

After a few unsuccessful attempts and some encouragement to continue, have Maggie find her bone and saunter off happily.

2. Review the puppet play with the children. Ask questions like the following:

- When Maggie first started looking, could she find her bone?
- Did she give up?
- Did she try again?
- Did she ever find it?

3. Summarize by saying something like, "When Maggie kept trying, she found her bone."

Variations for Toddlers:

Add a large cardboard block, towel, and book to the list of materials. Start the puppet play with the dog and her bone. The dog hides the bone behind the large block, plays with the ball, and then starts to dig. Speak for the dog saying, "I wonder where my bone is?" Dig around for it. Ask the children where she should look saying, "Should I look under the towel? Should I look next to the book? Should I look behind the block?" Encourage the children to cheer for Maggie when she finds it. Reiterate that Maggie found it when she kept looking.

Variations for Schoolagers:

This activity is not developmentally appropriate for most schoolagers.

Interview with a Spider

Goal:

Develop perseverance

Materials:

- spider puppet
- empty gift wrap tube or plastic rain gutter
- microphone (a block could substitute)

Procedure:

1. The spider in "The Itsy-Bitsy Spider" never gives up. Pretend to interview him in the puppet play below. Set the stage for the puppet to climb the plastic rain gutter or tube.

2. Have the children sing "The Itsy-Bitsy Spider" a time or two while you act it out using the puppet.

3. Tell the children you want to find out why the spider keeps climbing up the spout. Interview the spider, using the following script (or make up your own):

Interviewer: "This is your child care reporter here, coming from the bottom of the rain spout, where a spider continues to climb even after she is washed out. I wonder why she does that. Let's see if we can get a word with her and find out. Excuse me, Ms. Spider. I was wondering if you could answer a couple of questions for me."

Spider: "Who, me? Sure, I'll try!"

Interviewer: "Why do you keep climbing up the spout?

Spider: "I want to get to the top."

Interviewer: "But the rain keeps washing you out."

Spider: "Yeah, but I just try again."

Interviewer: "Why don't you give up?"

Spider: "I can't give up. I have to keep trying."

Interviewer: "Why do you have to keep trying?"

Spider: "If I don't try, I'll never make it to the top."

Interviewer: "What's at the top?"

Spider: "Hmmmm. I don't know. That's why I want to get up there. Now if you'll excuse me, I see the sun has come up and I have to try again." *(The spider starts humming the song to herself as she walks toward the spout.)*

4. When you have finished interviewing the spider, have the children sing the song again. When the rain washes the spider out, stop and ask, "Should she give up?" Summarize by saying, "The spider is really working to get to the top. She keeps trying, even when it is hard."

5. If you want to do more with this activity, have the children describe or draw what the spider finds when she finally reaches the top.

Variations for Toddlers:

Teach the words of the song to the children before adding the finger play. After they are familiar with the finger play, use the puppet to act out the spider going up the spout.

Variations for Schoolagers:

Schoolagers could be divided into small groups to draw a mural of what the spider finds when she reaches the top. Or the children could draw their own pictures, then share their pictures with a partner.

Drum and Sheet

33

Goal:

Develop perseverance; support the development of responsibility and the understanding of cause and effect

Materials:

- large light-colored bedsheet or parachute
- drum or other noise-making instrument

Procedure:

1. Give each child an opportunity to practice persistence in this drum and sheet activity. Have the children sit evenly spaced in a circle on the floor. Ask one child to go to the middle of the circle and get on her hands and knees. Spread the sheet over the child in the center. All the other children are to remain silent as the adult sneaks around and gives the drum to one of the children in the circle.

2. The child beats the drum and the child under the sheet crawls toward the drummer, using the sound as a guide. If she doesn't crawl to the right person the first time, encourage her to try again.

Variations for Toddlers:

Have toddlers ring a bell or shake maracas instead of beating a drum. Encourage the toddler who is under the sheet to find the child who is making the sound. When the location of the sound is discovered, have all the children in the circle encourage the child by saying, "Let's all clap for_____ . She found the sound."

Variations for Schoolagers:

Give three different instruments to the children. While they play their instruments, call out the name of one of the instruments. Have the child under the sheet crawl toward the location of the sound.

From Keeping the Peace: Practicing Cooperation and Conflict Resolution with Preschoolers(1989), by Susanne Wichert. Published by New Society Publishers, Gabriola Island, British Columbia, Canada. Used with permission.

Words of Encouragement

Goal:

Develop perseverance

Materials:

- puppet
- blocks
- chart paper
- markers

Procedure:

1. Explore ways for children to encourage themselves and others with this puppet play. Pretend the puppet is trying to stack blocks. Her blocks keep falling and she becomes discouraged. Say something like what she might be thinking, such as, "Oh, no! They've fallen down again. This never works for me. I'm just going to give up."

2. Interrupt by saying, "It looks like you are having trouble stacking the blocks." Encourage the puppet to keep trying. Say something like, "Keep trying! You'll learn how to do it. Maybe there's another way to stack them. How about putting the big blocks down at the bottom?"

3. Have the puppet try again. Ask the children to encourage the puppet by saying, "You can do it!" "Keep trying!" or "Keep practicing!" Show the puppet succeeding.

4. Review what took place in the puppet play. Ask questions like the following:

- "What was the puppet trying to do?"
  (*Build with blocks or stack them up.*)

- "What happened when she tried to stack the blocks?"
  (*They fell down or she couldn't do it.*)

- "What did she want to do when it was hard?"
  (*Give up or quit.*)

- "What did we say to help the puppet try again?"
  (*Keep going, you can do it, try again.*)
  Write down the encouraging words you use.

- "What happened when she kept trying?"
  (*She could do it, they didn't fall down, she got better.*)

5. Summarize by saying, "When we feel like giving up, it is important to try again. You can tell yourself or a friend not to give up by saying, 'Try again, you can do it.'" Read your list of encouraging words the children brainstormed.

6. Put out puppets and blocks for the children to retell the story during free play. Be sure to acknowledge the children when you notice that they are sticking with something they find difficult.

Variations for Toddlers:

Do the same puppet play. Have the children clap when the puppet tries again. Ask them to say, "You did it!"

Variations for Schoolagers:

Try to balance the blocks on the smallest block or on a pointed block. Have the children brainstorm ways to make the building more stable. Choose one to try. Try and try again until you succeed. Follow up with a commercial block balancing game such as Jenga or Blockhead.

Honking Geese

Goal:

Develop perseverance

Materials:

- chart paper
- markers

Procedure:

1. Give children an opportunity to discuss perseverance. Tell the following story:

"I want to tell you about a goose. *(Draw a single goose by making a "V" with the ends flared out. Start far enough down the paper so you can add more.)* She does not like to stay where it is cold. When it starts to get cold, she wants to fly south where it's warmer. But she doesn't want to fly alone. So she asks a bunch of her friends to come along. *(Draw additional geese in a "V" formation.)* The one in the front has a very hard job because she makes a path for the rest to follow. Her friends encourage her to keep going by saying 'honk, honk, honk.'"

2. Ask the group to list some of the encouraging words they could say to themselves or others when they are doing something hard. If they are not able to come up with phrases on their own, ask them to fill in the blank.

Keep ___*(going, trying)*___ !

Try ___*(again, harder, next time)*___ !

You can ___*(do it, make it work)*___ !

3. Ask the group to name some things that they find hard to do. Write them on the chart paper.

4. Summarize by saying, "Next time you are doing something hard like *(read the list they gave you)*, tell yourself not to give up. You can say some of the things we talked about like *(read their list of encouraging words)*."

Variations for Toddlers:

This activity is not developmentally appropriate for most toddlers.

Variations for Schoolagers:

Ask the children to draw a picture of something they find challenging. Have them write the words they will say to themselves in a bubble, like in a cartoon.

What preschoolers said when asked what they find hard to do:

Cleaning my room.

Going to bed.

Tying my shoes.

Catching butterflies.

Nintendo.

What preschoolers said when asked what they could say to encourage themselves or others:

Keep going.

Keep trying.

You can do it.

Try harder.

Don't give up.

Responsibility

Tyler acted responsibly when he started to clean the block area as soon as he heard the clean-up signal. He matched the blocks to the pictures on the shelves, stacking each where it belonged. He worked until all the blocks were put away before going to his spot at the table. When he noticed a block under his chair, he quickly picked it up and returned it to its place.

Children who are responsible recognize what needs to be done, understand how to do the task, and reliably complete it. At young ages, children can learn to care for their bodies, the materials they use, and their behavior. As they grow, they may also be responsible for schoolwork, managing small amounts of money, caring for younger children, and caring for the environment. Being responsible is a strength that is learned over time and in small steps. Children first need help learning to perform a job, then they need guided practice, and finally, opportunities to complete a task on their own.

When you help a child develop this strength, you help him grow to be a dependable adult. Following you will find suggestions for your environment, teachable moments, modeling, and activities that promote responsibility.

Environment

➤ Arrange your environment so children can be responsible for their own materials. Place toys and materials on low shelves where children can help themselves to the materials they need for play. This also makes it easier for children to return things to their places.

➤ Use visual aids to help children know where to put things away. For example, color code bins or baskets that belong on a certain shelf and label the box or bucket in which each toy belongs by taping a picture of the toy to the outside.

➤ Enlist the help of children in maintaining your environment. Give them the equipment they will need, like a whisk broom and dust pan, sponges and paper towels, or a carpet sweeper with a child-sized handle.

➤ Use a job chart to ensure that each child is learning and practicing a variety of responsibilities. Make a chart listing a number of tasks. For example, children can sweep under the sensory table, arrange the books on the bookshelf, set the table, and help to prepare snack. Put a pocket or piece of Velcro next to each job. Children place their name card or photograph in the pocket of the job they agree to perform. Put three or four pockets or pieces of Velcro by areas that are typically more work, like cleaning up the blocks, and have three or four children work together there. Periodically assign the jobs to the children so they get practice doing each.

➤ Allow children to do as much as possible for themselves when they are learning to do such things as zipping up their clothes, pouring their own water, or tying their own shoes. Build practice sessions into your schedule so children have ample opportunities to practice doing these things for themselves.

Teachable Moments

➤ Introduce a new toy or material by teaching children how to care for it. You might say, "Our new game will last a long time if we fold it up and put it on the shelf when we are done. That way it will be out of the way when we are sitting down for story." Or "If you use all your strength to throw the beanbag it might break our box. Then the fun would be done. Use half your strength."

➤ Whistle while you work. Make chores more fun by making them into a game or by adding a twist that helps motivate the children. Challenge the children to clean up all the blue things first or put one hand in their pocket while they clean.

- Talk about how good it feels when things are clean and cared for. You might say, "Wow! Does our room look nice! I feel proud when we take care of our things."

- Teach children how to do tasks you want them to complete. Provide detail and demonstration as you explain the tasks. For example, to teach a child to water the plants, you would need to show him where the watering can is, talk about what the temperature of the water should be, show him how to pour the water and when to stop pouring, discuss what to do if there is a spill, and let him know you expect him to return the watering can to its place.

- Offer support at the level the child needs. Some children will need physical help to complete the task. Others will need reminders and supervision. Some children will be able to perform the task independently.

- Simplify a task for a child who seems overwhelmed. Have the child do one part first, then the next. For instance, the housekeeping area can get so messy, cleaning it can seem like an enormous task. You might start cleaning by asking a child to gather all the plastic food and place it in a basket. Then ask him to stack the dishes on the shelf. Finally, have the child place the dress up clothes in the plastic tub.

- Help a distracted child focus on the task at hand with gentle reminders of what is expected. You might say, "You're almost done, keep working." Or post a chart that serves as a reminder for the child by showing the steps involved in the activity.

- Encourage the child to keep working until the task is completed. See the information in the section on perseverance to support your efforts.

Modeling

- Show how you care for something. Describe how it makes you feel. You might say something like, "This puppet is special to me so I always put it away when I'm done with it. I like to know that I'll be able to find it again when I need it."

- Be part of the team as you clean the room. Your participation can make a big difference.

Children's Books

Carlson, Nancy. *Harriet and the Garden*. Minneapolis: Carolrhoda, 1982.

Harper, Isabelle. *My Dog Rosie*. New York: Blue Sky, 1994.

Kraus, Robert. *Herman the Helper*. New York: Simon, 1974.

Miller, Margaret. *Where Does It Go?* New York: Greenwillow, 1992.

Oxenbury, Helen. *It's My Birthday*. Cambridge MA: Candlewick, 1993

Williams, Vera B. *A Chair for My Mother*. New York: Greenwillow, 1982.

36

Where Does This Belong?

Goal:

Develop sense of responsibility

Materials:

- variety of classroom materials: blocks, crayons, paper, plastic food, plastic plates, books, science materials, puzzle pieces, pegs

Procedure:

1. Help the children discover where toys and materials belong before requiring them to be responsible for clean up. Prepare for the activity by gathering a number of different materials that you have in your environment.

2. Gather the children. Ask them to look at different learning centers. Ask the same question about each center, "Is it clean or messy?" Then ask, "Whose job is it to clean up all the toys?"

3. Explain that in order to do a good job cleaning, everyone needs to know where things belong. Show one of the objects. Have the children point to where it belongs. Ask where it goes. In a basket, on the shelf, or _____ ?

4. Have one child place the object where it belongs. Repeat for all the objects you have collected.

5. After the children have considered where each object goes, ask them to choose or assign children to be responsible for cleaning up an area.

Variations for Toddlers:

Include toddlers in cleaning up the room. Give each toddler a specific item to put away or a task to do. Make clean up as much fun as dumping out the materials.

Variations for Schoolagers:

Think about individuals who may need help learning to clean. Talk with the individual about where things go or teach the child how to perform a particular cleaning task.

Taking Care of Babies

37

Goal:

Develop sense of responsibility; support empathy

Materials:

- dolls
- props for each child to act out caring for babies (diapers, empty powder bottles, washcloths, bottles, baby toys, and so on)

Procedure:

1. Practice ways to care for others by role-playing with a doll. Tell the children you want them to take care of their "baby." Provide them with the props they will need.

2. Describe situations that are likely to occur when caring for a baby and then ask the children what to do (see list below). Instruct them if they don't know.

- Your baby is crying. What could you do?
- Your baby is hungry. What could you do?
- Your baby has a dirty face. What could you do?
- Your baby needs a clean diaper. What could you do?
- Your baby wants to play. What could you do?

Variations for Toddlers:

In a role-play fashion, act out each situation. Say something like, "Oh dear, my baby is crying. I wonder what the problem is?" Ask the children to show you how to make the baby feel better in each situation. Comment on the responsible things the children do. You might say, "You shared the _____ with the baby." Or "The baby likes to have his face washed. He's giggling."

Variations for Schoolagers:

Many children will have lots of real-life experience caring for babies. Let them share their ideas, experiences, and concerns.

38

I'll Do My Part

Goal:

Develop sense of responsibility

Materials:

- three puppets
- plastic dishes
- pot
- spoon
- play food
- dish drying rack

Procedure:

1. Help children recognize how people count on them to be responsible. Set the stage for a puppet play with play dishes, a dish drying rack, and play food. Introduce the family of puppets: a parent and two children, Maria and Jacob. Tell a story similar to the one on the next page.

2. When you have finished the story, help the children think about the story by asking such questions as the following:

- What did Jacob refuse to do?
- What did Mom have to do before she could cook the supper?
- What almost happened because Jacob didn't do the dishes?
- Do you think Jacob did the dishes after he was done eating?

3. Allow the children to act out the story with the puppets and the props.

Variations for Toddlers:

Tell a similar puppet play about cleaning up toys. Keep the play short and do not use questions.

Variations for Schoolagers:

String together more disasters that could follow because Jacob didn't do the dishes. Ask the children to make up their own puppet plays about the consequences of not doing a job for which they are responsible (such as taking out the garbage, doing homework, or watching a younger child).

Mom: *I'm going to go out for a while. Jacob, it's your turn to do the dishes. Please finish them before I get back.*

Maria: *Ha ha, Jacob. You have to do the dishes today.*

Jacob: *I'm not doing them. I'm tired of doing them. You do them.*

Maria [laughs]: *I'm not doing them. It's your turn and if you don't…*

Jacob: *What could happen? I'm just going to pile them up in the dish rack like I washed them.* [He looks at the audience and puts his finger to his lips.] *Ssshhh! Don't tell my mom when she comes back.*

[Mom rushes in from shopping and sees the dishes in the drying rack]

Mom: *Jacob, you did the dishes. Thank you.*

[Mom lifts up a dish, looks at it, and frowns.]

Mom: *These dishes are still dirty. Now I'll have to do them.*

[Mom works quickly to do the dishes and thinks out loud.]

Mom: *Oh dear, I was hoping we could go to a movie after supper. Now I'm not sure there will be enough time.*

[Mom finishes the dishes, begins fixing supper, and continues to think out loud.]

Mom: *Oh dear, this spaghetti will take a long time to cook. I don't know if we will make it.*

[They all sit down to eat.]

Mom: *Jacob, I want you to think about what might happen because you didn't do your job.*

Jacob [sadly]: *We might not get to go to the movie. I'm sorry, Mom. I didn't think there would be a problem.*

[They finish their meal.]

Mom: *Now who will help me do the dishes?*

Weaving a Web

Goal:

Develop sense of responsibility;
support the understanding of cause and effect

Materials:

- large ball of yarn or string
- an area large enough for the children to sit in a circle

Procedure:

1. Give each child an opportunity to practice being responsible. Tell the children that they are all going to help make a giant spiderweb. Emphasize that each one will need to be responsible for their part of the web or it will fall apart.

2. Start by giving one child the ball of yarn. Tell him to place the ball of yarn in one hand and to hold onto the end of the yarn with the other hand. Then ask the child to roll the ball to another child without letting go of the end of the yarn.

3. The second child must also roll the ball while holding onto the yarn. Continue to roll the ball until each child is holding part of the web. Put a spider puppet in the middle of the web and tell the children that now the spider has a home. (*Note:* The children may need verbal and physical reminders to hold on to the string.)

4. Talk about each child having a job to do as they hold on to the string and help to make the spider's web. Ask, "What would happen if one person didn't do his job? Would the web be as strong?"

Variations for Toddlers:

This activity is not developmentally appropriate for most toddlers.

Variations for Schoolagers:

Schoolagers could throw the ball instead of rolling it. Help them keep from getting too carried away. Schoolagers can help untangle the web and rewind the ball of yarn. They might also enjoy designing spiderwebs around table and chair legs.

Recycle and Reuse

40

Goal:

Develop sense of responsibility

Materials:

- cardboard boxes
- a collection of recyclable materials
- garbage can

Procedure:

1. Use recycling boxes to introduce the concept of being responsible for the environment. Make a box for each type of material you might recycle, such as paper, aluminum, and plastic. Put a picture on the outside of the boxes in which they belong.

2. Collect a number of items used in your setting. Include "clean" garbage that you can safely use as props for this activity. Gather the children and talk with them about all the things that are thrown away throughout the day. Ask, "What do we do with garbage?" "Where does garbage go?" Pile the garbage you have collected in the center of the circle. Ask the children, "What might happen if we keep throwing all the garbage on the pile?" "How big will the pile of garbage get?"

3. Talk with the children about recycling. Explain that many of the things we use can be collected and reused.

4. Introduce the recycling boxes. Use the materials you collected for a sorting activity. Choose one of the materials and examine it. Talk about what it looks like and what it feels like. Ask if anyone knows what it is made of. Place it in the appropriate box. Repeat the activity until you have demonstrated with one or two things made of each recyclable material. Include a few things that cannot be recycled and need to go in the garbage.

5. Invite the children to sort the rest of the materials gathered during free play.

6. After the children have had an opportunity to practice with the collected objects, talk about where these boxes will be in the room. Ask them to think about anything that they are going to put in the garbage. Could it go in one of the recycling bins instead?

Variations for Toddlers:

This activity is not developmentally appropriate for most toddlers.

Variations for Schoolagers:

Read the poem, "Sarah Cynthia Sylvia Stout Would Not Take the Garbage Out" from Shel Silverstein's book *Where the Sidewalk Ends.* Introduce the recycling boxes (the sorting activity probably is not necessary). Schoolagers could make posters encouraging others to recycle too.

Jobs I Do

Goal:

Develop sense of responsibility; support self-esteem

Materials:

- chart paper
- stamp
- ink pad
- marker
- tape (optional)

Procedure:

1. Help children recognize ways in which they are acting responsibly. Prepare a chart with the heading "Jobs I Do At Home."

2. Talk about how everyone has jobs to do. Tell the children some of the jobs you do, like taking care of children and cleaning up toys.

3. Ask, "What jobs do you do at home?" Write or draw pictures of the jobs they list in the left-hand column of the chart. If you are uncomfortable drawing in front of the group, prepare simple pictures of jobs they are likely to mention. Be prepared for some ideas you hadn't anticipated. If the children need help with ideas, suggest the following:

- get diapers
- carry clothes
- pick up toys
- take out the garbage
- set the table
- make your bed

4. Tell the children that some of them may do many jobs on the list and others may do only one. Explain that it is okay if they don't do every job.

5. Ask all the children who do the first job on your list to stand up. Make a mark or put a stamp on the chart for each child standing. You can say, "This mark is for MiaYing; MiaYing, please sit down. This mark is for Sarah; Sarah, please sit down."

6. Repeat the procedure for each job on the list. Encourage the children to think hard about their jobs and to only stand up when it is something they do. Expect that some children will stand up for every item just for the fun of standing.

Variations for Toddlers:

Jobs toddlers might do include putting socks in the dirty clothes hamper, pulling on their own pants, washing their hands, brushing their hair, cleaning up spills, picking up toys, and getting a diaper. As you talk with the children, draw a picture of all the things they do to help. Affirm their responses by saying, "You're a big help" or "I bet that helps your mom/dad."

Variations for Schoolagers:

This activity will work for schoolagers in its present form. Extend it by asking the children to draw pictures of the chores they do at home and school.

Helping a Friend

Goal:

Develop sense of responsibility

Materials:

- individual pictures of children in your group
- yarn
- chart paper
- markers

Procedure:

1. Give children an opportunity to practice being responsible by arranging a way for them to help one another. Cut yarn to lengths that will make a necklace for each child. Tie a photograph of one child to each necklace.

2. Ask the children to develop a list of ways they can help one another. Their list might include actions such as these: tie a friend's shoes, zip up someone's jacket, get a napkin for someone, help someone clean up a game, teach a friend to do something if they don't know how, and hang up someone's artwork for them.

3. Tell the children that you are going to give them a special friend for the day. Give each child a necklace with their special friend's picture on it. It is their job to help that person throughout the day. If they forget who they are to help, they can look at the picture. Periodically remind the children to think of ways they can help their special friend.

4. At the end of the day, make three lists with the children: one naming all the things they did for their friend, a second saying how it felt to have someone help them, and a third identifying how it felt to help a special friend.

Variations for Toddlers:

Look for ways toddlers can help their peers. Make suggestions like, "Regina, please help Seng pick up the blocks" or "Rashima is good at bringing books for us to read. Rashima please get a book for Tyrone."

Variations for Schoolagers:

Schoolagers will enjoy the idea of being a secret helper. Assign one child to help another. Talk about helping children other than their special friend so they won't be easily guessed. Establish a minimum number of times they are to help their special friend so no one is ignored.

Cause and Effect

Andrea jumped up from the snack table when she saw Kiesha's cup tumble over. In an instant she had predicted that the spilled juice would get her wet and quickly moved out of the way.

Like Andrea, children have many everyday experiences with cause and effect. Children learn about actions and reactions by manipulating toys and materials, through trial and error, and by predicting, observing, and comparing. They also learn from the consequences that follow the choices that they make or the behaviors that they engage in. Adults help children learn this important strength when they use natural consequences as one of their guidance strategies. Children need many experiences with cause and effect to learn to anticipate what will happen.

Children who understand cause and effect can better predict what will take place and are able to foresee consequences of risky activities and behaviors. They learn to avoid hazards and keep themselves out of uncertain situations.

Some general ways to promote the understanding of cause and effect are listed below. Caregivers can support children's development of this skill by the way they set up the environment, by pointing out when one thing causes another during teachable moments, and by arranging activities.

Environment

➤ Provide activities in which children make predictions and test their accuracy. Science activities such as growing seeds, mixing colors, experimenting with objects that sink and float, and observing animals are among the many activities you could offer. For more ideas see *Mudpies to Magnets* by Rockwell, Sherwood, and Williams or *More Than Magnets* by Moomaw and Hieronymus.

➤ Talk about caring for your environment and materials. Ask, "What might happen if no one picked up the toys at clean-up time." Help them recognize that toys might get lost, dirty, or broken. Children might trip over things that aren't picked up, and they might not be able to find materials they need the next time they want to play.

➤ Let children be responsible for meeting as many of their own needs as possible. For example, children can get their own cup and napkin at snack time. Talk about what they will need to put their juice in and what they will need to wipe their face. When someone forgets, they will quickly remember once the juice is passed to them.

➤ Classroom pets can be used to talk about cause and effect. Discuss what would happen to the pet if no one fed it, gave it water, or cared for its other needs.

Teachable Moments

➤ Use natural consequences as part of your guidance approach to discipline. Avoid judgments and blaming when natural consequences happen. For example, if a child doesn't get ready to go outside with the other children, point out that she will have less time outside. Let the consequence follow without judgment or further comment. Children learn valuable "life lessons" from these natural consequences.

➤ Read a story but stop part of the way through. Ask the children to predict what will happen. Finish reading the story and see which of their guesses were right.

- Point out the consequences of a story character's behavior. For example, in the story about the Little Red Hen, the animals who didn't help with the work didn't get to help eat the bread.

- Be aware of and point out situations in which one action causes another. You might say, "When you push her, she cries," "Because your knee is scraped, it is bleeding and we need to wash it," or "When you shared the blocks, you built a huge castle."

- Wonder out loud during all sorts of activities. As you paint you might ask, "I wonder what will happen if I put yellow paint on top of this red?"

- Ask the children to make predictions. For example, you could ask, "What might happen if I put this magnet on plastic?"

- Ask the children to consider the consequences of the choices they make. Ask, "What might happen if you build your tower at the bottom of the slide?"

Modeling

- Use descriptive language as you work and play with the children. Talk out loud about things you are doing. For example, at the water table you might say, "When I pour more and more water into this cup, the water starts to spill out."

- Verbalize the natural consequences of your own behavior. When you realize you have left something behind, say something like, "I forgot to get the napkins so now I have to get up and get them," or "I am going to pick up all the little game pieces before the baby wakes up. Then she won't accidentally put one in her mouth."

Children's Books

Aardema, Verna. *Who's in Rabbit's House?* New York: Dial, 1977.

Burningham, John. *Mr. Gumpy's Outing.* New York: Holt, 1970.

Carlson, Nancy. *Loudmouth George and the Big Race.* Minneapolis: Carolrhoda, 1983.

———. *Harriet's Halloween Candy.* New York: Puffin, 1982.

Hobson, Sally. *Chicken Little.* New York: Simon, 1994.

Coloring the Coffee Together

Goal:

Develop an understanding of cause and effect

Materials:

- round coffee filters (not cone shaped)
- washable markers
- spray bottles filled with water

Procedure:

1. Help children experience cause and effect. Divide the group into pairs. Explain that they will be working together to make a picture. Show them the coffee filter and tell them how it is usually used. Then tell them that today they are going to color the filter.

2. Give the markers to one child in each pair and give the other child a spray water bottle. Lay the filter flat. Have the child with the markers color on the filter. When she is finished, have the children guess what will happen when it is sprayed. Then have the other child squirt the filter.

3. Have the children exchange materials and make a second picture.

4. When the filters are dry, hang them from a mobile or a clothes line in front of the windows.

Variations with Toddlers:

Let each child color on a filter, and then squirt the filter with water. Emphasize how you and the child worked together.

Variations with Schoolagers:

Let partners continue to work together to create their own colorful coffee-filter mobiles.

Wrecking Things

Goal:

Develop an understanding of cause and effect; support perseverance

Materials:

- foam or cardboard blocks
- string
- masking tape
- newspaper
- dowel

Procedure:

1. Explore cause and effect by experimenting with the wrecking ball. To prepare, wad sheets of newspaper into a ball. Tie a string around the ball. Leave one end of the string loose as you wrap masking tape around and around the ball. The tape will help the ball keep its shape. Suspend the ball from the ceiling or tie the loose end of the string around a dowel. Put the dowel between two chairs so the ball hangs off the ground.

2. Have children build a tower with foam or cardboard blocks. Use the ball to knock down the tower.

3. Help children determine where they need to place their building in order for the ball to knock it down. You may want to mark the spot with masking tape.

4. If the ball is hanging in the area where the children want to build their tower, talk with them about ways they can keep it aside until they are ready to let it swing.

Variations for Toddlers:

Practice making block towers with toddlers. Watch for the structure to become wobbly. Ask, "What is going to happen?" Or make newspaper balls for toddlers to roll at their foam block towers.

Variations for Schoolagers:

Each child could make their own wrecking ball. Decorate them with stickers or permanent marker.

Rolling Away

Goal:

Develop an understanding of cause and effect; support problem solving

Materials:

- plastic rain gutters about 4 feet long
- small cars and trucks
- different sized balls
- wheels in a variety of sizes (skate, plastic, from building sets, etc.)
- blocks
- masking tape

Procedure:

1. Help children practice making predictions. Place plastic rain gutters in the block area. Be sure the ends have no sharp edges. Invite the children to build a base for the rain gutters with large blocks. Put one end of the rain gutters on the blocks and roll down small cars.

2. Encourage the children to experiment with different degrees of incline to see if the cars go faster or slower.

3. Suggest that the children predict how far the car will go. Mark the location with masking tape. Then try it out.

4. Repeat the activity using balls or wheels.

Variations for Toddlers:

Build the ramps for the toddlers and let them experiment with the rolling action. Use comments like, "Where is the car? Where did it go? Here it is! We found it!"

Variations for Schoolagers:

Provide tools like tape measures, yard sticks, and rulers to measure the distance the object goes. Roll the object again and see if it goes the same distance each time. In addition, the children could make a chart showing which object goes the greatest distance.

Getting Through the Maze

Goal:

Develop an understanding of cause and effect; support problem solving

Materials:

- cover to a large box (a copy-paper box works well)
- Styrofoam or sponge strips
- marbles
- glue or hot glue gun

Procedure:

1. Explore cause and effect by learning to manipulate a marble through a maze. Make a maze by gluing Styrofoam or sponge pieces into a cover of a large box. Make the passageways large enough for marbles to go through.

2. Ask two children to use the maze. One child stands on each side of the maze. They are to get the marble from one end of the maze to the other by lifting and tilting the box cover to direct the marble.

Variations for Toddlers:

Make a simple maze for table tennis or golf balls. Let the toddlers do this activity with a teacher. Make several mazes so sharing is not an issue. Use words like tilt, lift, tip, and cooperate to verbalize what the children are doing.

Variations for Schoolagers:

Extend this activity by having the materials available for the children to make their own mazes. Make sure they have had multiple experiences with paper and pencil mazes prior to creating their own. Discuss maze-making strategies such as designing dead ends and crooked paths. Designing a maze is much harder than it appears!

Sponge It

47

Goal:

Develop an understanding of cause and effect

Materials:

- three to four different types of sponges (big-holed sponges, small-holed sponges, natural sponges, sponges cut into small pieces, dishwashing sponge with a handle, and so on)
- large sheets of easel or butcher paper
- primary colors of tempera paint in shallow containers

Procedure:

1. Provide children with an opportunity to cause changes as they paint. Divide the children into groups of three or four, depending on the size of your paper. Work with one group at a time.

2. Tell the children that they are going to make a group picture with sponges. Let each child choose a sponge. Show them the paint and how you paint with sponges. Ask them to guess what kind of impression each sponge will make. Will it be smooth? Will it cover the whole paper?

3. Let each child take a turn painting on the paper.

4. Ask thought-provoking questions like, "What happens if one child paints in the same spot as another? What happens if the colors overlap? What color will blue and red make?"

5. Emphasize how all the members of the group worked together to create a picture. Write the names of the group members on the painting and display their work. Write a short description of the process for parents to read and post it with the pictures.

Variations for Toddlers:

Use only one kind of sponge. Use a spring clothespin as a handle for children who may not want their hands to get dirty. Supervise closely and support clean-up efforts.

Variations for Schoolagers:

Discuss why the prints look different. Discuss what the sponge does (absorb and hold paint) and the role of the painter (to make an impression and decide where to place it).

Bears in Ice

48

Goal:

Develop an understanding of cause and effect

Materials:

- small objects (like teddy bear counters)
- ice cube trays
- chart paper
- markers
- jelly roll pan

Procedure:

1. Explore cause and effect as warm air melts ice. Freeze small objects (teddy bear counters work well) in ice cube trays. Remove the ice cubes from the trays and place on a jelly roll pan.

2. Gather the children and ask them to describe what they see and feel.

3. Have the children guess what will happen if the ice cubes are left out for a while. Help them be descriptive by asking questions like, "Will anything be different?" "Will the bears still be in ice?" "What will happen to the ice?" "What will it look like?" "Will anything else be different?" Accept any answers that children give. Ask follow up questions like, "Why do you think it will do that?" or "What makes you think so?"

4. Record their ideas on the chart paper. Write down or draw a picture representing all their ideas, whether they are likely to take place or not.

5. Encourage the children to check the ice cubes throughout the day. After a couple of hours, gather the children together again and have them examine what has taken place. Check their observations against their predictions listed on the chart. Circle the predictions that were accurate.

Variations for Toddlers:

Freeze larger objects in margarine containers. Let the children observe the changes that take place. Comment on the changes taking place. For example, you might say, "It's melting. The toy is coming out. Now there is a puddle."

Variations for Schoolagers:

Encourage the children to think of a variety of ways they could melt the ice faster. Try a few of their suggestions, like pouring hot water on the ice, placing them near the heating vent, or holding the ice in their hands.

What Might Happen?

Goal:

Develop an understanding of cause and effect; support problem solving

Materials:

Procedure:

1. Practice predicting what could take place in a variety of situations. Explain by saying, "We're going to play a game about 'What might happen if….' I'll give you a situation and you tell me what might happen."

2. Here are some situations to discuss with the children. Add your own ideas to make this activity more applicable to the children in your group.

- What might happen if you bought ice cream and you didn't eat it right away?
- What might happen if you forgot to feed your pet?
- What might happen if it was cold and you didn't put a coat on to go outside?
- What might happen if your mom or dad forgot to put gas in the car?
- What might happen if you forgot to turn the water off in the sink?
- What might happen if you dropped a glass on the floor?

3. Depending on your group, you may want to continue the activity by discussing some more threatening situations:

- What might happen if you walked in front of someone who was swinging?
- What might happen if you saw some candy on the ground and ate it?

- What might happen if you didn't stay by your mom or dad in a store?
- What might happen if you forgot to tell your mom or dad you were going to a friend's house to play?
- What might happen if your ball went into the street and you ran out to get it?

4. End the game before children show signs of fatigue or anxiety. Reassure them that they know a lot about staying out of danger.

Variations for Toddlers:

This activity is not developmentally appropriate for most toddlers.

Variations for Schoolagers:

Here are some situations to discuss for this age group. Add your own ideas to make this activity more applicable to the children in your group.

- What might happen if you didn't brush your teeth?
- What might happen if you left food in your bedroom?
- What might happen if you didn't bring your boots to school in the winter and it was time for recess?
- What might happen if you decided to play and didn't get your homework done?
- What might happen if you always wanted to be the boss when you were playing with your friends?

A Scary Movie

Goal:

Develop an understanding of cause and effect; support the identification and expression of feelings

Materials:

- audiotape of music from the sound track of a movie
- chart paper
- markers
- tape recorder

Procedure:

1. Help children predict danger by recognizing physical indicators. Make an audiotape of about eight 10-second cuts of music from movie sound tracks. Choose music that indicates a variety of moods or feelings. Some of the cuts should sound happy, some scary, some sad.

2. Talk about a children's movie you have seen that had some frightening parts. Say something like, "I saw the movie *Pinocchio* yesterday. I thought some parts were really scary." Discuss some of the scary movies the children have seen. Be prepared to hear about some movies that you feel are inappropriate for children. This is a time to let children talk about their feelings, not to judge whether the child should have been allowed to see a particular movie. Redirect discussion that gets too graphic or might scare other children.

3. Ask the children to show you what they look like when they are scared. Ask, "What happens to your body when you get scared?" The children may respond by mentioning some of the following: clench teeth, eyes get big, hands near mouth, shoulders tighten, tummy gets nervous, can't catch breath, heart pounds.

4. Tell the children that when you watch a movie and you get scared, you shut your eyes. Ask them what else they might do. Write down their ideas. You may hear some of the following: turn it off, run, sit with Mom or Dad, put your head in a pillow, and tell a grownup.

5. Tell the children that sometimes there are clues that something dangerous or scary is about to happen. Listen to the tape you prepared. Have the children dance to the happy parts. Ask them to stop and pretend to be afraid when they hear a scary part. Reiterate that they heard the clues and know the scary parts.

6. Summarize the activity by saying, "I want you to pay attention to clues that let you know you are getting scared." Review the list of indicators and what the children can do when they are scared.

Variations for Toddlers:

This activity is not developmentally appropriate for most toddlers.

Variations for Schoolagers:

Schoolagers won't want people to tease them about being afraid of things seen on television. Focus the discussion on real things that are frightening, like tornadoes or fires. Discuss what happens to such things as their pulse, their jaw, and their breathing when they are surprised by a fire drill or as a bad storm approaches. If you want to extend the discussion to television, talk about how special effects can make some things appear much more frightening than they actually are.

What children said they could do if they got scared during a movie:

Be brave, it's not real.

Put in a movie that isn't scary.

Reframing

At snack time, Tyler gets his cup and napkin. As he starts to move toward the table, he stops in his tracks. His bottom lip begins to quiver and he starts to cry. Tyler's child care provider moves close to him and asks, "What's the problem?" Tyler says, "I want the blue chair but Tina's already sitting there." His provider says, "I know you're disappointed, but there are lots of chairs. Maybe you would like to sit by your friend Ramon."

Tyler's provider is helping him learn to name his feelings and to reframe a problem. She understands Tyler's feelings about not getting his favorite blue chair and helps him look at the problem not as a tragedy but as an opportunity to sit by a friend. This type of flexible thinking is important in learning to problem solve, developing a positive attitude, and in coping with adversity.

Children also need to learn to frame problems in ways that allow them to take action to improve a situation rather than to think that they are the cause of the problem. For example, thinking "I keep falling off my bike because I'm no good at riding bikes," could be reframed as "I keep falling off my bike because I'm just learning. If I keep practicing I'll get better."

Adults can help children learn to reframe by doing the following:

- Encourage children to verbalize their thoughts by asking, "What is the problem?"

- Encourage children to look for alternative explanations by asking, "Why did that happen? Is there another reason?" or "What else might be happening?"

- Help children put the situation in perspective by saying something like, "I know you feel disappointed, but there are other places to sit."

- Develop a plan of action. For example, "Next time you might do _____ instead."

Reframing is heavily dependent on language and teachable moments. Watch for situations in which you can facilitate this type of learning. In addition, incorporate the suggestions for your environment, modeling, and activities that follow.

Environment

- Make looking at things in a new light very concrete for young children. Include kaleidoscopes, prisms, color paddles, binoculars, and magnifying glasses. As children explore, introduce the concept that "things can look different" with these lenses.

- Collect a number of different glasses, sunglasses with different tinted lenses, and eye glasses with the lenses removed. Use these to talk about how different things can look. Put them on at times when you want to look at something differently. Say, "I wonder what it would look like with these on" or "These might help me see it another way."

- Include ways for children to climb. At different heights, children experience seeing things from various points of view.

- Work with the children to rearrange your room. After they have had an opportunity to play in the newly arranged space, talk with them about what is different. Ask, "Are there any toys you play with more now that things look different to you?"

- Offer a number of puzzles. As children use them, wonder out loud, "What would this look like if we turned it around?" or "What would happen if we turned this piece upside down?"

Teachable Moments

> Watch for children who overgeneralize a problem. If they struggle with a task and then say that they are bad at everything, for example, help them reframe the situation. Say, "This is hard work. You will have to practice many times. Each time you try it will get a little easier."

> Offer another way for children to look at their problems. For instance, when a child complains that others aren't playing with him, help him look at ways he could join the group instead of waiting for an invitation.

> Help children understand the actions of others. Sometimes children misinterpret an accidental bump or shove. They believe the other child is threatening them. Their initial response is to retaliate. You might say something like, "Jesse was rushing to get in line and accidentally bumped you."

> Give children involved in a conflict a chance to tell what they believe is taking place. Listening to another person's explanation helps children learn someone else's perspective. Explore with children other reasons for a child's actions. For example, when a child complains, "He took my car," ask, "Why do you think he did that?" or "What's another reason?" Offer additional explanations for the behavior of others when the child can't think of any. For example, if a child says, "He just wanted to take mine," think with the child about other reasons. You might say, "Since you put the car down, maybe he thought you were done with it."

> Wonder out loud about what someone else is thinking. In the block area you could say, "I wonder what Brittany was thinking when she put this tube over here. Let's ask her." Brittany might then tell about how the tube was meant as a tunnel or a silo.

Modeling

> Look at a problem you encounter from a new perspective. For example, you might draw a picture and say something like, "I was trying to make a lamb, but it looks more like a pig. Maybe I'll just make it into a pig."

> Demonstrate how to find the positive in a situation. When plans need to change, you might say, "We don't get to do what we had planned, but that will give us time to do _____ instead."

Children's Books

Carle, Eric. *Little Cloud.* New York: Scholastic, 1996.

Hoban, Tana. *Look! Look! Look!* New York: Greenwillow, 1988.

Hutchins, Pat. *Changes, Changes.* New York: Aladdin, 1971.

LeGuin, Ursula. *Fire and Stone.* New York: Atheneum, 1989.

McGovern, Ann. *Too Much Noise.* Boston: Houghton, 1967.

Moss, Marissa. *Regina's Big Mistake.* Boston: Houghton, 1990.

Stevenson, James. *"Could Be Worse!"* New York: Greenwillow, 1977.

Stone, Jon. *The Monster at the End of This Book.* New York:
    Western, 1971.

51 Up High, Down Low, and On the Side

Goal:

Develop skill to reframe

Materials:

- large cardboard box
- variety of things to mount inside (colorful pictures, decorative wrapping paper, glow-in-the-dark stars, unbreakable mirror, and so on)

Procedure:

1. Give children an opportunity to view things from different perspectives with this box. Cut three- to four-inch holes in a large cardboard box at various positions (high, low, on the top, on the side, and so on). Leave the space directly across from each hole intact.

2. Mount something different across from each opening. An unbreakable mirror and glow-in-the-dark stars are especially fun. Magazine pictures or squares of decorative wrapping paper work too.

3. Encourage the children to explore the box and describe what they see in each opening.

Variations for Toddlers:

Construct the box as described above. Give cues for toddlers to find the stars, their face in the mirror, the kitty, and so on. Ask toddlers to tell you what they've found.

Variations for Schoolagers:

After providing a model perspective box, have schoolagers make their own using a shoe box. An adult will need to cut the holes.

Make Your Own Frame

Goal:

Develop skill to reframe; support optimism and hope

Materials:

- objects from nature (sand, twigs, shells, leaves)
- collage materials
- glue
- precut frames from heavy weight paper
- 2 or 3 commercial frames
- a completed piece of art from each child

Procedure:

1. Give children concrete experience in "framing."
To prepare, precut frames from heavy weight paper.

2. Show children how frames are used to set off a piece of art. Show two or three different types of commercial frames. Let the children know that frames can be decorative and that each is unique. Explain that they will be making their own special frame for one of their pictures.

3. Provide materials from nature for children to glue onto their frames. Let them create their own designs and arrange them in their own ways.

4. Use the completed frames to set off a piece of each child's artwork.

Variations for Toddlers:

Cut ovals from a piece of construction paper to make a simple frame. Place a frame over a photograph of each child (enlarge the photograph to 8 ½ by 11 inches, if possible). At group time, hold up the photos of each child and say, "We're glad you're here today." Everyone clap and say "Hooray!" Display the photos in a prominent place at the children's eye level.

Variations for Schoolagers:

This activity will work for schoolagers in its present form.

Choose a Frame

Goal:

Develop skill to reframe; support self-esteem

Materials:

- three or four frames
- children's artwork or a replica of a masterpiece
- chart paper

Procedure:

1. Help children experience the concept of reframing using their own artwork. Make three or four frames that are very different from one another. They can be made from heavy tagboard or a variety of materials. A collection of purchased wooden, metal, or plastic frames could be used too.

2. Prepare a chart that shows one of the frames in each column.

3. Show the children how to frame a picture. Use examples to talk about how different a picture can look depending on the frame. Set the frames out where the children can experiment. Ask them to try their pictures in the various frames and decide which they like the best.

4. Once the children have decided which frame they like best, have them put their name on the appropriate column of the chart.

5. After they have had a chance to put their names on the chart, count how many liked each frame. Talk about which column has more names and which has less. Accept each child's preference.

Variations for Toddlers:

This activity is not developmentally appropriate for most toddlers.

Variations for Schoolagers:

This activity will work for schoolagers in its present form.

Turn a Frown Upside Down

Goal:

Develop skill to reframe; support empathy

Materials:

- chart paper
- markers

Procedure:

1. Help children practice reframing using this optical illusion. Tell a story similar to the one that follows which illustrates how people may not be what they first appear.

Once upon a time there was a sad man. (Draw a picture of the sad man as shown). *He lived all alone and often-times had nothing to do and no one to talk to.*

Every day when the children would walk home from the school bus, the sad man would sit in a chair on his driveway and watch the children.

Treva noticed the sad man when she walked home from the bus. One day she asked her mother, "Mom, remember the man we were talking to at the neighborhood picnic?" Her mother said, "Does he live in the yellow house? His name is Willy." Treva asked, "Why is Willy always so sad?" Her mother said, "He lives alone and it's hard for him to get out to see his friends." Treva asked, "Can I talk to him?" Her mother said, "Of course. He is very nice. Daddy and I know him from when we do the neighborhood clean up."

The next day when Treva got off the bus, Willy asked Treva her name. Treva called from the bottom of his driveway, "My name is Treva." Willy didn't look quite so sad as he asked her, "How was school today?" Treva stopped for a moment and told him about the story they read and the picture she drew. Then she rushed home.

From then on Treva stopped at Willy's house each day and told him about school. One day when Treva got home her mother asked, "How was Willy today?" Treva exclaimed happily, "Willy is great, and you know what? He's not so sad anymore." (Turn the original picture upside down.)

2. Ask the children, "Why do you think Willy is happy now?"

Variations for Toddlers:

This activity is not developmentally appropriate for most toddlers.

Variations for Schoolagers:

Ask the children if they know any elderly people who might be lonely sometimes. Brainstorm ways to reach out to them. If possible, visit a nursing home and bring songs to share and artwork to decorate the rooms.

Illustration reproduced by permission from *You Can Be A Chalk Artist* (1978), by Art Barr. Published by Accent, Denver, Colorado. May not be further reproduced. All rights reserved.

55

What's Another Reason?

Goal:

Develop skill to reframe

Materials:

- multicultural dolls or puppets
- 2 or 3 baskets where children keep their personal materials
- books
- an easel
- props to support the role-plays you add

Procedure:

1. Explore the idea of reframing by looking for more than one way to explain the actions of others. Use dolls or puppets to act out the scenes on the facing page. Gather any props you might need to support your role-plays. Give the dolls names and introduce them to the group.

2. Add role-plays that fit your situation, such as someone building with blocks who thinks a newcomer will knock her blocks down.

3. Summarize by saying, for example, "Sometimes we get the wrong idea. This child had the wrong idea when she thought he wanted to take her things. Sometimes you might have the wrong idea too. Think of another reason."

Variations for Toddlers:

Do this activity at the water table with a few children at a time. Use rubber dolls to role-play one or two situations. Show how one doll is playing and another comes to play beside him. Comment, "Look, here comes Frankie. Frankie wants to play bubbles too. You are both playing side by side in the bubbles."

Variations for Schoolagers:

This activity will work for schoolagers in its present form.

Lisa is standing in front of the cubbies. Angelo approaches. Lisa thinks, "He's going to take all my stuff!"

Ask the children, "What is another reason Angelo might be coming to the cubbies?"

○

Lisa and Frankie are sitting side by side on the floor. Angelo comes and tries to squeeze between them. Frankie thinks, "He's trying to sit on my spot!"

Ask the children, "What's another reason Angelo might want to sit there?"

Frankie is looking at books in the reading area. Lisa comes toward him. He thinks, "She will take my book."

Ask the children, "What's another reason that Lisa might be coming to the book area?"

○

Lisa is drawing a picture at the easel. Angelo comes to the easel and stands close by. Lisa thinks, "He wants to take my turn!"

Ask the children, "What's another reason Angelo might come to the easel?"

56

You Could Be Happy

Goal:

Develop skill to reframe; support optimism and hope

Materials:

- squashed orange
- orange squeezer (optional)
- cup or juice glass
- orange juice
- chart paper
- markers

Procedure:

1. Explore the idea of reframing by looking for the positive in a variety of situations. Prepare a chart with two columns. Draw a sad face at the top of one column. Draw a happy face at the top of the other column.

2. Start by showing the children a squashed orange. Say that you are really disappointed because you wanted to eat that orange but now you can't because it's all squashed. Pretend to get an idea. Show the children how you can make orange juice out of the orange. Draw a picture of a squashed orange under the sad face. Then talk about how you ended up happy when you made orange juice. Draw a picture of orange juice under the happy face. Serve orange juice as part of this activity or for snack later the same day.

3. Tell the children there are many times they might feel disappointed because things don't work out the way they want. Draw or write the following situations in the first column of the chart (and add your own ideas):

- a rainy day
- a broken leg
- it's too cold to go outside
- no friends around to play with

4. Have the children help you think of ways to make disappointing situations better. Ask, "What could you do so you could be happy when…." Write their ideas in the second column.

5. Summarize by saying, "First we thought about things that would make us feel disappointed. Then we thought about things we could do so it wouldn't seem so bad." Read some of the ideas they had.

Variations for Toddlers:

Use puppets to role-play situations that make children in your care feel sad and happy. Here are a few ideas. With each situation, have the children show you what it looks like when they are sad and when they are happy.

Have the puppet talk about feeling sad when he wakes up early and it's dark all around him. Then turn it into a happy situation where the puppet notices that it is starting to get light and he sees some toys in his crib.

Show the puppet feeling sad when it is time to take a bath. Then turn it into a happy situation when the puppet finds some soap crayons and bath toys to bring with him.

Have the puppet talk about feeling sad when he has to take off his pajamas and get dressed. Turn it into a happy situation by having the puppet decide to leave on the pajama top to wear as a shirt.

Variations for Schoolagers:

Introduce this activity by reading a story about things to do on a rainy day. Follow up by discussing things that disappoint the children and ways to make the disappointing situations better. Summarize the discussion as in the fifth step above, and then invite the children to illustrate the concept. Give the children pieces of paper and invite them to use half of the sheet to draw a picture of something that disappointed them. On the other half, invite them to draw a picture of something they could do so it wouldn't seem so bad. Add captions.

Problem Solving

Stephanie was faced with a problem. She wanted to make her father a birthday crown, but each strip of paper she cut was too short to go around her head. She was sure it wouldn't go around her father's head. Yet she was uncertain how to make it bigger.

Problems like Stephanie's as well as problems that arise out of conflict are part of everyday life for a child. As children learn to solve problems they need lots of guidance and practice. Problem solving is a complex skill. It involves identifying a problem, thinking of ways to solve it, choosing the best idea, and trying it out. In order to take these steps, children need to understand cause and effect, control their impulses, think divergently, and make choices. In addition, when a problem involves a conflict, a child needs to know how to identify and express feelings.

To learn to solve problems, children need to observe others as they successfully solve problems, the assistance of adults as they first try problem solving, and many opportunities to try it on their own. Protecting children from challenges or solving conflict for them robs them of the chance to learn important skills.

Through conflict children learn to articulate their ideas about how to solve a problem. In addition, they broaden their repertoire of solutions as they listen to the ideas of others. By developing this strength, children gain the lifelong skills of resolving differences with others and finding solutions to their own problems.

Activities to help children identify and express their feelings begin on page 123. Activities focusing on cause and effect can be found on pages 169. A number of other resources provide further ideas on how to teach these component skills. Two examples are *Kids Can Cooperate: A Practical Guide to Teaching Problem Solving* by Elizabeth Crary and *Second Step: A Violence Prevention Curriculum* by Committee for Children.

Following you will find suggestions for your environment, examples of teachable moments, ways to model this skill, and activities that offer practice with impulse control, divergent thinking, and making choices. Because this strength is so complex, this section has more activities than other sections.

Environment

> Establish an environment in which children take safe risks. Children need to know that they can state an idea and try it out without being laughed at and that if it doesn't work, you will help them think of another. Say something like, "Try it. If it doesn't work, we'll think of something else." Encourage children to try their ideas in art projects, science and building activities, and pretend play.

> Offer choices for the children to make. Give choices of foods, activities, open-ended art projects, and which books to read. When children learn to make choices, they learn they have some control over what happens to them.

> Do activities that involve brainstorming. A few examples include thinking of all the things you need to pack to go on a trip, making a list of all the things to do in the snow, or brainstorming all the different ways there are to get from one place to another.

> Play games in which children practice controlling their impulses. Examples are statue tag and to stop dancing and freeze whenever the music stops.

> Make a poster listing the steps in problem solving. Use simple phrases or pictures to help children remember the steps. Put the hook side of a piece of Velcro after each step on the poster. Make several cards with check marks on them. Place the fuzzy side of the Velcro on the back of these. After the children complete a step, they can stick a check mark on the poster to help keep track of where they are in the process.

Steps in Problem Solving:

1. Identify the problem.

2. Gather information.

3. Generate solutions.

4.. Choose the best solution.

5. Implement the plan.

6. Evaluate how your plan is working.

7. Revise your plan as needed.

Teachable Moments

> Teach children to problem solve in all sorts of situations, not just when they are experiencing conflict. Use problem solving when deciding how to fix a broken toy, when thinking about how to build a fort out of blankets, or when deciding what to do about the noise level.

> Help children recognize when they are getting upset. You might say, "I can tell by your face (or your clenched teeth) that you are getting upset."

> Identify problems for children. Describe what you see, such as, "You are trying to get that to stick and it keeps falling," or "Michael and Josh both want the yellow truck," or "You can't agree about who will be the zookeeper first."

> Work through conflicts that occur in your setting. Obviously, there are times when you cannot stop the action to calmly work out a problem. Whenever you can, coach children involved in a conflict through the steps in problem solving. When you approach a situation in which two children are arguing, be careful not to assume you know what took place. Let each child express herself. As the children develop a list of suggestions, you

may find that their solutions are quite different from those you would develop. Trying out their ideas is part of the learning process. Help them try their ideas and evaluate them. You may find a successful solution you hadn't thought of before.

➤ Help children take a few deep breaths and calm down before problem solving. When their emotions are less intense, they are better able to attend to what you say.

Steps in Problem Solving

1. Identify the problem.

2. Gather information.

3. Generate solutions.

4. Choose the best solution.

5. Implement the plan.

6. Evaluate how your plan is working.

7. Revise your plan as needed.

Helpful Phrases

1. "I see _____."
   (Describe what you see.)

2. "Tell me about your problem."
   "How do you feel about that?"

3. "What could you do to work this out?"

4. "What might happen if you tried that?"
   "Is that okay with you?"
   "Which idea will you try first?"

5. "Try it."

6. "Is your idea working?"

7. "Is there another idea that might work better?"

Adapted from *So This Is Normal Too?* (1995), by Deborah Hewitt. Published by Redleaf Press, St. Paul, Minnesota, 800-423-8309. Used with permission.

> Provide suggestions as children brainstorm solutions. Ask, "Would it help to work on this at the table?" Be sure you are only offering a suggestion during problem solving and letting the children choose a solution for themselves. When you are not able to offer a choice, give a specific direction. For example, when you need the children to move their work to the table, you might say, "Please color at the table. You are not as likely to get bumped if you draw up there."

Modeling

> Expect that problems will be resolved. When you experience a challenge or difficulty, say something like, "I wonder how I can work this out? Maybe I could try..."

> Use a problem you are experiencing to show children how to think of many different solutions. If you try to make something and it doesn't work, say something like, "My first idea isn't working. I'll have to come up with another idea."

Children's Books

Berenstain, Stan, and Jan Berenstain. *The Berenstain Bears Get in a Fight.* New York: Random, 1982.

Crary, Elizabeth. *I Want It.* Seattle: Parenting Press, 1982.

Henkes, Kevin. *Bailey Goes Camping.* New York: Greenwillow, 1985.

Hutchins, Pat. *The Doorbell Rang.* New York: Scholastic, 1986.

Keller, Holly. *Geraldine's Blanket.* New York: Greenwillow, 1984.

Wood, Don, and Audrey Wood. *The Little Mouse, the Red Ripe Strawberry and the Big Hungry Bear.* New York: Scholastic, 1984.

Zolotow, Charlotte. *Mr. Rabbit and the Lovely Present.* New York: Harper, 1990.

One, Two, Three

Goal:

Develop skills used in problem solving

Materials:

Procedure:

1. Practice impulse control by explaining to the children that you are going to help them shake their wiggles out. Tell them you will count to three, then tell them what part of their body to shake.

2. Say, "One, two, three, shake your _____ with me." Fill in the blank with various body parts.

- hands
- head
- toes
- fingers
- tummy
- legs
- hair
- elbows
- ears

3. Help the children calm down by explaining that next you want them to keep each part still. Say, "One, two, three, keep your _____ still with me." Fill in the blanks with the same body parts as above.

4. Remind all the children that now that they have their wiggles out they can play more slowly and quietly or sit quietly to listen to a story.

5. Use this activity when you notice that a group or an individual needs help relaxing.

Variations for Toddlers:

Toddlers need to start by moving their whole body. Say, "One, two, three, _____ with me." Fill in the blank with *jump, shake, move,* and *wiggle.* Then use the jingle from the third step and fill in body parts: head, hands, and feet. After the children have mastered these, add arms, fingers, and legs.

Variations for Schoolagers:

Teach children to relax various parts of their bodies. When the children are sitting or lying down, ask them to tighten and release certain muscles. Go from the head down, squeezing and releasing each part three to four times. You might say, "I want you to squeeze your hands tight. Make them as tight as you can. Just a little longer. Now shake them out. Let them relax and leave them very still." Use a calm, quiet tone of voice to help create a relaxing atmosphere.

Blow Out the Candles

Goal:

Develop skills used in problem solving

Materials:

Procedure:

1. Practice relaxation and impulse control. Ask all the children to stop what they are doing and to look at you.

2. Explain that it is getting too loud or that everyone is getting "revved up." Tell them that you would like them to move more slowly and to use quieter voices.

3. Ask the children to hold up four or five fingers. Pretend that each finger is a candle on a birthday cake.

4. Direct them to draw in one big breath and to slowly blow out one candle. Put that finger down. Repeat for each "candle."

5. Use this exercise with the group or an individual when you recognize escalating behavior or emotions.

Variations for Toddlers:

Before giving toddlers directions for this activity, you will need to move close to each of them and touch them. Once you have their attention, you can give the explanation. After they have had practice with the activity, you may be able to ask them to stop the action and do this activity from wherever you are in the room.

Variations for Schoolagers:

Have the children hold their breath while you count to five, then slowly exhale.

Wait a Little Longer

Goal:

Develop skills used in problem solving

Materials:

- bell or whistle

Procedure:

1. Help children develop impulse control as they practice waiting. Explain that sometimes you have to wait. Give examples like waiting for a turn, waiting for someone to get done talking, and waiting for someone to get off the phone.

2. Tell the children you are going to practice waiting. Say, "I am going to ask you to pretend to do something. Don't start until I blow the whistle." Give the children the direction, but wait for a few seconds before blowing the whistle.

3. Have the children pretend any of the following actions (and add your own ideas):

- eating
- tying your shoes
- writing your name in the sky
- skating
- riding a bike
- being a lion
- being a robot

4. Affirm the children's behavior by saying, "You can be good at waiting. You can stop and wait."

Variations for Toddlers:

Ask toddlers to pretend that they are doing common actions, such as eating, drinking, dancing, washing their faces, combing their hair, or brushing their teeth. Let them know when they are doing a good job by saying, "Great job! You waited, then you pretended to eat."

Variations for Schoolagers:

Make the tasks a little more challenging, such as standing on one foot or tiptoeing. To make sure the children are concentrating, bring the whistle to your lips but do not blow it. Later in the game, let the children lead the activity and indicate when to begin.

Saving the Kitty

Goal:

Develop skills used in problem solving; support perseverance and the understanding of cause and effect

Materials:

- stuffed animal (kitten, if possible)
- tree or counter to be used as ledge
- props such as a toy ladder, rope, hiking boots, and fire truck

(This could be done as a flannel board activity.)

Procedure:

1. Introduce children to the idea of thinking of more than one solution before finding one that works. To prepare for this activity, place the stuffed animal on a counter or in a tree.

2. Explain that you are going to tell the children a story about a problem and how a group of children solved it. Tell the story that is on the facing page.

3. Before the conclusion of the story, show the children the four props. Ask them what would work to get Maybe down from the high place. Try each suggestion from the group. Have something go wrong with each one except the fourth. For example, "We could use the ladder, but the ladder is too short and won't reach the kitty. We could throw the rope up to the kitty, but Maybe won't or can't grab the rope. So the rope just sits there and is no help to Maybe. We could call the fire department, but their ladder breaks and they can't reach Maybe, or it takes them such a long time to get there that Maybe is in danger of falling." Use the last prop, the hiking boots, to tell how one of the friends decides to climb the tree and get Maybe down.

4. Make sure the story line shows the children working hard to solve the problem, and involve the group of children you work with as much as possible.

5. Once Maybe is rescued, finish the story.

Variations for Toddlers:

Simplify the story by eliminating all the props but one. Demonstrate how the children succeed in rescuing Maybe in the first try. Let them each use the prop to rescue the kitty.

Variations for Schoolagers:

Stop the story once Maybe is stuck in the tree. Have the children work alone or in pairs to draw a picture or write a brief ending to the story that describes how they would solve the problem. Ask them to show others in the group how they would rescue Maybe.

There once was a kitty named Maybe. Maybe had a problem. She loved to climb, but she was very afraid of heights. So she would climb up, up, up and then get stuck. When she looked down she would shake and shiver and meow. Eventually someone would have to rescue her.

Sherri and Malik were Maybe's owners. They loved her very much and tried to help her whenever she got up too high and frightened herself.

One Friday, Malik and Sherri were playing with some friends. All of a sudden Sherri stopped playing and said, "Listen...I think Maybe is in trouble. I hear her meowing." Her friends just laughed and told her she was wrong. But Maybe's cries became louder and louder. Finally, the children decided they would have to find out where Maybe was. They looked and looked. They looked in the house, they looked in the yard, they looked in the garage, but they couldn't find Maybe.

[Stop the story at this point and ask the children in your group where they think the children in the story should look. Look around the room until the children find the stuffed animal in the tree or on the ledge. Continue the story.]

Maybe was scared and shivering. She wasn't moving a muscle. The friends had to figure out how to get her down.

[Stop the story at this point for problem solving.]

Conclusion:

The children were so excited when Maybe was safely on the ground. They patted Maybe, got her a special bowl of milk, jumped up and down, and hugged one another. They could barely believe it when Maybe finished her milk and started walking toward another tree in the backyard.

Find Another Way

Goal:

Develop skills used in problem solving; support perseverance and reframing

Materials:

- large building blocks
- climbers
- barriers of any kind
- cardboard boxes
- tunnels
- other obstacle materials

Procedure:

1. Practice divergent thinking by developing an obstacle course that has more than one way to get through it. As you make the course, be sure to include a few spots in which the children can go more than one way and still get all the way to the end.

2. Let the children explore the course. Allow them to make choices about how they will move through the course and which way they will go. Then ask each child to go through in another way. Point out how each child solved the problem. Talk about how there were two ways to go and they could reach the finish going either way.

3. When interest flags, ask them to build an obstacle course together. Encourage them to "make more than one way." Have them invite their classmates or parents to go through it.

Variation: Build a tabletop obstacle course using small building blocks, dominoes, small cardboard boxes and tubes, and other materials you have available. Create tunnels, roadways, and interesting spaces for the children to explore. Have the children drive small cars through the course. Encourage them to find more than one way.

Variations for Toddlers:

Use only two or three pieces of equipment. Have only one place where there are two possible paths to take and point out how the children make different choices of how to go through it.

Variations for Schoolagers:

Schoolagers are likely to enjoy the challenge of designing an obstacle course. Invite younger children or parents to go through it. Have them draw a map of the courses they design. Put the maps into a booklet of obstacle courses that they can re-create.

Team Wrapping

Goal:

Develop skills used in problem solving; support perseverance

Materials:

- one large item for each group to wrap (like large stuffed animals)
- wrapping paper
- ribbon
- tape
- scissors

Procedure:

1. Give children practice in generating solutions and making choices. Begin by dividing the children into groups of three or four. Give each group an item to be wrapped. Large stuffed animals work well.

2. Explain that the children are to work together to wrap the items. Monitor each group to make sure that all members are involved in the activity and working cooperatively. The larger the item, the more likely it will be that all members of the group are needed to wrap it.

3. Talk with the groups about how they will solve the problems that they may face. How will they decide how much paper to use? How will they make the paper stay where they want it? What will they do about tails or ears that stick out? How will they work together?

Variations for Toddlers:

Let toddlers work in pairs or with a teacher to unwrap an already wrapped stuffed animal. Ask, "What can we do to get this open?" Use short encouraging statements throughout the activity like, "Keep working together, you'll get it," "You'll figure it out together," or "What good problem-solvers the two of you are."

Variations for Schoolagers:

Have the children make an item to be wrapped like a structure made out of tinker toys or a doll bed made out of cardboard boxes. Then ask them to wrap the item cooperatively. Exchange items with another group. Have the other group guess what the item might be from the shape of the package.

From *Keeping the Peace: Practicing Cooperation and Conflict Resolution with Preschoolers* (1989), by Susanne Wichert. Published by New Society Publishers, Gabriola Island, British Columbia, Canada. Used with permission.

Making Choices

Goal:

Develop skills used in problem solving; support empathy and perseverance

Materials:

- paper (11 by 18 inches or larger)
- primary colors of tempera paint
- paint brushes
- plastic grout spreaders with various sized grooves (available at hardware stores)

Procedure:

1. Give children an opportunity to practice making a number of choices. Assign partners. Give each pair a grout spreader and a piece of paper.

2. Tell the children that they are partners in making this picture. Explain that they are to paint on the paper and then use the grout spreader to make designs in the paint. Put the names of both children on the paper.

3. Explain that they will need to make a number of choices while they are working on this project. Ask them to settle the following questions:

- Who will paint and who will make the designs?
- Which color(s) will they use?
- Where should the colors appear on the paper?
- How should the designs be arranged (up and down, in a circle, all around)?
- Which size grooves should they use?
- How will they work together to hang their paper so it will dry?
- How will they share their painting when it is done?

4. Keep track of some of the choices they make. After everyone is done, describe some of the decisions. For example, "Tisha and Elijah decided to paint with blue and yellow. Kristen and Amanda decided they would each take a turn painting and scraping."

Variations for Toddlers:

Create a group picture. Let each child take a turn with much teacher assistance. Put the paint on a very large piece of butcher paper. Display at toddlers' eye level or use the group picture as the background for a bulletin board or as scenery for a puppet play.

Variations for Schoolagers:

If you have a wall or outdoor sidewalk that you can paint, give the children the opportunity to paint the wall or sidewalk in bright fluorescent colors using this technique.

Rag-Rolling Picture

Goal:

Develop skills used in problem solving; support empathy and perseverance

Materials:

- old rags rolled and tied with string
- paper (11 by 18 inches or larger)
- oblong cake pans
- tempera paints

Procedure:

1. Give children an opportunity to practice making choices. Have the children form pairs. Give each pair a rolled rag and a piece of paper. Put the names of both children on the paper.

2. Tell the children they are to work together to create a picture. Explain that they are to create a design by rolling the rag in the paint and then rolling the paint-filled rag on the paper. As they work they will need to make a number of decisions together, including the following:

- How many colors to use?
- Which colors to use?
- Who will roll the rag in the paint?
- Will they roll the rag on the paper or drag it?
- When will they stop painting?
- How will they work together to hang it so it will dry?
- How will they share their painting?

3. Keep track of some of the choices the children make. After everyone is done, describe some of the decisions that were made. For example, "Tamara and Oris decided that one person would take the painting home for a week and then bring it back for the other to take home. Samuel and Meng decided to cut their picture in half so they could each have part of it."

Variations for Toddlers:

Create a group picture. Let each child take a turn with much teacher assistance. Put the paint on a very large piece of butcher paper. Display at toddlers' eye level or use the group picture as the background for a bulletin board or as scenery for a puppet play.

Variations for Schoolagers:

This activity will work for schoolagers in its present form.

Goal:

Develop skills used in problem solving

Materials:

- poster with stoplight
- two puppets
- one truck
- any book

Procedure:

1. Introduce children to the steps in problem solving. To prepare, make a large poster with a stoplight on it. Write the steps of problem solving in the lights.

Red = Stop
What is the problem?

Yellow = Slow Down and Think
What can you do?
What's the best idea?

Green = Go
Try your idea.

2. Explain to the children that the stoplight can help them when they have a problem. Review what each color on the stoplight typically means as well as its special problem-solving meaning.

3. Put on a puppet play where two puppets want the same toy. An example follows.

This is Ellie. This is George. George and Ellie are playing with trucks. Let's watch and see what they are doing. Ellie is driving the truck. "Zoom, zoom!" goes Ellie's truck. Here comes George. George wants the truck. George pulls on Ellie's truck. Ellie pulls back.

4. Tell the children that Ellie and George can use the stoplight to help them solve their problem. Use the stoplight to discuss their problem.

Red = Stop

Ellie and George need to stop. They have a problem. They both want the truck at the same time.

Yellow = Slow Down and Think

Tell the puppets, "You need to slow down and think about what you can do." Have George say, "We could share or take turns playing with the truck." Have Ellie say, "We could get another one."

Ask the puppets, "What's the best idea?" Have George and Ellie think that the best idea is to take turns. (For a group that is advanced or has had experience with problem solving, expand the discussion to cover who will have the first turn.)

Green = Go

Tell the puppets, "Okay, try your idea." Have Ellie drive the truck to George and have George drive it back to Ellie. Back and forth they take turns with the truck.

5. Put on another puppet play about a problem. Use the stoplight again as you problem solve. For example, Shana is reading a book. Emillio wants to read the book too. Emillio tries to sit right next to Shana and look at the book at the same time. Shana doesn't like it. Use the stoplight and the steps in problem solving to work it out.

6. Post the stoplight in your room. Refer to it when children need help problem solving.

Variations for Toddlers:

Toddlers will need some preparation for this activity. Discuss what each color on a stoplight means. For example, say, "Red means stop, yellow means slow down, and green means go." Play Red Light, Green Light. Then put on the puppet play suggested earlier.

Variations for Schoolagers:

Adapt this for schoolagers by using more complex problems. For example, two children are playing school and both want to be the teacher. Or two children always get to be the catcher or the pitcher when they play baseball at recess, and everyone else has to be in the outfield. Or two children are playing a board game and one gets mad because he doesn't think he will win.

Ways to Be Friendly

Goal:

Develop skills used in problem solving; support empathy

Materials:

- chart paper
- marker
- copies of book pages found on the next page
- enlarged copy of the book for the book area
- scissors
- stapler

Procedure:

1. Tell the children you want them to pretend they have a problem. Say, "You want to be friends with another child but you aren't sure how to start." Ask the children to tell you some ways to be friendly. Give an example like, "Friends say hello to one another. Accept their ideas, but if their ideas are vague, probe a little further by asking, "What does that look like?" or "Tell me what you would do."

2. Write down their answers on chart paper.

3. Pass out copies of the book pages found on the next page. Tell the children, "Here are some pictures that show some of your ideas and other ideas about being friendly too."

4. Have the children cut out each picture. Include blank pages so the children can draw their own ideas. Staple them together in book form.

5. Explore the books with the children. Ask them to look for various pictures. For example, say, "Find the picture with the child who is smiling at his friend."

6. Encourage the children to use their books when they need help thinking of a way to be friendly. Summarize by saying, "There are many ways to show people you want to be friendly. When you need an idea, look at your book. Choose one of the ideas and try it."

7. Make a big book for your book area by enlarging the pictures, decorating them, and stapling the pages together.

Variations for Toddlers:

Make this into a big book and read it with the children. In addition, laminate pictures from magazines that show people being friendly. Have toddlers point to things in the pictures that show friendship. For example, "Put your finger on the picture of two friends sitting side by side."

Variations for Schoolagers:

Schoolagers can make their own books. Have them choose captions for their pages from the list of ways to be friendly. They can illustrate each page. Ask schoolagers to choose one of the actions to carry out each day.

> **Kids' responses when asked, "How can you be friendly?"**
>
> *Play nice.*
>
> *Say nice words.*
>
> *Trade toys.*
>
> *Hug.*
>
> *No fighting.*

The Best Idea

Goal:

Develop skills used in problem solving

Materials:

- picture cards with problem situations found on the next page

Some children may need to begin learning to problem solve by making choices between two options. This activity gives children an opportunity to gain experience evaluating the options. In each situation, one of the actions that the children could take is clearly destructive and the other is constructive. Although we provide one constructive suggestion, there are others that would be possible. If your group is ready for it, you can explore other appropriate options. As children gain experience with problem solving, they will be better able to generate a number of solutions. This activity is the first in a series of three ("The Best Idea," "When I Have Trouble," and "What Could You Do") that are designed to take children from simple to more complex problems and problem solving.

Procedure:

1. Let children practice deciding which of two actions is the best choice. Then give them an opportunity to generate additional solutions. Explain that sometime they may have a problem and they will have to decide what is the best thing to do. Tell the children that you are going to practice deciding on the best idea.

2. Show a picture card of a problem situation. Give the children two possible solutions to the problem. Have the children decide which is the best. Why? What might happen if the other option takes place? Extend the activity by asking, "What else could be done?"

3. Summarize by saying, "Sometimes we have to decide what is the best idea. We need to think really hard about what might happen and which is the best idea."

Variations for Toddlers:

This activity is not developmentally appropriate for most toddlers.

Variations for Schoolagers:

Schoolagers will need more complex problems than those found here. Let the children list problem situations. Ask them to generate a number of different solutions. Then consider the consequences of each suggestion. Discussion may lead to the realization that none of the solutions may work perfectly.

Two children want the same toy at the same time.

Choices: This boy can grab the toy or he can wait for a turn.

Which is the best idea? Why? What might happen if he grabs the toy? What else could he do?

This girl wants a turn on the jumper but someone else is already using it.

Choices: She can push her off or say, "I'd like a turn."

Which is the best idea? Why? What might happen if she pushes her off? What else could she do?

This girl accidentally broke something.

Choices: She can try to hide it or tell a grownup it was an accident.

Which is the best idea? Why? What might happen if she tries to hide the broken pieces? What else could she do?

This boy is mad.

Choices: He can say, "I'm mad!" or he can kick the door.

Which is the best idea? Why? What might happen if he kicks the door? What else could he do?

When I Have Trouble

Goal:

Develop skills used in problem solving

Materials:

- book
- chart paper
- markers
- copies of book pages found on the next page
- scissors
- staplers

Procedure:

1. Help children learn a number of different solutions to problems. Introduce the activity by doing a role-play where you and a child, an assistant, or even a puppet have trouble sharing a toy or a book. Pretend that the other person had the book and you want a turn with it. Approach the other person and say, "I want to read that book."

2. Ask the children what you can do to solve the problem. Write down their ideas.

3. Present a second problem. Role-play that you and another person are sitting next to each other while someone is reading a story. Pretend to bother the other person by tugging at her or talking to her.

4. Ask the children what could be done to solve the problem. Write their ideas down. Comment on how many ways they thought of to solve the problem.

5. Explain to the children that they will be making a book about what to do when you have trouble. Tell them it shows some of the ideas they have thought of and some new ones.

6. Pass out copies of the book pages. Have the children cut out each picture. Staple them together in a book form.

7. Summarize by saying, "There are many things you can do when you have trouble. When you need an idea you may look at your book."

Variations for Toddlers:

This activity is not developmentally appropriate for most toddlers.

Variations for Schoolagers:

Instead of the role-plays listed above, role-play a problem situation that occurs in your setting. Maybe one child could say, "I don't want to be your friend anymore" or "Your picture is stupid." Leave some pages blank for the children to add their own ideas and solutions.

What Could You Do?

Goal:

Develop skills used in problem solving; support the development of responsibility and the understanding of cause and effect

Materials:

Procedure:

1. Give the children an opportunity to practice divergent thinking skills by telling them that they are going to think of all the things that they could do when they have a problem.

2. Ask the children to think of all the things they could do in the following situations:

- You found a toy that isn't yours.
- You want to play but no friends are around.
- You need to tell your mom something but she's on the phone.
- You accidentally break a toy.
- You're looking at a book and a page falls out.
- You're pouring juice and it spills.
- Your baby brother or sister is crying and no one else is around.
- Your friend falls off her bike and starts to cry.

3. Summarize by saying, "You have lots of good ideas about solving problems."

Variations for Toddlers:

This activity is not developmentally appropriate for most toddlers.

Variations for Schoolagers:

Encourage many different solutions to each problem. Stress that there is usually more than one way to deal with a problem.

Optimism and Hope

When Brittany first told of her father's accident, she spoke in a voice that was barely audible. She said that he had been in a terrible accident and now was in the hospital too sick to see her. Her voice cracked as she reported that they weren't going to go on the vacation they had planned. Brittany found it difficult to perform even routine tasks and just went through the motions of most activities.

After days in the hospital, her father's condition improved and so did Brittany's spirits. As her father began to recover, her hope was restored. Along with it, her energy and playfulness returned. She gave updates of his condition with more enthusiasm and excitedly reported to her provider, "Daddy might be able to come home soon. If he keeps doing his exercises, he might be able to take me to the park by my birthday."

While hope and optimism can be influenced by the situations children encounter, it is also related to a child's temperament and can be influenced by surrounding people. We need hope in order to believe that things will work out and to keep us going as we work toward solutions to problems. Seeing that effort brings the results you seek also builds hope.

Fortunately, many children can find hope in events or conditions they encounter. They hope to go to the pizza place for supper, or they hope a special friend can come to their house, or they hope for a certain toy for their birthday. This hope and optimism gives them a reason to look forward to the many things they have yet to experience and allows them to look for the good in daily occurrences.

Adults can foster a sense of hopefulness by providing an optimistic model, offering encouragement, and presenting experiences in which children will gain a sense of pleasure. Following are general ideas for ways providers can influence the development of an optimistic outlook through the environment, interactions with the children, and activities.

Environment

> Create an environment that is appealing to children, a place where you would want to spend time. Consider what the physical space looks like from the child's perspective. Are there things that interest each child? Are the materials culturally relevant to the children? Is it a place they would feel comfortable spending a number of hours each day? Are there things of beauty like statues, ceramic vases, reprints of artwork, and cloth or weavings from different cultures?

> Communicate a spirit of fun throughout your activities. Let laughter fill your rooms so children look forward to attending your program.

> Include plenty of opportunities for children to engage in dramatic play. This is a source of joy for young children no matter what their experiences might be. It offers some children a chance to temporarily escape from difficult situations.

> Make a time line for your group. Record special events you experience together and post activities that are yet to come. This gives children things to look forward to and a visual way of tracking when they will happen.

> Plan celebrations. Many children need reasons and occasions to celebrate. Celebrate the small things, including a lost tooth, a new accomplishment, and a sunny day.

> Read for enjoyment. In addition to stories that support the development of the ten strengths, read books just for fun. Children will begin to develop a lifelong habit of reading that can help reduce stress.

Teachable Moments

> Find time to enjoy the children and their playful activities. Adults often worry about preparing the next activity or enforcing the rules, missing the pleasant experiences they could share with the children.

> Help develop the special interests of the children in your group. These interests may turn into lifelong hobbies.

> Teach children to take a break when things aren't going well. Say, "Try again after nap. Maybe things will go better after you are rested," or "Let's take a break and get some wiggles out. When we come back maybe it will be easier." Use reflective listening if the child is expressing disappointment. For example, if a child says, "This just isn't working for me," you might respond by reflecting back, "Your project isn't going how you thought it might." Help the child name his feelings by saying something like, "You look really disappointed and frustrated."

Modeling

> Set an optimistic tone. Expect that you will be able to work problems out together. Look for ways to salvage a situation or activity that has not turned out as planned. Be hopeful that things will work out.

> Demonstrate how to be hopeful. For example, if a child tells about someone they know who is sick, respond by saying, "I hope he will feel better soon," or "We hope that she is getting stronger every day."

> Look on the bright side of situations. You might say, "I couldn't find the book I was looking for at the library, but I found another one of our favorites."

> Use humor throughout the day. Don't be afraid to laugh at your own mistakes and at things that take place. Laughter can help to ease difficult situations and offers a positive release of emotion.

Children's Books

Brandenberg, Alexa. *I Am Me*. San Diego: Red Wagon, 1996.

Carlson, Nancy. *Take Time to Relax*. New York: Viking, 1991.

Feelings, Tom, and Eloise Greenfield. *Daydreamers*. New York: Puffin, 1981.

Holabird, Katharine. *Angelina Ballerina*. New York: Potter, 1983.

Kraus, Robert. *Leo the Late Bloomer*. New York: Windmill, 1971.

McLerran, Alice. *Roxaboxen*. New York: Lothrop, 1991.

Wells, Rosemary. *Moss Pillows: A Voyage to the Bunny Planet*. New York: Dial, 1992.

Up, Up, and Away!

Goal:

Develop a sense of optimism and hope; support problem solving

Materials:

- quiet background music

Procedure:

1. Help children learn to relax with this imaginary bubble ride. Be sure children have had experience blowing and watching bubbles before trying this activity. Begin by playing soft background music.

2. Ask the children to curl up into a ball.

3. Tell the children, "We are going to pretend to blow a bubble that is big enough for you to ride inside. When you are in the bubble, you can ride high up in the sky and float around the room. When the music stops, your bubble will slowly fall to the ground."

4. Instruct the children to take a deep breath and to slowly blow it out. As they blow they are to imagine their bubbles growing bigger and bigger. Take three or four big breaths.

5. Pretend to climb inside the big bubble and move around the room as if floating in the sky above the building. In a quiet, calming voice, describe what you might see (the climbing equipment, the play area, or the tree you read stories under).

6. Repeat this activity two or three times and pretend to fly above different things each time, like their homes, the zoo, or a flower garden.

Variations for Toddlers:

Give toddlers experiences with bubbles. Blowing them and watching them float can be relaxing. Trying to run and catch them can be a fun break from other types of play. Use a variety of things as bubble wands, such as cookie cutters, berry baskets, and margarine lids with a hole or shape cut out. Make bubble solution using 1 cup water, 2 teaspoons dish detergent, ½ teaspoon sugar, and 1 teaspoon glycerin (available at drug stores). Mix together gently.

Variations for Schoolagers:

This activity will work for schoolagers in its present form.

My Favorite Place

Goal:

Develop a sense of optimism and hope

Materials:

- pictures of places people may visit (house, meadow, lake, apartment building, a ball game, and so on)
- chart paper
- drawing paper
- markers or crayons
- *The Perfect Spot* by Robert J. Blake (optional)

Procedure:

1. Help children recognize places that they find relaxing. Introduce the activity by showing pictures of places that people find relaxing and enjoyable. Show a picture of your favorite place. Describe what it is like and tell why you like it. Or read *The Perfect Spot* by Robert J. Blake.

2. Ask the children to list some of the places they like to go. Write down the places they describe. Ask the children what their special place is like. For example, someone might like to go to dance class because there are lots of mirrors.

3. Tell the children that lots of people have a place they like to go or that feels special to them.

4. Ask each child to draw their special place. If drawing is frustrating for some children, let them dictate a description of their favorite place while you write it down. Then they can color or paint how they feel when they are at their special place.

5. At the bottom of the picture, have the children write a sentence or two about the place they draw. Write a caption for those who are unable to write their own.

Variations for Toddlers:

Toddlers may tie special places to special people such as their mom, grandma, or dad. Ask toddlers about their favorite cuddle time. Do they cuddle in the morning, at night with a good book, on the couch as they watch television? Find or draw pictures of the cuddling places the children talk about. Mount them at toddlers' eye level for further discussion. Talk about how they feel when they cuddle. Do they feel warm, calm, safe, happy?

Variations for Schoolagers:

This activity will work for schoolagers in its present form.

Just Imagine

Goal:

Develop a sense of optimism and hope

Materials:

- drawing paper
- markers or crayons
- magic wand

Procedure:

1. Help children develop a sense of optimism and hope for themselves and their futures. Put a heading at the top of drawing paper that helps them think positively about one aspect of their future. For example, "When I'm a grownup, I'm going to…."

2. Tell the children that sometimes it is fun to pretend you are somebody else.

3. Say, "Let's pretend this is a magic wand. I'm going to take this wand and wave it to turn you into something different. Abracadabra, pretend you are a kitty." Pretend to be other things too, such as a galloping horse, a mouse, a robot, and a baby. End by having the children pretend to be a grownup.

4. Ask, "What would it be like to be grownup? What kinds of things would you do?" You might hear such things as read books, tuck children into bed, work, cook supper, and so on.

5. Have the children draw pictures of themselves as grownups. Write a caption for those who are unable to write their own. If the children in your group aren't ready to draw, let them continue to act out what they might do. Children could each have a turn acting it out as the others in the group guess what they are doing.

Variations for Toddlers:

Break this into two separate activities for toddlers. On the first day, pretend to be animals with which the children are familiar. Help them act out what the animal might do. For example, a kitty might purr, play with a toy, drink milk, and curl up in a ball to sleep. On the second day, pretend to be a grownup. Act out waking up, eating breakfast, taking care of children, going to work, and going to the grocery store. Add your own ideas too.

Variations for Schoolagers:

This activity will work for schoolagers in its present form. Be prepared for some children who might view this as an opportunity to be powerful and controlling. They might draw pictures of themselves as adults who punish their children. Talk with these children individually. Find out why the adult is punishing someone. Ask if there is another way they might teach a child to behave.

> **What kids said when asked, "What kinds of things will you do when you are a grownup?"**
>
> *Have a baby.*
> *Buy breath mints.*
> *Get married.*
> *Be in the circus.*

73

Some Really Great Things

Goal:

Develop a sense of optimism and hope; support self-esteem and the identification and expression of feelings

Materials:

- large sheet of butcher paper
- drawing paper
- crayons
- markers
- colored pencils
- personal photographs (optional)

Procedure:

1. Help children develop an optimistic attitude by encouraging them to think about things that they really enjoy. Begin by talking about some things that you think are really great. It might be your pet, a good meal you have had, your family, a trip you took, or something that you saw. If possible, show photographs to help the children see what you are talking about.

2. Ask the children to draw a picture of something they think is great. Label their pictures for them if they are not able to write a caption for themselves.

3. To make a group mural, paste the individual pictures to a large sheet of butcher paper (or the children can draw directly on the butcher paper). As you put the pictures together, talk about how happy you are to have experienced, to have seen, or to be a part of these great things.

4. At the top of the mural, write a heading like "Some Great Things!" At the bottom you could add a subtitle "We are GREAT-ful."

Variations for Toddlers:

This activity is not developmentally appropriate for most toddlers.

Variations for Schoolagers:

Allow schoolagers to decide on their own title for the group mural.

I See a Good Thing

Goal:

Develop a sense of optimism and hope;
support reframing

Materials:

- decorated toilet paper or paper towel tube
- plain tube for each child
- decorative materials (ribbon, sequins, yarn, colored noodles, and so on)
- glue

Procedure:

1. Help children develop an optimistic attitude by looking for the good. Explain that you are going on a search. You are going to be looking for things that are good and you will need the group's help.

2. Help the children begin to think about what might be good by saying, "Let's look around the room. Think of things that you like; things you think are fun; find good work someone has done; or find something that is good. Everyone get an idea."

3. Use a tube that you've already decorated as a spyglass. Look through it and say, "I see _____ . It's a good thing. What do you see?" Pass the tube to a child.

4. Include as many children as are interested in offering ideas. Some children may want to pass. Expect repetition of some ideas.

5. Extend the activity by having the children decorate a spyglass to take home.

Variations for Toddlers:

Have toddlers name things they see in the room. Give them the words to use if they need help labeling things. Another time have them find something in the room that they like.

Variations for Schoolagers:

Write down the things the children say are good and post them. Extend this activity by going outside and looking for good things.

Hopewheels

Goal:

Develop a sense of optimism and hope

Materials:

- large sheet of heavy paper
- markers
- crayons

Procedure:

1. Provide children with an opportunity to practice articulating their hopes by making hopewheels. Cut one large circle out of heavy paper for each child. Draw five or six spokes from the center of each circle.

2. During free play, ask each child to come over and fill out a hopewheel with you. Define the concept of hope by saying something like, "Hope is what we would like to have happen." Ask each child what they hope for. Rephrase the question for some children by saying, "What are some things that you would like to have happen?" Write down each answer on one of the spokes.

You could do one hopewheel for the entire group rather than individual wheels. Make a large circle out of butcher paper and make one spoke for each child in your group. Ask each child to tell you what he hopes for. Write it on one of the spokes. Let the children take turns decorating their section of the wheel.

3. Let the children decorate their individual wheels after you have written down their ideas.

Variations for Toddlers:

Define the concept of hope for the children by saying, "Hope is what we want to have happen." Have the toddlers glue precut magazine pictures onto the wheel. Label the wheel "Hopewheel." Make sure the pictures depict positive situations, events, emotions, and people. Talk about the pictures as the children are working.

Variations for Schoolagers:

Schoolagers will be able to write their own hopes on the spokes and share them with the large group. Extend this activity by doing another hopewheel focusing on their hopes for the community.

A New Ending

Goal:

Develop a sense of optimism and hope; support reframing

Materials:

- blank audiotape
- tape recorder

Procedure:

1. Practice replacing negative thoughts with positive ones by using the common experience of a bad dream. Tell a story about a girl who had a scary dream similar to the one on the following page.

2. Ask the children, "What would be a better way to end this dream?" Retell the last part of the story. Say, "She stopped to look at the cereal and when she looked up...What did she see?" Encourage a number of different responses. You may hear endings like these: she saw her mother, her mother asked what kind of cereal she would like to buy, she saw the tooth fairy. Tape-record the various endings.

3. Play back the new endings.

4. Tell about a second dream where a boy climbs to the top of a tree and is too scared to climb back down. Have the children tape-record new, happy endings to this dream too. Summarize by telling the children that they can make new endings to their scary dreams too.

Variations for Toddlers:

This activity is not developmentally appropriate for most toddlers.

Variations for Schoolagers:

Ask schoolagers to list other things they can do when they have a nightmare.

> **Children's new endings to the dream about the boy who couldn't climb down from the top of a tree:**
>
> *Someone brought a trampoline and he bounced down.*
> *He saw a rainbow.*
> *He climbed on a bird and flew down.*

Once upon a time there was a little girl who had a scary dream. She was dreaming that she and her mother were shopping for groceries and she stopped to look at the cereal on the bottom shelf. When she looked up, she couldn't see her mother. Her heart started pounding, and she was very frightened.

The dream was so scary that the little girl woke up. Even when she was awake she felt scared. She talked to her mom about the scary dream, and her mom said, "Don't worry, it was only a bad dream." That helped a little, but she still needed to do something so she could get back to sleep. Each time the scary ideas from the dream came back, she pushed them away by thinking of a better way to end the dream.

Appendix One: Working with Children with Special Needs

Adapted from work by Dr. Joan K. Blaska (Professor, St. Cloud State University).

General Reminders

- Demonstrate genuine respect for the child and his or her abilities and disability.

- Work with the parents as partners. Invite and respect their input.

- Consider the child's developmental age as well as the chronological age when selecting materials and activities.

- Select activities that allow children to be in control, or make adaptations so the children have more control.

- Use a multisensory approach both in the materials and the methods you choose.

- Promote independence whenever possible.

- Use your state's Center for Independent Living as a resource. Seek information from disability rights advocates and peer counselors. Talk to adults who share the child's disability.

- Describe to children what is going to happen next, and provide assistance only when necessary.

- Ask the child if she needs help.

- Consult with an early childhood special education teacher when working with preschool children.

For children who are blind or visually impaired

- Use actual objects that children can touch whenever possible, instead of photographs or drawings.

- Use objects with a variety of shapes and textures.

- Identify the objects the child uses, describing what the objects look like and what action is occurring.

- When reading stories, have small replicas of the animals or main objects in the story to pass around for the child to feel (e.g., dog, horse, brush, cup). Do this with textures and smells, as well.

- For each verbal prompt, use a physical prompt as well, until verbal prompts can be used independently.

- Use child's name when giving verbal directions.

- Use normalized language. Even though a child who is blind will need to feel and object to identify it, the child should be asked if he or she wants to "see" or "look at" the object.

- If the child is partially sighted, stand so the child does not have to look into a glare or light.

- Use a sighted partner for some activities, as appropriate. Be sure that the sighted partner is not in a "helping" role the majority of the time. In addition, be sure to provide partnered activities that allow the blind or visually impaired child to be in the role of helper.

- Organize the environment so it has a predictable order and is free from "trip and fall" hazards.

For children with visual impairments, it is particularly important to provide activities for

- body awareness (name body parts and show where they are),

- object manipulation (manipulate a variety of objects, starting with larger and progressing to smaller),

- tactile discrimination (feel many textures, describing and matching),

- auditory discrimination (identify the sound), and

- auditory localization (identify location of sound).

To better understand these children and to keep your expectations appropriate, remember:

- Self-initiated mobility is usually delayed (i.e., creeping, crawling, standing by furniture).

- Language develops differently but by age five is generally the same as sighted children's language.

- Language frequently includes echolalia (repeating of sounds or words).

225

- "Blindisms" (inappropriate self-stimulating mannerisms) often become habitual and need to be addressed.

For children who are Deaf or hearing-impaired

- Get the child's attention before speaking.

- Face the child when speaking so your face can be seen for lip-reading and facial expressions.

- Stand still when you are speaking.

- Simplify instructions by using simple words and fewer words.

- Speak at your normal rate and loudness.

- Combine visuals (e.g., objects, modeling) with words whenever possible.

- Demonstrate or model the activity to clarify expectations.

- Have a hearing child next to a Deaf or hearing-impaired child to promote modeling.

- Have the child sit in the front of a classroom or near the teacher.

- If the child appears confused, repeat yourself or say the same thing in a different way.

- Learn American Sign Language or pidgin sign, if appropriate. Know the difference between signed English and ASL; become familiar with Deaf culture and the Deaf community.

- Understand the use of hearing aid or the phonic ear, as needed.

- Understand alternative modes of communication, when needed.

- When using a record player or musical instrument, allow child to "feel the beat" by putting her hand on the instrument or stereo speaker.

Be aware of the following:

- Deaf children's English vocabulary is generally smaller and their sentences are often shorter than hearing children's.

- Errors in English articulation and structure are common.

- Children who are Deaf or hearing impaired often have difficulty understanding what has been said to them verbally.

- Work closely with a speech/language clinician.

For children with motor impairments

- Understand the positioning needs of the child and develop the skills to position the child appropriately as approved by the physical therapist or physician.

- Have appropriate equipment available (e.g., provide tables at the appropriate height for children in wheelchairs or other equipment).

- Be willing to change classroom procedures (e.g., allow all students to sit in chairs during group so everyone is in a chair). Provide an inclusive, accessible environment, schedule, and activities. Find some way to make every activity and opportunity available to each child.

- Give the child with the disability choices, as appropriate (e.g., sit on the floor with other students or remain in wheelchair or other equipment).

- Substitute sitting or lying position for a standing position, when appropriate.

- Provide appropriate rest during movement activities.

- Work closely with the physical therapist, occupational therapist, or physician.

For children with cognitive or developmental disabilities

- Provide short, clear directions.

- Use words that the child will understand.

- Repeat directions whenever necessary.

- Accompany verbal directions with modeling and demonstration.

- Teach concrete concepts and ideas.

- Present information to as many senses (hearing, seeing, taste, touch, and smell) as possible.

- Expect to repeat concepts and explanations more often; plan for repetition and extended practice with materials or concepts.

- Continue prompting (giving physical or verbal help) as needed, then reduce prompts gradually, providing the least amount of prompts needed for success.

- Pair with another child who can model the skill or activity.
- Break the skills down into small teachable steps as needed.
- Provide positive reinforcement for small steps of progress.
- Provide positive reinforcement for good effort.

For children with emotional or psychiatric disabilities or behavioral difficulties

- Provide clear expectations and consequences.
- Structure the environment; provide a predictable routine.
- Provide consistent expectations and consistent behavior.
- Use physical prompts.
- Reinforce appropriate behavior.
- Alternate sitting and moving activities. Provide choices as much as possible. Help the child identify her own needs for quiet time or physical activity, and then choose an activity to meet them.
- Get the child's attention with direct eye contact before speaking.
- Evaluate all aspects of the programs to determine if you have programmed appropriately and have appropriate expectations.
- Develop specific behavior programs as needed. When program is developed, be consistent in following it.

For children with speech and language delays

- When a child makes an articulation error, model the appropriate pronunciation. The child should not be asked to repeat words. (Child says, "Bwoo fith." Teacher responds, "You see a blue fish.")
- When a child speaks using one or two word utterances, model an expanded sentence. (Child says, "Blue." Teacher says, "Yes, that's a blue truck.")

- When a child labels something incorrectly, model the appropriate label without asking the child to repeat you or indicating that she is wrong. (Child says, "Red." Teacher says, "It looks like you have a blue block.")
- Provide short, clear directions (one or two steps).
- Simplify instructions by using easy and fewer words.
- Use words the child will understand.
- Repeat information when necessary; ask the child if he or she understands.
- If child appears confused, say the same thing in a different way or by using different words.
- Be aware of the skills the child is working on with the speech clinician so you can follow through in the classroom and have appropriate expectations.
- Work closely with a speech/language clinician.

For children with a chronic illness

- Have a clear understanding of how the chronic illness is affecting the child's development (i.e., is there cognitive delay or a motor delay?).
- Refer to the strategies above for the disability or disabilities that the illness is causing.
- Be certain the health needs of the child are being met (e.g., medications are taken, appropriate rest is provided).
- Be aware of any medication the child is taking and possible side effects (i.e., fatigue, nausea, low appetite, hyperactivity).

References

Bailey, D.B., and M. Wolery. *Teaching Infants and Preschoolers with Disabilities.* 2nd ed. Columbus: Merrill, 1992.

Cook, R.E., A. Tessier, and V.B. Armbruster. *Adapting Early Childhood Curricula for Children with Special Needs.* 2nd. ed. Columbus: Merrill, 1991.

Deiner, P.L. *Resources for Teaching Children with Diverse Abilities.* 2nd ed. New York: Harcourt, 1993.

Fewell, R., and S.R. Sandall. "Curriculum Adaptation for Young Children: Visually Impaired, Hearing Impaired, Physically Impaired." *Topics in Early Childhood Special Education* (1983) 2 (4), 51-63.

Appendix Two: Activity Goals

Primary Goal = ◆
Secondary Goal = X

The Ten Strengths

Activities	Self-Esteem and Competence	Cultural Competence	Empathy	Perseverance	Responsibility	Identification and Expression of Feelings	Cause and Effect	Reframing	Problem Solving	Optimism and Hope
Bears in Ice							◆		X	
The Best Idea									◆	
Blow Out the Candles									◆	
Choose a Frame	X							◆		
Coloring the Coffee Together							◆			
Drum and Sheet				◆	X		X			
Feelings Word Book						◆	X			
A Feelings Guessing Game						◆				
Fill 'Er Up				◆						
Find Another Way				X				X	◆	
Finger Paint Mix-Up	X	◆								
Gender Stereotypes		◆								
Getting Through the Maze							◆		X	
Helping a Friend					◆					
High Stepping	X	◆								
Honking Geese				◆						
Hopewheels										◆
Hot Lava			◆		X				X	
How Am I Feeling?			◆			X		X		
How I Helped			◆					X		
I Feel Loved	◆	X								
I'll Do My Part					◆					
I'll Guide Your Hand			◆	X			X		X	
I Might Explode						◆	X			
I See a Good Thing								X		◆
I Was So Mad						◆			X	
Interview with a Spider				◆						
Jobs I Do	X				◆					
Just Imagine										◆
Look What I Can Do Now	◆									X
Looking for Clues						◆				
Make Your Own Frame								◆		X
Making Choices			X	X					◆	
My Favorite Place										◆
Name the Feeling						◆				
A New Ending								X		◆

228

The Ten Strengths

Primary Goal = ◆
Secondary Goal = X

Activities

Activity	Self-Esteem and Competence	Cultural Competence	Empathy	Perseverance	Responsibility	Identification and Expression of Feelings	Cause and Effect	Reframing	Problem Solving	Optimism and Hope
One, Two, Three									◆	
Rag-Rolling a Picture			X	X					◆	
A Really Big Puzzle	◆	X								
Recycle and Reuse					◆					
Rolling Away							◆		X	
Saving the Kitty				X			X		◆	
Say Something Friendly			◆							
A Scary Movie						X	◆			
Showing Love	◆	X								
Some Like It, Some Don't		X	◆			X				
Some Really Great Things	X					X				◆
Sponge It							◆			
Stop Light									◆	
Taking Care of Babies			X		◆					
Tasting Bread		◆								
Team Wrapping				X					◆	
Tell Me What to Draw	◆			X					X	
Things I'm Good At	◆									
Turn a Frown Upside Down			X					◆		
The Turnip				◆					X	
Up High, Down Low, and On the Side								◆		
Up, Up, and Away!									X	◆
Wait a Little Longer									◆	
Walk In Someone Else's Shoes		X	◆							
Ways to Be Friendly			X							
We All Celebrate	X	◆								X
We All Have Drums		◆								
Weaving a Web					◆		X			
What About the Spider?			X		◆			X		
What Could You Do?					X		X		◆	
What Could You Do to Help?			◆		X				X	
What Language Is That?		◆								
What Might Happen?							◆		X	
What's Another Reason?								◆		
When I Have Trouble									◆	
Where Does This Belong?					◆					
Where's My Bone?				◆						
Words of Encouragement				◆						
Wrecking Things				X			◆			
You Could Be Happy								◆		X

Appendix Three: Teaching Strategies

Free Play Activities

Choose a Frame, 184

A Feelings Guessing Game, 123

Feelings Word Book, 126

Fill 'Er Up, 148

Find Another Way, 200

Getting Through the Maze, 172

Helping a Friend, 165

High Stepping, 114

Look What I Can Do Now, 105

Name the Feeling, 124

A Really Big Puzzle, 101

Recycle and Reuse, 163

Rolling Away, 171

Tasting Bread, 117

Team Wrapping, 201

Things I'm Good At, 106

Up High, Down Low, and
   On the Side, 182

Walk in Someone Else's Shoes, 135

What Language Is That? 116

Wrecking Things, 170

Large Group

Bears in Ice, 174

The Best Idea, 208

Drum and Sheet, 151

Honking Geese, 153

I Might Explode, 128

I Feel Loved, 103

I See a Good Thing, 221

I Was So Mad, 127

Let's Tell the Teacher What
   to Do, 104

When I Have Trouble, 210

Looking for Clues, 125

A Scary Movie, 176

Some Like It, Some Don't, 136

Ways to Be Friendly, 206

We All Celebrate, 115

Weaving a Web, 162

What Could You Do? 212

What Might Happen? 175

Where Does This Belong? 158

You Could Be Happy, 188

The Arts

Coloring the Coffee Together, 169

Finger Paint Mix-Up, 113

Hopewheels, 222

How I Helped, 137

I'll Guide Your Hand, 138

Just Imagine, 219

Make Your Own Frame, 183

Making Choices, 202

My Favorite Place, 218

Rag-Rolling Picture, 203

Showing Love, 102

Some Really Great Things, 220

Sponge It, 173

We All Have Drums, 118

What About the Spider? 130

Role-Plays

Hot Lava, 139

How Am I Feeling? 134

Say Something Friendly, 142

Taking Care of Babies, 159

The Turnip, 146

What Could You Do to Help? 140

Puppet Plays

Interview with a Spider, 150

Stoplight, 204

What's Another Reason? 186

Where's My Bone? 149

Words of Encouragement, 152

Stories

I'll Do My Part, 160

A New Ending, 223

Saving the Kitty, 198

Turn a Frown Upside Down, 185

Charts

Gender Stereotypes, 119

Jobs I Do, 164

Transition Activities

Blow Out the Candles, 196

One, Two, Three, 195

Up, Up, and Away! 217

Wait a Little Longer, 197

Appendix Four: Resources

Advocacy

American Humane Association
Children's Division
63 Inverness Drive East
Englewood, CO 80112-5117
(303) 792-9900
www.amerhumane.org

Children's Defense Fund
25 E Street NW
Washington, DC 20001
(202) 628-8787
www.childrensdefense.org

For the Children
3615 Superior Avenue
Building 31, 4th Floor
Cleveland, OH 44114
(216) 431-6070

National Association for the Education of Young Children (NAEYC)
1509 16th Street NW
Washington, DC 20036-1424
(800) 424-2460
www.naeyc.org/naeyc

National Association of Child Advocates
1522 K Street NW
Washington, DC 20005
(202) 289-0777
www.childadvocacy.org

Career Development

Center for Career Development in Early Care and Education
Wheelock College
200 The Riverway
Boston, MA 02215-4176
(617) 734-5200 ext. 21
ericps.crc.uiuc.edu/ccdece

Council for Early Childhood Professional Recognition
2460 16th Street NW
Washington, DC 20009-3575
(800) 424-4310

National Center for the Early Childhood Work Force
733 15th Street NW, #1037
Washington, DC 20005
(202) 737-7700

National Institute for Early Childhood Professional Development
NAEYC
1509 16th Street NW
Washington, DC 20036
(800) 424-2460 ext. 386 or 388
www.naeyc.org/naeyc

Child Abuse and Neglect

National Clearinghouse on Child Abuse and Neglect Information
PO Box 1182
Washington, DC 20013-1182
(800) FYI-3366
www.calib.com/nccanch

National Committee to Prevent Child Abuse
332 South Michigan Avenue, #1600
Chicago, IL 60604
(312) 663-3520
www.childabuse.org

National Safe Kids Campaign
1301 Pennsylvania Avenue NW, #1000
Washington, DC 20004
(202) 662-0600
www.safekids.org

Child Care

National Association for Family Child Care (NAFCC)
206 6th Avenue, #900
Des Moines, IA 50309-4018
(800) 359-3817
www.assoc-mgmt.com/dms/users/nafcc

National Child Care Association
1016 Rosser Street
Conyers, GA 30012
(800) 543-7161
www.nccanet.com

National Child Care Information Center
301 Maple Avenue West, #602
Vienna, VA 22180
(800) 616-2242
ericps.crc.uiuc.edu/nccic

National School Age Care Alliance
1137 Washington Street
Boston, MA 02124
(617) 298-5012
www.nsaca.org

National Association of Child Care Resource and Referral Agencies
1319 F Street NW, #606
Washington, DC 20004
(202) 393-5501

Children with Disabilities

Council for Exceptional Children
1920 Association Drive
Reston, VA 20191
(800) CEC-READ

ARC National Headquarters
500 East Border Street, #300
Arlington, TX 76010
(800) 433-5255

National Association of Private Schools for Exceptional Children
(202) 408-3338
www.spedschools.com/napsec

Diversity

All One Heart
www.alloneheart.com

Black Community Crusade for Children (BCCC)
25 E Street NW
Washington, DC 20001
(202) 628-8787
www.childrensdefense.org

Children of Lesbians and Gays Everywhere (COLAGE)
2300 Market Street, #165
San Francisco, CA 94114
(415) 255-8345
www.colage.org

Council on Interracial Books for Children
1841 Broadway
New York, NY 10023
(212) 757-5339

Gay and Lesbian Parents Coalition International (GLPCI)
PO Box 50360
Washington, DC 20091
(202) 583-8029
www.glpci.org

National Association for the Advancement of Colored People (NAACP)
Washington Bureau
1025 Vermont Avenue NW, #1120
Washington, DC 20005
(202) 638-2269
www.naacp.org

National Black Child Development Institute
1023 15th Street NW, #600
Washington, DC 20005
(202) 387-1281

People of Every Stripe
PO Box 12505
Portland, OR 97212
(503) 282-0612

Family Support

Families and Work Institute
330 7th Avenue
New York, NY 10001
(212) 465-2044
www.familiesandwork.org

Family Resource Coalition
20 North Wacker Drive, #1100
Chicago, IL 60606
(312) 338-0900

Family Support Network
21902 2nd Avenue West
Bothell, WA 98021
(425) 487-4009
www.familynetwork.org/wecare

National Council on Family Relations
3989 Central Avenue NE, #550
Minneapolis, MN 55421
(612) 781-9331
www.ncfr.com

National Parent Information Network
University of Illinois
Children's Research Center
51 Gerty Drive
Champaign, IL 61820-7469
(800) 583-4135
ericps.ed.uiuc.edu/npin

National Parent Teacher Association
700 North Rush Street
Chicago, IL 60611
(302) 670-6783
www.pta.org

Parents Anonymous, Inc.
The National Organization
675 West Foothill Boulevard, #220
Claremont, CA 91711
(909) 621-6184

Single Parents Association
(800) 704-2102

Zero to Three/National Center for Infants, Toddlers and Families
735 15th Street NW, #1000
Washington, DC 20005
(202) 638-1144
www.zerothree.org

Health

American Academy of Pediatrics
Division of State Government Affairs
141 Northwest Point Boulevard
PO Box 927
Elk Grove Village, IL 60007
(847) 981-7666
www.aap.org

American Medical Association
515 North State Street
Chicago, IL 60610
(312) 464-5563

American Psychological Association
750 1st Street
Washington, DC 20002
(202) 336-6046

Children's Health Environmental Coalition
PO Box 846
Malibu, CA 90265
(310) 573-9608
www.checnet.org

Children's Health Fund
317 East 64th Street
New York, NY 10021
(212) 535-9400

Healthy Mothers, Healthy Babies
409 12th Street SW
Washington, DC 20024-2188
(202) 863-2458

National Association of WIC Directors
1627 Connecticut Avenue NW, #5
Washington, DC 20009
(202) 232-5492

The Brass Ring Society
(800) 666-9474
www.worldramp.net/brassring

Homelessness

Coalition for the Homeless
89 Chambers Street
New York, NY 10007
(212) 964-5900
www.homeless.24x7.com

**National Law Center on Homelessness
and Poverty**
918 F Street NW, #412
Washington, DC 20004
(202) 638-2535

Hunger

Bread for the World
1100 Wayne Avenue, #1000
Silver Spring, MD 20910
(301) 608-2400
www.bread.org

Children's Hunger Fund
PO Box 7085
Mission Hills, CA 91346
(800) 708-7589
www.chf2serve.org

Food Research and Action Center (FRAC)
1875 Connecticut Avenue, #540
Washington, DC 20009
(202) 986-2200

Mentoring

Big Brothers Big Sisters of America
National Office
230 North 13th Street
Philadelphia, PA 19107
(215) 567-7000
www.bbbsa.org

Girls, Inc.
30 East 33rd Street, 7th Floor
New York, NY 10016
(212) 689-3700
www.girlsinc.org

One to One Partnership, Inc.
2801 M Street NW
Washington, DC 20007
(202) 338-3844
www.mentoring.org

Poverty

Bureau for At-Risk Youth
PO Box 760
Plainview, NY 11803-0760
(800) 99-YOUTH

Head Start Bureau
ACYF Head Start Bureau
PO Box 1182
Washington, DC 20013
www.acf.dhhs.gov/programs/hsb

Substance Abuse Prevention

Campaign for Tobacco-Free Kids
1707 L Street NW, #400
Washington, DC 20036
(202) 296-5469
www.tobaccofreekids.org

Center on Alcohol Advertising
2140 Shattuck Avenue, #1206
Berkeley, CA 94704
(510) 649-8942

Join Together
441 Stuart Street, 6th Floor
Boston, MA 02116
(617) 437-1500
www.jointogether.org

National Inhalant Prevention Coalition
1201 West 6th Street, #C-200
Austin, TX 78703
(800) 269-4237
www.inhalants.com

Violence Prevention

Center on War and the Child
PO Box 487, Department F
Eureka Springs, AR 72632
(501) 253-8900

Children's Creative Response to Conflict
PO Box 271
Nyack, NY 10960
(914) 358-4601

Coalition for Quality Children's Media
535 Cordova Road, #456
Santa Fe, NM 87501
(505) 989-8076
www.cqcm.org/kidsfirst

Concerned Educators Allied for a Safe Environment (CEASE)
17 Gerry Street
Cambridge, MA 02138
(617) 864-0999

Educators for Social Responsibility
23 Garden Street
Cambridge, MA 02138
(617) 492-1764

Families Against Violence Advocacy Network
Institute for Peace and Justice
4144 Lindell Boulevard, #408
St. Louis, MO 63108

Growing Communities for Peace
16542 Orwell Road North
Marine on St. Croix, MN 55047
(612) 433-4303

National Alliance for Nonviolent Programming
1864 Banking Street
Greensboro, NC
(910) 370-0407

National Coalition on Television Violence (NCTV)
PO Box 2157
Champaign, IL 61820
(217) 384-1920

The Television Project
11160 Veirs Mill Road, #277
Wheaton, MD 20910
(310) 588-4001

Youth Development

National 4-H Council
7100 Connecticut Avenue
Chevy Chase, MD 20815-4999
(301) 961-2820

YMCA of the USA
101 North Wacker Drive
Chicago, IL 60606
(312) 977-0031
www.ymca.net

YWCA of the USA
350 5th Avenue, 3rd Floor
New York, NY 10118
(212) 273-7800

Appendix Five: Children's Books

1. Self-Esteem and Sense of Competence

Carlson, Nancy. *I Like Me!* New York: Scholastic, 1988.

Corey, Dorothy. *Will There Be a Lap for Me?* Morton Grove, IL: Whitman, 1992.

Henkes, Kevin. *Sheila Rae, the Brave*. New York: Greenwillow, 1987.

Hutchins, Pat. *My Best Friend*. New York: Greenwillow, 1993.

Moose, Barbara. *Mama, Do You Love Me?* San Francisco: Chronicle, 1991.

Morris, Ann. *Loving*. New York: Willam Morrow, 1990.

2. Cultural Competence

Ashley, Bernard. *Cleversticks*. New York: Crown, 1991.

Carlson, Nancy. *Arnie and the New Kid*. New York: Puffin, 1990.

Kissinger, Katie. *All the Colors We Are*. St. Paul: Redleaf, 1994.

Martin, Bill, Jr. *White Dynamite and Curly Kidd*. New York: Holt, 1986.

Morris, Ann. *Shoes, Shoes, Shoes*. New York: Lothrop, 1995.

Pellegrini, Nina. *Families Are Different*. New York: Holiday House, 1991.

Surat, Michele Maria. *Angel Child, Dragon Child*. New York: Scholastic, 1983.

3. Identification and Expression of Feelings

Berry, Joy. *Let's Talk About Feeling Angry*. New York: Scholastic, 1995.

Carlson, Nancy. *Harriet and the Roller Coaster*. New York: Puffin, 1982.

Crary, Elizabeth, and Shari Steelsmith. *When You're Happy and You Know It*. Seattle: Parenting Press, 1996.

Hazen, Barbara Shook. *Fang*. New York: Atheneum, 1987.

Lewin, Hugh. *Jafta*. Minneapolis: Carolrhoda, 1983.

Mayer, Mercer. *I Was So Mad*. New York: Western, 1983.

4. Empathy

Campbell, Alison, and Julia Barton. *Are You Asleep, Rabbit?* New York: Lothrop, 1990.

Cohen, Miriam. *Jim's Dog Muffins.* New York: Greenwillow, 1984.

de Paola, Tomie. *Now One Foot, Now the Other.* New York: Putnam, 1980.

Gackenbach, Dick. *What's Claude Doing?* New York: Clarion, 1984.

Mayer, Mercer. *Just For You.* New York: Western, 1975.

5. Perseverance

Brown, Marc. *D.W. Flips!* Boston: Little Brown, 1987.

Carle, Eric. *The Very Busy Spider.* New York: Philomel, 1984.

Keats, Ezra Jack. *Whistle for Willie.* New York: Viking, 1964.

Piper, Watty. *The Little Engine That Could.* New York: Platt, 1976.

Schlichting, Mark. *The Tortoise and the Hare.* Novato, CA: Living Books, 1993.

6. Responsibility

Carlson, Nancy. *Harriet and the Garden.* Minneapolis: Carolrhoda, 1982.

Harper, Isabelle. *My Dog Rosie.* New York: Blue Sky, 1994.

Kraus, Robert. *Herman the Helper.* New York: Simon, 1974.

Miller, Margaret. *Where Does It Go?* New York: Greenwillow, 1992.

Oxenbury, Helen. *It's My Birthday.* Cambridge, MA: Candlewick, 1993.

Williams, Vera B. *A Chair for My Mother.* New York: Greenwillow, 1982.

7. Cause and Effect

Aardema, Verna. *Who's in Rabbit's House?* New York: Dial, 1977.

Burningham, John. *Mr. Gumpy's Outing.* New York: Holt, 1970.

Carlson, Nancy. *Loudmouth George and the Big Race.* Minneapolis: Carolrhoda, 1983.

———. *Harriet's Halloween Candy.* New York: Puffin, 1982.

Hobson, Sally. *Chicken Little.* New York: Simon, 1994.

8. Reframing

Carle, Eric. *Little Cloud.* New York: Scholastic, 1996.

Hoban, Tana. *Look! Look! Look!* New York: Greenwillow, 1988.

Hutchins, Pat. *Changes, Changes.* New York: Aladdin, 1971.

LeGuin, Ursula. *Fire and Stone.* New York: Atheneum, 1989.

McGovern, Ann. *Too Much Noise.* Boston: Houghton, 1967.

Moss, Marissa. *Regina's Big Mistake.* Boston: Houghton, 1990.

Stevenson, James. *"Could Be Worse!"* New York: Greenwillow, 1977.

Stone, Jon. *The Monster at the End of This Book.* New York: Western, 1971.

9. Problem Solving

Berenstain, Stan, and Jan Berenstain. *The Berenstain Bears Get in a Fight.* New York: Random, 1982.

Crary, Elizabeth. *I Want It.* Seattle: Parenting Press, 1982.

Henkes, Kevin. *Bailey Goes Camping.* New York: Greenwillow, 1985.

Hutchins, Pat. *The Doorbell Rang.* New York: Scholastic, 1986.

Keller, Holly. *Geraldine's Blanket.* New York: Greenwillow, 1984.

Wood, Don, and Audrey Wood. *The Little Mouse, the Red Ripe Strawberry and the Big Hungry Bear.* New York: Scholastic, 1984.

Zolotow, Charlotte. *Mr. Rabbit and the Lovely Present.* New York: Harper, 1990.

10. Optimism and Hope

Brandenberg, Alexa. *I Am Me.* San Diego: Red Wagon, 1996.

Carlson, Nancy. *Take Time to Relax.* New York: Viking, 1991.

Feelings, Tom, and Eloise Greenfield. *Daydreamers.* New York: Puffin, 1981.

Holabird, Katharine. *Angelina Ballerina.* New York: Potter, 1983.

Kraus, Robert. *Leo the Late Bloomer.* New York: Windmill, 1971.

McLerran, Alice. *Roxaboxen.* New York: Lothrop, 1991.

Wells, Rosemary. *Moss Pillows: A Voyage to the Bunny Planet.* New York: Dial, 1992.

Appendix Six: Bibliography

Addams, Jane. "One World." *Teaching Tolerance* 7, No. 1 (1998): 65.

Allen, Juliet V. *What Do I Do When?* San Luis Obispo, CA: Impact, 1983.

Angelou, Maya. *The Complete Collected Poems of Maya Angelou.* New York: Random, 1994.

Anthony, James, and Bertram Cohler. *The Invulnerable Child.* New York: Guilford, 1987.

Baldwin, James. *The Fire Next Time.* New York: Dell, 1962.

Ballantine, Betty, and Ian Ballantine, eds. *The Native Americans.* Atlanta: Turner, 1993.

Barr, Art. *You Can Be a Chalk Artist.* Denver: Accent, 1978.

Bassett, Margot, Carrie Stengel, and Mattie Weiss. *Indian Boarding School—History Day Performance.* Minneapolis Public School, 1995. Videocassette.

Bennett, Lerone, Jr. *Before the Mayflower: A History of Black America.* Chicago: Johnson, 1969.

Berg, Steve. "In Fargo N.D., 'State of Union' Is Not So Bad," *Star Tribune,* 27 January 1998.

Bisson, Julie. *Celebrate! An Anti-Bias Guide to Enjoying Holidays in Early Childhood Programs.* St. Paul: Redleaf, 1997.

Black, Kathy. *In the Shadow of Polio: A Personal and Social History.* Reading, PA: Addison-Wesley, 1996.

Blake, Robert J. *The Perfect Spot.* New York: Philomel, 1992.

Bredekamp, Sue, ed. *Developmentally Appropriate Practices.* Washington, DC: NAEYC, 1986.

Bremner, Robert H., ed. *Children and Youth in America: A Documentary History.* Vol. 1. Cambridge: Harvard University Press, 1970.

Brodkin, Margaret. *Every Kid Counts: 31 Ways to Save Our Children.* New York: Harper, 1993.

Brownlee, Shannon. "The Biology of Soul Murder." *US News and World Report* 121 (1996): 71-73.

Cecil, Nancy Lee. *Raising Peaceful Children in a Violent World.* San Diego: Lura Media, 1995.

Center for the Child Care Workforce. *Biography of Marcy Whitebook.* Washington, DC: Center for the Child Care Work Force, 1998.

Chang, Hedy Nai-Lin, Amy Muckelroy, and Dora Pulido-Tobiassen. *Looking In, Looking Out: Redefining Child Care and Early Education in a Diverse Society.* San Francisco: California Tomorrow, 1996.

Cherry, Claire. *Think of Something Quiet.* Belmont, CA: Pitman, 1981.

Children's Defense Fund. *A Brief Biography of Marian Wright Edelman.*
Washington, DC: Children's Defense Fund, 1998.

———. *The State of America's Children: Yearbook 1996.*
Washington, DC: Children's Defense Fund, 1996.

Children, Youth and Family Consortium. *Seeds of Promise* 1 (April 1996).

Chumbawamba. "Tubthumping." *Tubthumper.* New York:
Universal Records, 1997.

Cisneros, Sandra. *The House on Mango Street.* New York: Vintage, 1984.

Clark, Dick. *Preparing Youth for the 21st Century: Third Conference,
February 16-19, 1996.* Washington, DC: The Aspen Institute, 1996.

Clinton, Hillary Rodham. *It Takes a Village and Other Lessons
Children Teach Us.* New York: Simon, 1996.

Cohn, Victor. *Sister Kenny: The Woman Who Challenged the Doctors.*
Minneapolis: University of Minnesota Press, 1976.

Committee for Children. *Second Step: A Violence Prevention Curriculum.*
Seattle: Committee for Children, 1991.

Compas, Bruce. "Coping with Stress During Childhood and
Adolescence." *Psychological Bulletin* 101 (1987): 393-403.

Coontz, Stephanie. *The Way We Never Were: American Families
and the Nostalgia Trap.* New York: Basic Books, 1992.

———. *The Way We Really Are.* New York: Basic Books, 1997.

Copage, Eric B. *Black Pearls for Parents.* New York: Quill, 1995.

Cowen, E., and W. Work. "Resilient Children, Psychological Wellness
and Primary Prevention." *American Journal of Community
Psychology* 16 (1988): 591-607.

Cowen, E., P. Wyman, W. Work, and G. Parker. "The Rochester
Child Resilience Project: Overview and Summary of First Year
Findings." *Development and Psychopathology* 2 (1990): 193-212.

Crary, Elizabeth. *Kids Can Cooperate: A Practical Guide to Teaching
Problem Solving.* Seattle: Parenting Press, 1984.

———. *Pick Up Your Socks...and Other Skills Growing Children Need!*
Seattle: Parenting Press, 1990.

Deloria, V., Jr. "The Application of the Constitution to American
Indians." In *Exiled in the Land of the Free.* Edited by O. Lions,
J. Mohawk, V. Deloria Jr., L. Hauptmann, H. Berman, D. Grinde Jr.,
C. Berke, and R. Venables, 282-315. Santa Fe: Clear Light, 1992.

Derman-Sparks, Louise, and the A.B.C. Task Force. *Anti-Bias Curriculum:
Tools for Empowering Young Children.* Washington, DC: NAEYC, 1989.

Earle, Alise Morse. *Child Life in Colonial Days.* New York: Macmillan, 1961.

Edelman, Marian Wright. *The Measure of Our Success: A Letter to My
Children and Yours.* Boston: Harper, 1992.

Egeland, Bryon. "A Prospective Study of High Risk Families: Antecedents
of Child Maltreatment." *Wilder Research Center Report.* 1991.

Egeland, B., D. Jacobitz, and L. Sroufe. "Breaking the Cycle of Abuse."
Child Development 59 (1988): 1080-1088.

Eisenberg, Nancy. *The Caring Child*. Cambridge: Harvard University Press, 1992.

Elkind, David. "The Child Yesterday, Today, and Tomorrow." *Young Children* 42 (1987): 6-11.

——. *Ties that Stress: The New Family Imbalance*. Cambridge: Harvard University Press, 1994.

Erickson, Martha Farrell. "Raising Children Well." *News* July/August (1996): 1+.

Far West Laboratory, in Collaboration with California Department of Education. *Ten Ways to Culturally Sensitive Child Care*. Highland Laboratories, 1992. Videocassette.

Farber, E., and B. Egeland. "Invulnerability Among Abused and Neglected Children." In *The Invulnerable Child*. Edited by E. Anthongy and B. Cohler, 253-287. New York: Gilford, 1987.

Freedman, Russell. *Kids at Work: Lewis Hine and the Crusade Against Child Labor*. New York: Clarion, 1994.

Garmezy, N. "Resiliency and Vulnerability to Adverse Developmental Outcomes Associated with Poverty." *American Behavioral Scientist* 34 (1991): 416-430.

Garmezy, N., and A. Masten. "Stress, Competence, and Resilience: Common Frontiers for Therapist and Psychopathologist." *Behavior Therapy* 17 (1986): 500-521.

Gilgun, J. "Resilience and the Intergenerational Transmission of Child Sexual Abuse." In *Family Sexual Abuse: Frontline Research and Evaluation*. Edited by M. Q. Patton, 93-105. Newbury Park: Sage, 1990.

Goleman, Daniel. *Emotional Intelligence*. New York: Bantam, 1995.

Gonzalez-Mena, Janet. *Multicultural Issues in Child Care*. Mountainview, CA: Mayfield, 1993.

Greenleaf, Barbara Kaye. *Children Through the Ages: The History of Childhood*. New York: McGraw, 1978.

The New Grolier Multimedia Encyclopedia, 1993.

Hamburg, David A. *Today's Children*. New York: Random, 1992.

Hatkoff, Amy, and Karen Kelly Klopp. *How to Save the Children*. New York: Fireside, 1992.

Heidemann, Sandra, and Deborah Hewitt. *Pathways to Play: Developing Play Skills in Young Children*. St. Paul: Redleaf, 1992.

Hewitt, Deborah. *So This Is Normal Too? Teachers and Parents Working Out Developmental Issues in Young Children*. St. Paul: Redleaf, 1995.

Hewlet, Sylvia Ann. *When the Bough Breaks: The Cost of Neglecting Our Children*. New York: Basic Books, 1991.

Hiner, N. Ray, and Joseph M. Hawes, eds. *Growing Up in America: Children in Historical Perspective*. Urbana, IL: University of Illinois Press, 1985.

Hirschfelder, Arlene, and Martha Kriepe de Montano. *The Native American Almanac: A Portrait of Native America Today*. New York: Prentice, 1993.

Honig, Alice Sterling. "Stress and Coping in Children."
    Young Children 41 (1986): 47-59.

hooks, bell. *Ain't I a Woman: Black Women and Feminism*. Boston:
    South End, 1981.

Hoxie, Frederick E. *Encyclopedia of North American Indians*.
    Boston: Houghton, 1996.

Hyson, Marion C. *The Emotional Development of Young Children: Building
    an Emotion-Centered Curriculum*. New York: Teachers College, 1994.

Jampolsky, Gerald. *One Person Can Make a Difference: Ordinary People
    Doing Extraordinary Things*. New York: Bantam, 1990.

Joseph, Joanne M. *The Resilient Child: Preparing Today's Youth
    for Tomorrow's World*. New York: Plenum, 1994.

Joslin, Sesyle. *What Do You Say, Dear?* New York: Harper, 1986.

Katz, Lilian, and Diane E. McClellan. *Fostering Children's Social
    Competence: The Teacher's Role*. Washington, DC: NAEYC, 1997.

Katz, Lilian. "The Professional Early Childhood Teacher."
    Young Children 39 (1984): 3-10.

Kaufman, J., and E. Zigler. "Do Abused Children Become Abusive
    Parents?" *American Journal of Orthopsychiatry* 57 (1987): 186-192.

Ketz, Louise, ed. *A Dictionary of American History Revised*. Vol. 7.
    New York: Scribner, 1996.

Kingbird, Joe. *Historical Timeline*. Unpublished manuscript, 1997.

Koplow, Lesley, ed. *Unsmiling Faces: How Preschools Can Heal*.
    New York: Teachers College, 1996.

Koplewicz, Harold S. *It's Nobody's Fault*. New York: Times, 1996.

Kotlowitz, Alex. *There Are No Children Here: The Story of Two Boys
    Growing Up in the Other America*. New York: Doubleday, 1991.

Kusz, Natalie. *Road Song*. New York: Farrar, 1990.

Kyrios, Michael, and Margot Prior. "Temperament, Stress, and Family
    Factors in Behavioral Adjustment of 3 to 5-Year-Old Children."
    International Journal of Behavioral Development 13 (1990): 67-93.

Leach, Penelope. *Children First: What Society Must Do—And Is Not
    Doing—For Children Today*. New York: Vintage, 1994.

Leffert, Nancy, Peter Benson, and Jolene Roehlkepartain. *Starting Out Right:
    Developmental Assets for Children*. Minneapolis: Search Institute, 1997.

Levin, Diane E. *Teaching Children in Violent Times: Building a Peaceable
    Classroom*. Cambridge, MA: Educators for Social Responsibility, 1994.

Photographs by Levin, James, and Editor Jackie Carter, *Helping*.
    New York: Scholastic, 1993.

Lindsey, Duncan. *The Welfare of Children*. New York:
    Oxford University Press, 1994.

Lomawaima, K. Tsianina. *They Called It Prairie Light: The Story of Chilocco
    Indian School*. Lincoln, NE: University of Nebraska Press, 1994.

Luthar, S., and E. Zigler. "Vulnerability and Resilience: A Review of Research on Resilience in Childhood." *American Journal of Orthopsychiatry* 61 (1991): 6-22.

Lyon, Gabrielle. "An Unconditional Embrace." *Teaching Tolerance* 7, No. 1 (1998): 11-15.

Marsolek, Karen. *Science Curriculum.* Anoka, MN: Anoka-Hennepin I.S.D. Community Education Learning Readiness Preschool Program, unpublished.

Masten, Ann. "Resilience: Lessons from Children Who Overcome the Odds." *Early Report* 16 (1989): 1+.

Masten, A., K. Best, and N. Garmezy. "Resilience and Development: Contributions from the Study of Children Who Overcome Diversity." *Development and Psychopathology* 2 (1991): 425-444.

McCracken, Janet Brown. *Valuing Diversity: The Primary Years.* Washington, DC: NAEYC, 1993.

McClellan, J., and E. Trupin. "Prevention of Psychiatric Disorders in Children." *Hospital and Community Psychiatry* 40 (1989): 630-636.

Meltzer, Milton. *Cheap Raw Material.* New York: Viking, 1994.

Moomaw, Sally, and Brenda Hieronymus. *More Than Magnets: Exploring the Wonders of Science in Preschool and Kindergarten.* St. Paul: Redleaf, 1997.

Morris, Ann. *Bread, Bread, Bread.* New York: Lothrop, 1989.

———. *Loving.* New York: Lothrop, 1990.

Mrazek, Patricia J., and David A. Mrazek. "Resilience in Child Maltreatment Victims: A Conceptual Exploration." *Child Abuse and Neglect* 2 (1987): 357-366.

National Commission on Children. *Next Steps for Children and Families: Strengthening and Supporting Families.* Washington, DC: National Commission on Children, 1993.

National Educational Service. *Reclaiming Youth at Risk: Our Hope for the Future.* Bloomington, IN: National Educational Service, 1996.

Neugebauer, Bonnie, ed. *Alike and Different: Exploring Our Humanity with Young Children.* Washington, DC: NAEYC, 1992.

Oehlberg, Barbara. *Making It Better: Activities for Children in a Stressful World.* St. Paul: Redleaf, 1996.

Olson, James S., and Raymond Wilson. *Native Americans in the Twentieth Century.* Chicago: University of Illinois Press, 1984.

Owens, Karen. *Raising Your Child's Inner Self-Esteem.* New York: Plenum, 1995.

Pellegrini, D. "Psychosocial Risk and Protective Factors in Childhood." *Developmental and Behavioral Pediatrics* 11 (1990): 201-209.

Postman, Neil. *The Disappearance of Childhood.* New York: Delacorte, 1982.

Prutzman, Priscilla, Lee Stern, M. Leonard Berger, and Gretchen Bodenhamer. *The Friendly Classroom for a Small Planet: Children's Creative Response to Conflict Program.* Gabriola Island, British Columbia, Canada: New Society, 1988.

Ramsey, Patricia. *Making Friends in School: Promoting Peer Relationships in Early Childhood.* New York: Teachers College, 1991.

Rifken, Jeremy. *The End of Work.* New York: Putnam, 1996.

Riley, Patricia, ed. *Growing Up Native American.* New York: Avon, 1993.

Rockwell, Robert, Elizabeth Sherwood, and Robert Williams. *Mudpies to Magnets.* Beltsville, MD: Gryphon, 1987.

Rutter, M. "Psychosocial Resilience and Protective Mechanisms." *American Journal of Orthopsychiatry* 57 (1987): 316-331.

———. "Resilience in the Face of Adversity." *British Journal of Psychiatry* 147 (1985): 598-611.

Seaman, P. David, ed. *Born a Chief: The 19th Century Hopi Boyhood of Edmund Nequatewa.* Tucson, AZ: University of Arizona Press, 1993.

Search Institute. "40 Developmental Assets Among Minnesota Youth." *Update.* Minneapolis Public Schools, 1996.

Seligman, Martin E. P. *The Optimistic Child.* Boston: Houghton, 1995.

Shapiro, Joseph, Dorian Friedman, Michele Meyer, and Margaret Lofton. "Invincible Kids." *U.S. News and World Report.* 121 (1996): 63-71.

Sheets, Rosa Hernandez. "Nations Within." *Teaching Tolerance.* Fall 1997: 11-15.

Sherman, Arloc. *Wasting America's Future: The Children's Defense Fund Report on the Costs of Child Poverty.* Boston: Beacon, 1994.

Shusterman, Neal. *Kid Heroes: True Stories of Rescuers, Survivors, and Achievers.* New York: Doherty, 1991.

Silverstein, Shel. *Where the Sidewalk Ends.* New York: Harper, 1974.

Skolnick, Arlene. *Embattled Paradise: The American Family in an Age of Uncertainty.* New York: Basic Books, 1991.

Smith, Charles A. *The Peaceful Classroom: 162 Easy Activities to Teach Preschoolers Compassion and Cooperation.* Beltsville, MD: Gryphon, 1993.

Smith, Jane. *Patenting the Sun: Polio and the Salk Vaccine.* New York: Morrow, 1990.

Smith, Maureen. "Tougher Stuff." *Update.* Minneapolis Public Schools, 1989.

Strand, Deborah S. "Case Study: Supporting Resilience in Males." Master's thesis, Augsburg College, 1994.

Strickland, R., ed. *Felix S. Cohen Handbook of Federal Indian Law.* Charlottesville, VA: Michie, 1982.

Struteevant, William C., and Wilcomb E. Washburn, eds. *History of Indian-White Relations.* Washington, DC: Smithsonian, 1989.

Szasz, Margaret. *Education and the American Indian: The Road to Self-Determination, 1928-1973.* Albuquerque, NM: University of New Mexico Press, 1974.

Trattner, Walter. *Crusade for the Children: A History of the National Child Labor Committee and Child Labor Reform in America.* Chicago: Quadrangle, 1970.

Utter, Jack. *American Indians: Answers to Today's Questions.* Lake Ann, MI: National Woodlands, 1993.

Valentine, Glenda. "Editors Note." *Teaching Tolerance* 7, No. 1 (1998): 4.

Walker, Alice. *Anything We Love Can Be Saved.* New York: Random, 1997.

Wall, Steve, and Harvey Arden. *Wisdom Keepers.* Hillsboro: Beyond Words, 1990.

Wallerstein, Judith S., and Sandra Blakeslee. *Second Chances: Men, Women, and Children a Decade After Divorce.* New York: Ticknor, 1989.

Washburn, Wilcomb E. *The American Indian and the United States: A Documentary History.* Vol. 1. New York: Random, 1973.

Washburn, Wilcomb E., Volume Editor, and William C. Struteevant, General Editor. *History of Indian-White Relations.* Washington, DC: Smithsonian, 1988.

Washington, Margaret, ed. *Narrative of Sojourner Truth.* New York: Vintage, 1993.

Waters, Frank. *Brave Are My People.* Santa Fe: Clear Light, 1993.

Weinreb, Maxine L. "Be a Resiliency Mentor: You May Be a Lifesaver for a High-Risk Child." *Young Children* 52 (1997): 14-20.

Werner, Emmy E. "High-Risk Children in Young Adulthood: A Longitudinal Study from Birth to 32 Years." *American Journal of Orthopsychiatry* 59 (1989): 72-81.

Werner, Emmy E., and Ruth S. Smith. *Overcoming the Odds.* Ithaca, NY: Cornell University Press, 1992.

———. *Vulnerable But Invincible.* New York: McGraw, 1982.

Wichert, Susanne. *Keeping the Peace: Practicing Cooperation and Conflict Resolution with Preschoolers.* Gabriola Island, British Columbia, Canada: New Society Publishers, 1989.

Winn, Marie. *Children Without Childhood.* New York: Pantheon, 1983.

Wub-e-ke-niew. *We Have the Right to Exist.* New York: Black Thistle, 1995.

Wyman, P., E. Cowen, W. Work, and G. Parker. "Developmental and Family Milieu Correlates of Resilience in Urban Children Who Have Experienced Major Life Stress." *American Journal of Community Psychology* 19 (1991): 405-426.

Yellin, Emily. "Around the Freedom Table." *Teaching Tolerance* 7, No. 1 (1998): 47-53.

York, Stacey. *Big As Life.* 2 vols. St. Paul: Redleaf, 1998.

Zinn, Howard. *A People's History of the United States.* Rev. ed. New York: Harper, 1995.